LITTLE STROKES

LITTLE STROKES

WALTER C. ALVAREZ, M.D., D.Sc.

Emeritus Professor of Medicine,
University of Minnesota (Mayo Foundation)

FOREWORD BY
Michael E. De Bakey, M.D.

J. B. LIPPINCOTT COMPANY
PHILADELPHIA AND TORONTO

Foreword

"Stroke has been for many years a tragically neglected disease. The health professions have shown very little interest in it; the public has accepted it with resignation." This straightforward, perhaps even blunt, statement from the report of the President's Commission on Heart Disease, Cancer and Stroke is an accurate summation of the current status accorded this crippling and fatal disease. The distressing lack of awareness of and interest in stroke is predicated for the most part on the widely accepted misconception that stroke is simply a way of dying, that little can be done about it.

Almost ironically, the facts indicate something altogether different. For example, many strokes—indeed, most strokes—can be predicted, as indicated by Dr. Alvarez in this text. Three of every four patients with occlusive stroke display symptomatic signs which warn of the impending attack. A high percentage of these symptoms are attributable to occlusion of the vessels supplying blood to the brain. And often these lesions are as amenable to surgical correction as are occlusive lesions in other areas of the body. Secondly, sophisticated rehabilitative programs have been developed through which surviving victims of stroke can be restored to relatively normal, active and productive living. Through intensive rehabilitative care, as many as 80 per cent of such patients can be made self-sufficient rather than totally dependent upon family, friends and society. Equally important, exciting new avenues of research offer hope for the prevention and treatment of stroke within the foreseeable future. Among these promising developments are new drugs to improve circulation to the brain; alteration of blood-clotting mechanisms; control of fat metabolism and hypertension; and blood-vessel surgery.

So, it is not enough to say that the facts fail to substantiate the long-held misconceptions regarding stroke. Rather, it is obvious that the facts completely shatter any notions that the physician must sit quietly and idly by as this "inevitability" takes its course, and in its course, takes life.

Stroke is a problem of significant magnitude. In the United States alone in 1963 more than 200,000 persons died as a result of stroke. As a cause of death stroke ranks third in this country. And, although stroke is more a disease of the aged than are heart disease and cancer (killers ranking first and second), by no means can it be considered solely as being limited to the aged. In fact, one-fifth of all stroke deaths in 1963 claimed individuals under 65 years of age. This fact, which might at first seem insignificant, means that 20 per cent of all people who die of stroke are taken during the most productive years of their lives. In this respect, stroke is the number five killer. Other statistics as to the staggering economic burden imposed by the hundreds of thousands of surviving stroke victims who are not self-sufficient and as to the loss in manpower and productivity simply add force to the thesis that the problem of stroke must be attacked head-on and immediately.

It must be said to Dr. Alvarez's credit that he has for many years tried to point up the importance of stroke and the means of dealing with it. He long has campaigned to educate both the profession and the public to an awareness of this crippler and killer. Only when both the profession and the public come fully to appreciate such information as we have already and are continuing to gain can the problem be dealt with adequately. This, then, is the underlying philosophy leading to the presentation of this book.

MICHAEL E. DE BAKEY, M.D.

Preface

This little volume is unique. After a year of searching through a great medical library I can say that this is the only book ever written to describe one of the commonest diseases of man—one that until 15 years ago usually went undiagnosed. It is the disease which in millions of cases either slowly or quickly pulls down an arteriosclerotic person to his or her death.

I here take pleasure in thanking my dear wife, who for a solid year typed and typed and retyped the manuscript of this book, and slaved to get every item in the big bibliography correct.

I gladly thank also Miss Georgia Price, of the Northwestern University Medical Library, for her skill in helping me find the hundreds of books and articles that I wanted to read.

WALTER C. ALVAREZ, M.D.

Contents

LITTLE STROKES

He who would talk about the medical art must speak so that the layman can understand.

Hippocrates, *on* ANCIENT MEDICINE

We see many patients who have a series of transient or "little strokes" which may range in severity from slight numbness or weakness of the side of the face, or slight difficulty with speech, to hemiplegia; and which may last for from a few minutes to several days, with complete recovery.

Irving S. Wright and Ellen McDevitt (1955)

I believe that you will agree that the subject . . . is one of the most important in all of medicine, and it deserves our closest attention. Vascular disease . . . ranks first in frequency and gravity amongst all diseases of the brain.

R. D. Adams (1956)

Nothing could be more important to the clinician than the nature of the transient cerebral episodes which have been variously attributed to vascular spasm, vascular insufficiency, and ischemia associated with arteriosclerosis.

B. J. Alpers (1959)

Other uncounted thousands experience transient stroke-like attacks which are never reported, and which never reach the attention of a physician.

Robert A. Kuhn (1961)

Although in the form of apoplexy and heart disease arteriosclerosis kills four times as many civilized people as cancer, it has not aroused the crusading spirit of the public.

Irvine Page (1961)

Nothing has been so injurious to philosophy as this circumstance, namely, that familiar and frequent objects do not arrest and detain men's contemplation, but are carelessly admitted, and their causes never inquired after.

Francis Bacon, NOVUM ORGANUM, FIRST BOOK (1620)

1

Introduction

In writing this book, my object has been to acquaint my readers with what I have learned through a half century of study of those commonly seen syndromes which, for the sake of simplicity, convenience, brevity and ease of comprehension, I call the *Little,* the *Brief,* and the *Silent* strokes. Perhaps I should add two more names—the *Prodromal* strokes, and the *Progressing* strokes. Surely, the usually brief and often harmless episodes should have a different name from that of the big ones which produce aphasias and hemiplegias.

WHY SOME PHYSICIANS NEVER SEE PATIENTS WITH LITTLE STROKES. Because some of my friends may now say, "But wait, I never saw anyone with a little stroke," I should explain that in the past the patients with this common disease rarely had their troubles correctly diagnosed because they almost never told their physician of the dizzy, vomiting, blackout or falling spell which suddenly, one day, worked a distressing change in them; and perhaps left them with an uncomfortable abdomen. A common story is that of a healthy, hard-driving, efficient, and perhaps outstanding executive who *suddenly one day* became an ailing, dull, tired, and forgetful invalid who could no longer work.

But when the man went to a physician, his brain was functioning so poorly that he failed to mention his inability to get anything done, and complained only of his least important symptoms. As a result, when an x-ray examination showed some spasm in his duodenal cap, an ulcer was diagnosed and operated on; or when nothing was found, the man was told that all that was wrong with him was that he had become too anxious about his health. The doctor then prescribed a tranquilizer, and that was that. Worse yet, in many a case I have seen the patient—with his crippled brain—operated on for a "chronic appendix" or a silent gallstone.

1

Time and again when at a consultation I have tried to show the family doctor that the old scar of a peptic ulcer could not possibly account for a formerly able man's dull face, his slow answers to questions, his loss of memory, or his inability any longer to do productive work, I have failed. I have failed partly because no one had ever taught my friend the great need for noting the tremendous significance 1. *of a face much duller than it should be for the person's position in life;* 2. a dulled wit, with slow and inadequate answers to questions, and 3. poor grooming, with perhaps gravy on the man's coat. I have failed to convince the doctor also because no one had ever taught him that when a man is too dull or too forgetful to give his history, the facts must be obtained by questioning his wife, or grown children, or perhaps a business associate— *and unless this is done, the correct diagnosis will rarely be made.*

Commonly, when I ask the man's wife what happened, she will say, "Since the day when he fell out of his chair or had that frightening dizzy spell, he has been a changed man—so changed I now hardly know him. He, who used to be so kindly, is now irritable and irascible and unreasonable."

Usually then, I turn to the patient and ask, "What did you think was happening to you when you had that dizzy spell?" And when he answers, as he is likely to do, "I thought I was having a stroke, and expected to die any minute," the diagnosis of a brain injury has been made, and there cannot be much question about it.

Why the Failure of the Patient To Realize What Has Happened to Him? For years I marvelled at the inability of patients—badly disabled mentally by a little stroke—to realize what a terrible thing had happened to them. I wondered how a formerly able business man, or an eminent lawyer or physician could go about, unconcerned, when he was unkempt, perhaps dirty, and perhaps reeking of dribbled urine. I wondered until one day I found an article by Parkes Weber (1942) quoting neurologists who had noticed that certain patients who had been blinded, and paralyzed on one side by a big stroke, were so unable to sense the big change in themselves that they denied that there was anything wrong with their eyes or their still weak and flabby hand. Evidently some part of the brain which makes a person conscious of the state of his body can be destroyed.

As I write this, a brilliant, nationally known editor who, a while ago, suffered a big stroke, tells me that today, although he has recovered well, he has no consciousness of his left arm and hand, and does not know where the hand is, unless he looks to see. I imagine that some of the persons who have had a severe little stroke have a bad case of this type of agnosia, or lack of knowledge of what their body is like.

Why Have Physicians So Often Failed To Note the Big Changes

IN THE APPEARANCE AND ABILITY OF A ONCE ABLE MAN? Just as I have marvelled at the inability of the president of a big corporation to see that he was in my office unwashed, dirty, poorly shaved, and badly dressed, so, on many occasions, I have marvelled at the failure of his eminent internist to notice the man's bad grooming. How could the doctor have failed to see the great abnormality, and how could he have failed to realize what it meant in terms of injury to the man's brain? How could he have sent the man away with a clean bill of health, or how could he have hoped to cure him with an appendectomy?

The answer, I think, was given us long ago by that great French neurologist, Charcot, who used to say that we human beings usually "see only what we are ready to see, and what we were once taught to see." I might add that it is very hard for most of us to see or notice or realize the importance of something that we cannot quickly fit into the store of knowledge that we already have. To illustrate: back in 1914, when I would tell a physician that waves go down the digestive tract, apparently because of a gradient of forces that I had demonstrated; the man would look at me blankly, because he had never heard of a gradient. But if I talked to an engineer, he would say immediately, "How interesting, and how logical; surely there should be a gradient of forces." He accepted the idea instantly because all his life he had known about gradients, many of which influenced the flow of water, or something that he had had to move.

Around 1895, when physicists had learned that if they did not want to have their photographic films fogged, they must keep them away from the Crooke's tubes (much like x-ray tubes) then being much experimented with—they just moved the films away! It was only Roentgen who had the curiosity and genius to ask, "But how are the films being fogged?"

OUR ASTOUNDING LACK OF INTEREST IN STROKES. Some 40 years ago, when I began to search for articles on little strokes, I looked first in big books on brain diseases, neurology, pathology, and arteriosclerosis, and was discouraged when, commonly, in the index, there was no such word as "*stroke*." Then I looked under *cerebral arteriosclerosis*, and, again, usually I found either nothing or very little. In one huge book I found 8 lines; and in another book of 600 pages on diseases of the brain I found 10 lines.

In one of our best big texts on the problems of aging (1942) I found nothing on cerebral arteriosclerosis, and nothing on strokes of any kind! Dr. Purves-Stewart (1947, in his big text, p. 455) had only a short paragraph on "intermittent cerebral claudication." As Dr. Tracy Putnam once said (1938, p. 563) the study of cerebral thrombosis "is usually omitted in textbooks on neuropathology."

WHY HAS THE WORD "STROKE" AND THE CONCEPT OF STROKE BEEN SO

UNIVERSALLY AVOIDED? Obviously, the word "stroke," and even more often the words "little strokes" have, for the last century, up to about 1950, been rigidly avoided in medical circles, and strictly tabooed. Even in the Transactions of the Second Congress on Cerebrovascular Accidents, I could not find a mention of "little strokes."

When a physician is called to see a man who has just had a slight stroke why does he commonly diagnose a heart attack? Why does Mr. Herbert Marks—statistician for the Metropolitan Life Insurance Company—have to say that, because of this tendency of us physicians to avoid the diagnosis of a "stroke," the country's vital statistics on strokes and coronary attacks must be far from accurate? Dr. Robert A. Kuhn has corroborated this statement (1961). In Japan, where the people do not seem to have our horror of the word "stroke," the apparent incidence of strokes is high while that of heart attacks is low.

I never knew how disgraceful it can be (in the eyes of some people) to have a stroke until, some 40 years ago, when, as I was taking care of a lovely woman recovering from a big stroke, she kept asking me why God had struck her down so cruelly? What could she have done to have made Him so angry with her? Actually, this 65-year-old college graduate had served God devotedly all her days, first as a minister's daughter, then as a missionary in China, then as the wife of a minister, and finally as the president of a large association that every month kept raising large sums of money for God's work. As I said to her, "No; God did not strike you; all that happened was that, with your unusually high blood pressure, an artery on the surface of your brain." But I doubt if she believed me; and if I could not convince this well-educated woman, I can imagine how many millions of our people must suspect that when a friend or neighbor is felled by a stroke, God has caught him in some secret skulduggery and hence punished him severely.

This idea of a stroke's being a punishment is found in the Old Testament (I Samuel 25:36-38) where we learn that Nabal one evening drank so heavily that next day he had a bad hangover. And 10 days later "the Lord smote Nabal so that he died." There we have the Biblical idea that God struck and killed a man for even so minor a sin as an evening's drinking of a bit too much wine!

I suspect it is because we physicians know about this ancient idea that we are inclined to avoid a diagnosis which has such unpleasant connotations. What is sad about this is that, until 15 years ago, we rarely mentioned one of the commonest diseases of aging men and women, and when we did mention it, we called the big strokes CVA's, and the little ones, perhaps, "Momentary ischemic episodes due to vasomotor spasm, excited by impulses arriving by way of the cervical sympathetic chain of nerves."

In Chapter 4 I list some 170 names for little strokes. I hope all neurologists and angiologists will glance through this list just long enough to feel a bit horrified. We might remember what Hans Selye said a while ago, that we physicians are lucky that a gene got called a gene and not—more scientifically—a "catalytoid autoperpetuating chromonematoblast."

For 35 years my friends in medicine, when on very rare occasions they said anything about little strokes, assured me that there were no such things. Hence, when recently, during 16 months I searched the literature, I was reassured on finding the writings of some 275 men or groups of men who had described or mentioned little strokes. At first glance, this may suggest that the disease was well known, but if the reader will look through Chapter 6, he will see that I started with the ancient Greek, Caelius Aurelianus, and the great Richard Bright (1836). After this, during the next 114 years, there might be one or two writers on little strokes each year. Then, about 1950, the dam burst, and since then there have been many articles each year.

A few of the early writers described little strokes so beautifully that it is impossible for me to understand how their work came to be completely, or almost completely, unnoticed. Even Sir William Osler's fine paper (1911), so far as I can remember, was never mentioned by anyone.

Around 1880, the eminent Hughlings Jackson was wondering why transitory paralyses had for so long been ignored. In 1885, the great Frenchman, Trousseau, said that the little spells are so common, and knowledge of them is *"so well established, and so well accepted that one shows poor grace in appearing to doubt it."*

In 1933, Critchley—a great English expert on diseases of the aged—wondered at the lack of interest of physicians in little strokes. Engel, in 1950 (p. 59) remarked on how common these strokes are. Wilson, Rupp, Riggs and Wilson (1951) said that all of us "see cases in which transient neurologic symptoms develop." As I said above, about 1950, the taboo was broken, and since then, most angiologists have been writing about the many "ischemic spells" they see every week. Unfortunately, most clinicians seem still to be ignoring the subject.

To me it is interesting that during the last 100 years laymen seemed to be much more willing to speak of little strokes than were physicians. For instance, when Walt Whitman kept having brief spells of paralysis—through the years 1864 to 1873—he would write to Burroughs, "It is probable I have had several strokes, but I am feeling as I write about the same as is now usual for me." In 1873, he wrote to his mother, "I have had a slight Stroke."[*]

In that tragic story, *"The Dismissal"* (1962, Pantheon books), the lay

---

[*] C. E. Feinberg, Arch. Int. Med., 114:835-842, 1964.

writer Jurgen Thorwald tells how the mind of the great lung surgeon, F. Sauerbruch, went to pieces under the impact of many small strokes. Long before he died his assistants noticed that even at the operating table he would have sudden brief blackouts, and soon his work became so bad that he would cut a big artery and kill a patient.

As Heard said in 1910, laymen have always known about the little strokes, while we doctors usually denied their existence. Some 230 years ago, as Dean Swift was slowly petering out with a much disturbed brain, he said he was dying like an old tree, at the top. Lord Byron made a similar remark about himself. Dr. Irvine Page published in his fine book, "Strokes" (1961) the following little poem by Swift which certainly suggests little strokes—what with the change in the face, the vertigo, the failing memory, the decaying ability, and the stubbornness. Page says that the "Gloomy Dean" was then 72, and had had a stroke. Fairly obviously, he was talking about his own experience.*

> Poor gentleman, he droops apace,
> You plainly see it in his face,
> That old vertigo in his head
> Will never leave him til he's dead.
> Besides, his memory decays,
> He recollects not what he says . . .
> For poetry he's past his prime,
> He takes an hour to find a rime;
> His fire is out, his wit decay'd,
> His fancy sunk, his muse a Jade.
> I'd have him throw away his pen,
> But there's no talking to some men.

DR. SAMUEL JOHNSON AND HIS LITTLE STROKE. The Eaton Laboratories recently noted that the famous Dr. Samuel Johnson woke at three in the morning of June 17, 1883, with ". . . a confusion and indistinctness in my head which I suppose lasted about half a minute." Because he could not speak, he realized he had suffered a stroke.

He tested his mental functions by making a prayer in Latin verse, and was cheered when he found he could do this. But still he could not talk. Then he penned a note with some difficulty, remarking that his hand made wrong letters.

His difficulties with speech and writing soon cleared away, but edema, gout, asthma, dropsy, emphysema, and heart failure went ahead and finished him off in a year and a half.

To show how well many lay people understand little strokes, I often tell of the sweet old lady who said that Death was taking little bites of

---

* See also, *The Portable Swift*, edited by Carl van Doren, Viking Press, 1948; also, that rare book, *The Closing Years of Dean Swift's Life, his unpublished poems, and some remarks on Stella*, by W. R. Wilde, Dublin, 1849.

her; every time she had a frightening dizzy spell she was left a bit more tottery, a bit more forgetful, and a step nearer the grave. Remarkable is a letter to the Editor of *The Lancet* by an able woman who tells how her research-working father kept slipping down hill mentally until he became demented.† His physician refused to recognize the progressive change in the man—a change due perhaps to a brain atrophy.

GENERAL PRACTITIONERS HAVE LONG KNOWN OF LITTLE STROKES. Around 1930, when I began talking often before medical societies about the little strokes, the men who most quickly and easily accepted the idea were fine old general practitioners. I remember one such man who, after I had spoken, came up to the platform and said; "How correct you are; right now I must have two dozen such patients under my care, petering out step by step with those dizzy spells you describe; why couldn't I have guessed what they were due to, and what they meant?"

Here is a letter I received in 1946 from dear old Dr. Paul P. Halleck —a dedicated doctor of the old school—then the Director of a state mental hospital. He wrote: "I read that paper of yours (in *Geriatrics*) over and over again—three times—because that was the 'dope' for which I had been seeking vainly for so long. You put all those vague syndromes and episodes into a definite picture with real meaning. And what a relief it was. I suppose that in the Mental Hospital I have seen a thousand of those spells, yet I never felt quite certain of their significance, even though I was very suspicious that they were small strokes."

Thirty years ago I loved the honesty of an able neurologist who, in all friendliness, used to tell me that he did not believe a word of my writings on little strokes. Then, one day, in he came to apologize. He said that some nights before, he had wakened with a "horrible commotion in his brain." Knowing that he was having a stroke, he quickly opened his eyes to make sure that he could see; he spoke out loud, to make sure he was not aphasic or deaf; he swallowed, to see that his bulb was working; he moved his arms and legs, and he pinched his skin. Then he said to himself, "Thank God, it is only one of Walter's crazy little strokes," and with this, he turned over and went happily back to sleep.

The great Russian, Ivan Turgenev, died in 1883 with a series of spells, which his physician called "little strokes."

Recently (Postgrad. Med.) Dr. Morris Fishbein wrote that Marcello Malpighi, the first great histologist, in 1694, had a big stroke from which, in 40 days, he largely recovered; but his biographer noted that, as so often happens, he "failed in memory and reason, he wept often, and he suffered from indigestion, and slight fits of giddiness."

WHY A GASTROENTEROLOGIST WAS COMPELLED TO BECOME INTERESTED IN LITTLE STROKES. To those of my neurologist friends who may feel un-

† Lancet 1:1012-1015, 1950.

easy about a man of my meager neurologic attainments trying to diagnose little strokes, I will say that, during my 25 years at the Mayo Clinic, I could not avoid handling hundreds of patients with this disease who asked for a stomach specialist because their main distress or pain was in their abdomen. They came to me in such large numbers that I could not possibly have turned them over to the able men in our then much over-worked neurologic section. Besides, these patients so rarely had a neurologic sign such as anyone could find with a pin and cotton and a rubber hammer that my neurologic friends almost always reported "negative examination." As that able British physician, G. W. B. James, said so wisely, back in 1926, these patients in the early stages of their disease are *"rich in symptoms, but poor in signs."*

Only when I found a person whose repeated dizzy episodes, or spells of weakness could conceivably have been due to a carotid obstruction, a mild epilepsy, a late and mild polio, a brain tumor, or an atypical multiple sclerosis, did I feel justified in bothering the neurologists with appeals for help.

I regret the lack here of necropsy reports. I wish I could present here a necropsy report on every one of my patients, but during my 56 years of largely consultant practice in San Francisco, Rochester, and Chicago, most of my patients came to me from a distance—just for a diagnosis—and very few of those with little strokes ever remained near me long enough to die. Hence it is that I cannot say what the lesions were in their brains, or exactly where they were. But through the years I have felt that my inability to get this much desired information should not keep me from recording *the clinical details of the syndromes,* or from studying them. I felt I could do this bit of *clinical* research for the good of medicine, while I left the problems of neurology, angiology, and pathology to specialists in those fields.

WHAT DOES THIS BOOK TEACH? I think this book can show all of us who teach that we must now try to get our younger brethren in medicine to recognize quickly and surely the significance of the syndromes I describe in this book—if only so that when the young graduates see people suffering from the distressing results of a brain injury, they will not do as so many have done in the past—and try to cure a brain-injured patient by removing some harmless organ of his that looks a bit peculiar in an x-ray film. If, in the next few years, we who teach will only save several hundred thousand patients with little strokes from unnecessary & unfortunate operations, we will have accomplished much.

2

How I Became Interested
in Little Strokes

One handicap I may have in writing now about cerebral arteriosclerosis is that, for 30 years of my life, from 1910 to 1940, the bulk of my clinical work and research was done in the field of gastroenterology. I can therefore imagine some of my old friends asking, "What on earth is the man doing now, writing about little strokes?"

Actually, any gastroenterologist worth his salt must be somewhat of a neurologist and a psychiatrist. All my life I have never wanted to be so confirmed a gastroenterologist that I could not, or would not, sometimes get deeply interested in the troubles of that large group of my patients who kept coming in with abdominal discomforts or pains for which no cause could be found in the abdomen.

During my many years at the Mayo Clinic, I worked in a section in which most of the patients came with a digestive or abdominal complaint, but perhaps a third turned out to have some nervous or "functional" syndrome. I soon found that many of the older persons with a crippled brain, were suffering from the effects of little or brief or silent strokes. All of these people I had to try to comfort and help; and so I had to learn all I could about their disease by talking to them and their relatives. I soon learned that I had to make the diagnosis from a glance at the patient, and a history, obtained from a relative or business associate. Eventually, around 1940, it dawned on me that my main interest in medicine had changed, and most of the patients I was seeing needed some psychiatric help. They had gotten into a gastroenterologic section by *mistake*, usually because they had developed abdominal discomfort or pain.

The Young Physician Is Inclined to Accept Any Diagnosis Given Him. During my years at the Mayo Clinic I was constantly being dis-

9

tressed by my difficulty in getting a new assistant to see that he must not, unthinkingly, accept as the diagnosis anything given him by a laboratory girl or an x-ray man—and preferably something that could be operated on. Commonly, I could not convince him that the removal of a silent gallstone that had never produced a single symptom could clear up a bad nervous breakdown, or banish a burning pain in the skin of the left hip.

Worse yet, when, with the answers to a few questions asked of a man's wife, I would show my assistant that the fellow's symptoms had all come suddenly with a fall to the ground, perhaps followed by a few minutes of coma, and that the illness could be caused only by some damage to the brain—still he might feel that the obvious thing to do, first off, was to operate on the gallstone or on a supposed duodenal ulcer, or on a somewhat knobby uterus. He just could not see that with the finding of a gallstone he had not even begun to solve the diagnostic problem facing him; he could not see that it was up to him to start again and try to make a diagnosis *that would explain the symptoms.* He could not see why I kept fussing about a problem which he felt sure he had solved and hence need not look at again.

WHY HAVE LITTLE STROKES BEEN SO RARELY MENTIONED BY NEUROLOGISTS? When, for 30 years, I had been writing and lecturing about little strokes, and only a very few men had mentioned or accepted my work, I became puzzled. My friends the neurologists practically never diagnosed the mild little strokes—but this I could understand because they never saw the patients with mild episodes such as left no residue of the type which would have told the patient or his family physician that it was a neurologist who was needed.

Around 1922, Dr. Henry Woltman, the able Chief of the neurologic section of the Mayo Clinic, wrote two excellent articles on little strokes, but he was too far ahead of his time; and so, in spite of his eminent position in the world of neurology, no one, so far as I have been able to find ever noticed his work. I am sorry to say I did not learn of it until a few years ago, when I was lucky enough to run onto his papers.

Lately, as I searched the literature I found here and there descriptions of what I call either "*severe* little strokes," or "*brief* strokes." A beautiful example of a brief stroke is the one that early one morning struck down a spry, 81-year-old banker friend of mine. With his aphasia and hemiplegia, things looked bad for him, but by evening he was so well that he took friends out to supper, and then to the theater! In the literature there are many case-reports like that.

WHY HAVE THE GASTROENTEROLOGISTS FAILED TO WRITE ABOUT THE LITTLE-STROKE PATIENTS THEY MUST CONSTANTLY BE SEEING? Recently, I got to asking myself, if so often I keep seeing patients with little strokes —because they thought they should consult a "stomach specialist"—then all of my gastroenterologic friends must also be seeing such patients; and if so, why do they never talk or write about them, and why did the editors of "gastro" journals—my old friends—resolutely refuse to publish any paper on the digestive syndrome often produced?

With a little thinking, I got the answer. As I said in Chapter 1, the patient with a little stroke that has produced "a constant misery" in his abdomen rarely thinks to tell his physician about the *sudden onset* of his trouble, with perhaps a woozy spell or a fall to the floor; and he rarely mentions the great change in his character and ability. Left to himself he will talk only of his stomach-ache. Obviously, then, unless the gastroenterologist whom the patient consults gets a hunch from the man's dull face, or asymetrical mouth, or poor grooming, or slow wit; and unless then he turns to the wife to get the essential story, he will not recognize one little-stroke-patient in a year.

To show what can happen: one day a distinguished "stomach specialist" asked me to see with him a middle-aged woman with a "duodenal ulcer" which was not responding to treatment. When, after asking a few questions, I saw that the poor woman was too dull to give me a history, I turned to her fine, intelligent husband and said, "Surely your wife was not always this slowed-up and forgetful?" And he said, "Oh, no; she used to be a wonderful woman, very bright and able and attractive. This illness came suddenly on July 17th, at 7:30 in the morning. As she was getting breakfast, she slumped to the floor. I got her onto the davenport where she kept asking me again and again, 'What happened? What happened?' Ever since, she has been so mentally crippled that I have had to bathe her, dress her, and take care of her like a baby!"

Unfortunately, my eminent physician friend could not adjust his thinking quickly enough to a new idea, and so he ignored the dullness of the somewhat decerebrate woman, and the statement of her husband, and clung doggedly to the x-ray diagnosis of ulcer.

Another case of this "x-ray duodenal ulcer type," out of dozens that I could here present, is that of the president of a big company. Again, as so often happens, I was asked to see him because his "ulcer would not heal." When I quickly saw that I could not get much of a history out of such a dull-looking and slow-thinking man, I turned to his intelligent young second wife and asked her what had happened to him, and if it had happened suddenly? She said, "Yes; two months ago he had a frightening dizzy spell, after which he felt so tired and unable to work that I took him to Florida for a rest; but soon after we got there, he crashed to the floor of the bathroom. He picked himself up, and said he was all right, but I was so frightened that I brought him home. A few days later, again while shaving, he fell to the floor. He got up and said it was nothing, but ever since then he has kept complaining of a pain in his abdomen, and he has not been able to go to his office." After a few months of rest, this man, who evidently had had three little strokes, recovered his health. That was 6 years ago, and his wife tells me that he is still feeling well and is able to work. He never had any symptoms of an ulcer.

Following are two more case-reports that will show how *absolutely essential* it is for the physician to ask a relative of a dulled patient to give the story. One day a banker came with a letter from his home physician, saying that the man had an intractable duodenal ulcer. Noticing immediately that the fellow neither looked like a banker nor talked like one, I took his two grown sons into another room and asked them if they had noticed anything mentally wrong with their father. They said, "Most certainly, yes; following some severe dizzy spells, he has lost all of his old good business judgment, and has been making one 'crazy investment' after another. Right here in Rochester, as soon as he arrived, he bought a run-down third-class hotel, which will be only a loss and a nuisance. We really ought to take him into court and have him declared incompetent, but we can't bear to do such a thing to our father."

In the second case, the point that interested me much was that *in the absence of a relative* of the much-dulled patient, I had to spend several hours, spread over 10 days, trying to get an understandable history. The man was a bachelor of 55, an explorer for minerals, who had come from New York to Rochester—*alone*—and that was what caused me all the trouble. Eventually, after much listening to his vague rambling talk, I got the hint I needed. He, who, all his life, had traveled alone through wild parts of Asia and Africa, without feeling any fear, after several "little mental earthquakes"—each of which had "shaken him up badly"— had become so afraid of being alone that he had begged his sister to come and stay with him! After getting this information, I soon dug out the details about a series of little strokes. Then I telephoned his secretary, and got from her more details about the man's sudden and marked loss of ability—that had put an end to his usefulness.

THE DOCTOR WHO WAS TOO BUSY TO MAKE AN EASY DIAGNOSIS. One day an able and much overworked internist asked my opinion as to the cause of a woman's puzzling syndrome of great abdominal distress and loss of ability to work. Studies of her abdominal organs had shown nothing abnormal. Noting a slight assymetry of her mouth, I asked, "Did these symptoms of yours come suddenly?" And she said, "Why, yes; I was perfectly well until March 5th, when, at 5 P.M., I fell to the floor, and was 'out' for a few minutes. When I waked, my face was pulled over to one side, and for a few days my hand on that side was clumsy. Ever since then I have been utterly miserable." With this, the doctor asked, "Why didn't you tell me you had had a stroke?" And she answered, "I started to tell you, sir, but, in your hurry, you said, 'Just answer my questions,' and that is what I did."

A family doctor ought to make the diagnosis of a little stroke more easily than does a consultant because for years he knew the man, and hence should be able to see the great change that one day came over him. Obviously, a *family doctor* should more easily recognize a little stroke than does a consultant who is much handicapped by the fact that *he has never seen the man before.* The general practitioner knew the patient so well before the coming of his bad dizzy spell that it should have been easy for him to see the big change that followed an "episode." Also, the family doctor is more likely than is a specialist to talk to the man's wife or perhaps his partner, and thus to learn from them that the poor fellow has become terribly slowed-up. And yet, many a time I have had a nice old family doctor bring me a patient of his with a great dullness which he had failed to notice.

That the family doctor can sometimes make the correct diagnosis from looking at the patient was shown me when I was called in consultation to see a university president, who one morning awoke vomiting, mentally confused, and very ill. Taken to a hospital, he was put through the usual diagnostic mill, and when amoebas were found in his stools, the doctors thought they had made the diagnosis, and gave the man a course of anti-amoebic treatment. When this did no good, the specialists wanted to try another course, but the family demurred. To me, it seemed obvious at a glance that the dull, apathetic, and uncommunicative man before me must have had a severe injury to his brain. When I asked the fine old family doctor about this, he said, Yes, he had noticed the great change in the man's intelligence and had immediately made the diagnosis of a severe "little stroke." A few weeks later the president had a big stroke that ended his days.

But at times even the family doctor can fail to note what he should have seen. One day in 1920, I was called by the busiest general practitioner then in San Francisco to see with him a man of 60 who, for years, had been California's leading corporation attorney. Because the man's main complaint was that of abdominal pain, many x-ray and laboratory studies had been carried out, and nothing wrong had been demonstrated. What I saw instantly was a dull and dying man. When I asked his son when the tremendous change had come, he said that his father had been a brilliant, keen, and wonderfully dynamic man until a day some two weeks before, when twice, while presiding at a big meeting at Yale University, he had fallen out of his chair. After getting home, he wasn't able even to go to his office, let alone to do any work there. He never did any work again, but drifted into a senile dementia. The family physician, who could see no sense at all in my diagnosis of two little strokes, went ahead and removed the man's appendix.

SURGICAL MISTAKES. To show what sometimes happens when a good history is not taken: one day there came into my office a sad-looking, depressed, chronic alcoholic whose wife told me the story of a little stroke which had produced mainly abdominal pain. Because his surgeon did not get the tell-tale story of a few minutes of aphasia (that came just before the first attack of pain) he wasted his time exploring the man's abdomen. He found nothing wrong. I could tell dozens of such stories. An important diagnostic point is that an abdominal pain that is widespread and constant, perhaps for years, is arising in the brain.

A FAMILY THAT WANTED TO SUE A HOSPITAL. An interesting story is that of a man who recently was brought to me. His lawyer told me that the patient's family was going to sue a hospital because in it his client had been badly poisoned by an intravenous injection. Knowing that the patient was the founder and owner of a large general store, I asked his wife when he had changed and become dull and silent, and she said, "Suddenly, when he was poisoned. Since then he hasn't been able to read even the newspaper. He is so unreasonable and irascible that he is a terrible problem to me."

A little more questioning and I learned from the wife that the reason her husband was taken to the hospital was that he had become very ill after a bad woozy spell in which, for a few minutes, he had not been able to talk clearly, and had been weak in one leg! This bit of information was a big surprise to the lawyer. Even he—a layman—could see immediately what that meant. The wife went on to say that at the hospital her husband collapsed while getting the intravenous injection, and after this he lay in a coma for two days.

Fortunately for the man's doctor and the hospital, I was able quickly to get the family to see that the man's serious illness began *before* he received the intravenous injection, and with this they saw that they had no reason to sue.

WHAT I LEARNED FROM MY 10-YEARS' ACQUAINTANCE WITH A VERY ABLE MAN WHO DIED SLOWLY FROM A LONG SERIES OF LITTLE STROKES. I gained my first acquaintance with little strokes in the years from 1901 to 1911, as I watched an able man go down hill to his death with a series of severe little shocks. Each one, when it came, pushed him a bit nearer to the grave. Here was a former Greek scholar and college president—one of the finest orators I ever listened to. In his early years, he had been a charming and lovable Irishman, and a most devoted husband; and then, at the age of 33 years, he had had some sort of a spell which, over-night, changed him and weakened his formerly strong body and mind so much that he had to take a long vacation. Six years later another similar spell knocked him out badly, and six years after that another spell was so devastating that he had to give up his work and take a year's rest. His doctors never made a logical diagnosis.

After his extended vacation, he took another responsible position. Along the way, his wife would tell me of the great mental changes that had come with each of his spells. He had become irritable and irascible, and he had lost his business judgment. With a loss of control of his epiglottis, he used often to choke terribly at mealtimes, and his formerly perfect table manners degenerated. He might drool saliva and talk thickly as many a man does after a big stroke. His children—not knowing that their father's brain was being badly damaged—lost all respect for him.

Formerly a careful dresser, he lost interest in bathing, changing his linen, and keeping his clothes clean and pressed. One evening he went to a meeting in his carpet slippers! His business associates, noticing these things, wondered if he was drinking or taking some drug. Then, he had another atypical stroke that nearly killed him.

In 1909, he had the first spell that convinced me that my diagnosis of little strokes was correct. He woke one morning with a paralyzed leg. Fortunately, in a couple of hours it's strength returned. He worked on until 1911 when he died suddenly of a big stroke.

Very interesting to me was his wife's alarm when on a six-weeks' journey, he never wrote her once! For some men this might not have meant much, but for a devoted husband who had formerly always written every day when on a journey, it meant a great deal.

Another remarkable fact this man's illness taught me: on occasions, when two old cronies of his dropped in for a visit, for two hours he could be his old brilliant and entertaining self; but after his friends left, he would slump. I used to say that he was like a man living in an ill-furnished basement who, with a big enough stimulus, could get up for a while into one of the beautiful parlors upstairs. Also, when this man went to see his physician, during the brief interview, he could be his old charming self. This fact can explain why his doctor never suspected what was wrong. Only members of the family and a few close friends knew the tragedy of the change in the man, and the terrible problems that his wife had to face and struggle with at home.

THE BRAIN-INJURED PATIENT DOES NOT KNOW WHAT A SPECTACLE HE IS MAKING OF HIMSELF. One fact that was enough to convince me that this man had suffered serious damage to his brain was that obviously he did not know what a spectacle he was making of himself when he went out on the street in his untidy state. As I searched the old literature for a mention of little strokes, I found only one or two writers—one of them

Richard Bright (1836)—who mentioned the untidiness of these brain-injured people. In many cases this one feature—a lack of good grooming —is highly diagnostic. I remember a wealthy woman who, after a little stroke, came into my office in old and unsuitable and dirty clothes. She was in an agitated depression.

I remember also when, on two occasions, I met old friends—formerly eminent consultants—who were walking on the street in dirty clothes. One of them was reeking of ammonia due to dribbled urine, and the other had a big urine-stain on his trousers.

3

A Classification of Strokes

A Chinese sage once said so truly that the beginning of wisdom is the the calling of things by their right names. Today, we know, of course, that a stroke can be the result of a hemorrhage, a thrombosis, an embolism, a rupture of a tiny aneurysm, possibly a spasm in a blood vessel, a sudden fall in blood pressure—such as happens when a heart suffers a big coronary infarct or a spell of ventricular fibrillation, or a long Adams-Stokes block. Also, a stroke can be due to an obstruction in an internal carotid or in the basilar artery, or it can be due to a sprinkling of minute hemorrhages, such as are found in cases of a severe hypertensive encephalopathy. Many a bad stroke comes at night during sleep, or it comes during a confinement or the administration of an anesthetic.

In this book I use the term *little stroke* for the brief often dizzy spell that seldom leaves any "neurologic residue," but occasionally affects the person's memory and takes away some of his ability. I use the term *brief stroke* for the episode that starts out as a big stroke, but is gone in a few hours or days. By a *silent stroke* I mean one that comes during sleep, or one that, when it comes during the day, produces no mental distress or (at the time) recognizable symptoms. A *progressing stroke* is one which starts like a little stroke and then keeps getting progressively worse (De Bakey).

I admit that the term little stroke seems inappropriate when a spell leaves the patient a bit of human wreckage, but we need a special term that will show that the man did not have the usual big stroke with an aphasia and a hemiplegia. At times we should use the term *prodromal stroke*. Dr. W. F. Hoyt, in 1963, told of persons who suffer from brief spells of a minute or more in which there is a sudden dimming of vision— a "gray out" which he feels is a common forerunner of a stroke.

DIFFERENT DEGREES OF SEVERITY OF LITTLE STROKES. Nine out of ten of the little strokes I see are so mild that I may not feel sure of the nature of the first dizzy or "tipsy" or vomiting spell, unless I can learn that it was associated with a momentary loss of consciousness, aphasia, weakness in a leg, clumsiness of a hand, or a definite change in memory, character, or ability. Remarkable are the often silent strokes that produce only a sudden big drop in the person's weight, or a quick big drop in his blood pressure, or usher in a long period of severe insomnia.

LACK OF PAIN WITH STROKES. Curious is the lack of pain felt by many persons when they suffer a big or a little stroke. Perhaps this is due to the insensitivity of the substance of the brain (Penfield). Men have told me that when a big stroke suddenly felled them to the ground, they felt only the sudden loss of strength in the arm and leg.

Very interesting was the fact that after an intelligent man of 65 had been chatting with me in my office for a half-hour, and had gotten up to leave, he and I were much surprised when, because of a paralyzed leg, he crashed to the floor. He then said that, as he had sat, he had felt nothing; and certainly, when the brief stroke came, there was no change in his voice, or his facial expression. Fortunately, he recovered in a few minutes and walked out to catch a bus!

SEVERE LITTLE STROKES. A person who has had a severe little stroke may have fallen out of his chair or may have experienced a brief blackout. Next day he may find that he is slow in reading, and when he writes, he leaves out words, or he writes words other than the ones he thought he was writing. His hand-writing may have changed so much that the bank has to send for him to leave with them a new specimen of his signature. For long I have found this story of changed hand-writing pathognomonic of a stroke.

In some cases the man may suddenly get a severe and long-lasting sensation of a burning, or terrible itchiness, or great sensitiveness in some part of his skin, or a lasting pain in his chest.

SOME BRIEF STROKES. R. D. Adams (1954) told of a 78-year-old physician who, one day, suffered aphasia for 20 minutes. It left no residuum. Later, three months before his death, he had trouble with speech for 6 days, and then his right arm became weak. Again he recovered, but, later, he died of angina pectoris. Adams' Case 5 was that of a 65-year-old woman with much hypertension and a diabetes. She had frequent little strokes with dizziness, blurred vision, slight confusion and weakness. The spells lasted from 1 to 5 minutes and cleared, leaving no residual. She had over 50 such spells. Necropsy showed recent softening in the brain stem, the cerebellum and the thalamus. In Adams' Case 8, a 74-year-old woman had had an aphasia, a hemiplegia, and a hemianesthesia on the right, that cleared in 48 hours.

Typical of a brief stroke was a case described by G. W. Pickering (1948). He told of a man of 52, previously well, who while down town, suddenly developed an aphasia and a hemiparesis. Half an hour after reaching his home, *he recovered suddenly,* and for a time thereafter, remained well. Many other men have written of such episodes that ended suddenly about the time the patient reached his home, or a hospital; I have seen a few of them.

LITTLE OR BRIEF STROKES DUE TO OBSTRUCTION IN AN INTERNAL CAROTID, OR A VERTEBRAL, OR THE BASILAR ARTERY

In 1937, and again about 1950, many men became interested in the types of severe little or brief strokes which often come in a series, and which are due to an obstruction in either an internal carotid or a vertebral or the basilar artery. Interestingly, over a century ago, a number of men realized that obstruction of an artery running up through the neck to the brain could cause brief or little strokes. The earliest of such writers that I have found was Richard Bright, who, in 1836, suspected that some of the little strokes he saw were due to obstruction of a carotid, or possibly a vertebral artery.

Drs. Michael E. De Bakey, E. S. Crawford, G. C. Morris, Jr. and D. A. Cooley (1961) quoted W. S. Savory, who, they say, described the case of a young woman with obliteration of the main arteries in both arms and in the left side of the neck.*

Chao, Kwan, Lyman and Loucks (1938) said that during their thorough search of the literature they found articles on obstruction in the neck arteries written as early as 1822. They gave a fine bibliography of the early articles, such as those of J. Yeloly (1822); W. S. Savory (1856); E. Frankel (1880); J. Dejerine and E. Huet (1888); A. R. von Weismayr (1894); A. Hogerstedt (1897); W. Erb (1904); J. S. Roeder (1927); Wüllenweber (1928) and many others.

I have read that F. Penzoldt wrote in 1881; Mehnert had an Inaug. Diss. in 1888, and Lucas had an Inaug. Diss., in 1894. See Brissaud and Massary (1898), Goras (1901), and H. Oppenheim (1911). Chiari (1905) studied 400 necropsied patients, examining the carotids and finding many stenosed. J. R. Hunt (1914) had a splendid article. He pointed out that if the external carotid is obstructed, there is no pulsation in the temporal artery on that side. He spoke of the pallor of the optic disc on the affected side. Osler, in an early edition of his textbook, had a section on thrombosis of the arteries supplying the brain.

---

* Trans. Med. Chir. Soc., London, 39:205, 1856.

Millikan and Siekert (1955) in their fine paper on the carotid artery syndrome gave much of the early literature, quoting W. R. Gowers (1875), L. G. Guthrie and Stephen Magow (1908), and W. B. Cadwalader (1912). Pal (1905) wrote about thrombosis of the basilar artery.

J. B. McMullen (1963), in a most interesting article full of the history of the subject, wrote that Broadbent (1875) recognized trouble in the brain due to disease of the innominate artery.

Splendid, of course, is the paper by Moniz, Almeida and DeLacerda (1937). It may come as a surprise to those who once thought that the internal carotid syndrome was discovered about 1950, to learn that in 1924, in Paris, Moniz gave a most interesting lecture on carotid arteriography, and in 1937, he and his associates were able to report 537 angiographic studies. In 1940, Moniz wrote a big book on the subject in German, and later, he wrote another book in Portuguese.

The Usual Symptoms of Obstruction in an Internal Carotid Artery. On studying many case histories of patients who had had trouble with an internal carotid artery, I soon found that the diagnosis can be strongly suspected when the person tells of a ("stuttering series")—often in close succession—of severe little strokes, perhaps with blindness in one eye, weakness in the opposite hand, and a brief spell of aphasia. Always when I have heard this story, I have sent the patient quickly to an angiologist. The blindness is due probably to the fact that a branch of the carotid artery runs to join the ophthalmic artery. Occasionally, I have been the more suspicious of disease in an internal carotid artery when an ordinary roentgenogram showed marked calcification of the artery where it enters the skull.

In the book on arteriosclerosis recently published by the National Institutes of Health the symptoms of "carotid ischemia" are listed as unilateral weakness, numbness, dysphasia, confusion, ipsilateral monocular blindness, homonymous field defects, headache, and perhaps focal epileptic seizures (see their bibliography). Millikan and Siekert (1955) mentioned homolateral impairment of vision in spells, with a decrease in retinal blood pressure on the side of involvement, and a decreased pulsation of the carotid artery.

Denny-Brown advised making light pressure on the eye-ball of the affected side during an ophthalmologic examination. This may cause the retinal vessels to pulsate, while more pressure will empty them. Manual compression of the unobstructed internal carotid artery on the side of the paralysis will cause blanching of the vessels in the fundus of the opposite eye. See Carter's book on cerebral infarction which is excellent in its description of diagnostic procedures. Groch *et al.* (1960) have used ophthalmodynamometry and palpation of the internal carotid artery in the pharynx—to help in the diagnosis. Van der Drift (1961) doubted the value of such palpation.

Crevasse, Logan and Hurst (1958) said that in their experience with the carotid artery syndrome, they saw a visual disturbance with contralateral hemiplegia in 15 per cent, aphasia in 50 per cent, and no symptoms in 15 per cent. Louis and Lewis (1963) commented on the rarity of an objective sensory loss in cases of thrombosis of the proximal carotid.

Men interested in obstructions of the carotid and vertebral arteries should read the report of Sir Astley Cooper's exhaustive studies on the results of tying these arteries (1836). See also Hunt's (1914, p. 706) remarkable account of the early studies of this subject; also his fine bibliography.

The Great Ability of Some Persons to Stand Obstruction in the Neck Arteries. Kameyama and Okinaka (1963) were surprised at the amount of occlusion one can sometimes find in an internal carotid artery, or even in both carotid arteries, in a person who has not suffered any signs of infarction of any part of the brain. The Japanese workers were much impressed with the often-seen ability of the collateral circulation to protect the brain from injury. However, among 67 patients with severe stenosis in their cervical arteries, 38 suffered "recurrent episodes of cerebral vascular insufficiency," perhaps when there was a drop of their systemic blood pressure.

A most remarkable case is that of David E. Doniger (1963), who wrote about a 48-year-old woman who suffered little in spite of the fact that she had a complete occlusion not only of both her internal carotids but of her basilar artery! For a while she had some visual phenomena, suggesting an episodal bilateral occipital lobe dysfunction, and she had two episodes of right hemiparesis. But each time, without any operation, she quickly recovered, and was left with only a small defect in her visual field. For a while, she had some weakness of her right leg, but this cleared, and soon she was back at work as a choir leader.

Ten years before, at the age of 38, this woman had had 4 attacks of complete blindness during a three-week period. She would black out for from 10 to 15 minutes, and during this time she would feel giddy, and her gait would be unsteady. In two attacks she had some numbness of the right hand, but between episodes, she was free from symptoms. One marvels how a woman like this, after once "blocking up," could go for 10 years without further trouble, and then get by so well after an "episode." One morning she woke with numbness of her entire right side, including her mouth, tongue and the inside of her throat. Her speech was thick, and she had trouble finding words. For a brief time she had incontinence of urine. But in a few weeks she was well.

This one case is sufficient to show what a large amount of obstruction can be found in the neck arteries of a few people, without its having produced symptoms severe and permanent enough to need relief by an operation. Denny-Brown (1951), Lord Brain (Book, 1964) and Kirgis, Llewellyn, and Peebles (1960) pointed out that there are persons who can tolerate a complete occlusion of one internal carotid artery, and who then either go on without any symptoms, or they have them for a while and then recover without treatment. Like Doniger, Kuhn (1960 and 1961) and Groch, Hurwitz and McDowell (1960) found that in some persons *both* internal carotid arteries can be obstructed without the production of much trouble in the brain.

Kirgis *et al.* (1960) studied 300 circles of Willis, and found many peculiarities which may perhaps explain why obstruction of the internal carotid can produce different syndromes, or no symptoms at all. McMullen (1963) quoted Fisher and Friedman (1959) who found obstruction of the internal carotid in 17 children. Denny-Brown (1960) tied one internal carotid artery in monkeys, usually without producing any injury to the brain. Some persons with carotid obstruction will have a series of minor strokes and will then get well, while others can suddenly suffer a big stroke.

In 1963, F. A. Faris, C. M. Poser, D. W. Wilmore, and C. H. Agnew went at the problem in another way; they made angiographic studies of the neck arteries of 43 apparently healthy volunteers in a penitentiary. The men ranged in age from 40 to 65 years. The remarkable fact is that these apparently normal men had about as much carotid atherosclerosis as was found in a group of 68 prisoners with symptoms of cerebrovascular insufficiency. In the two groups there were only slight differences in radiologic abnormalities. As Dr. De Bakey has said, these tolerations of obstruction in the internal carotids are probably due to an excellent collateral circulation (1964, p. 337).

De Bakey, Crawford, Morris, and Cooley (1961) studied 985 patients with signs of occlusive disease in their carotids or other arteries. Lesions were demonstrated in 41 per cent. Operations were performed in 372 cases. Some of the lesions were inoperable. Transient attacks of cerebral ischemia were described by 160 patients, or 43 per cent. There was a "persistent progressive stroke" in 27 patients, or 7 per cent.

Some 47 per cent of these patients with obstructions in extra-cranial arteries had hypertension, and 40 per cent had heart disease. Ninety-three per cent of the patients survived their operation, and 85 per cent were relieved of the symptoms they had had.

Fields, Edward, and Crawford (1961) studied 16 cases of complete occlusion of both internal carotid arteries, and 6 patients continued to enjoy good health. They must have had a good collateral circulation. Soon 7 more cases of double obstruction were found in 179 patients studied.

In the majority of the 280 cases in which the circulation could be restored, there were no more little strokes, and there was relief of, or improvement in, symptoms of neurologic deficit. Complete hemiplegia and aphasia were relieved in some instances (p. 161).

As Drs. Crawford, De Bakey, Blaisdell, Morris, Jr., and Fields (1960, p. 93) said, although extracranial occlusive lesions may be shown in 40 per cent of patients with cerebral arterial insufficiency, the "functional significance of these lesions *may be doubtful*, except in the more advanced cases." Very important is the statement that lesions that block less than half of the artery lumen did not produce obstruction. Hence, Dr. De Bakey (in 1960) believed in operating only when there was more than 50 per cent obstruction.

Naturally, in the face of such observations, some workers in this field have lost some of their early enthusiasm, and have concluded that they must use more caution in interpreting some of the radiologically demonstrated slight arterial narrowings. Unless wisdom is used, the operation may not work the desired miracle.

Drs. S. Louis and B. Lewis (1963) concluded that disease of the middle cerebral artery is more likely to produce injury to the brain than is disease in the internal carotid artery. See also G. T. Hultquist (1942), who studied the carotids in 1300 necropsied persons. O'Doherty (1963) studied the collateral channel between the external and internal carotid arteries by way of the ophthalmic artery.

ANGIOGRAPHY. According to Fields, Crawford, and De Bakey (1959) 16 per cent of patients with a stroke, studied with angiography, were found to have occlusion of a carotid artery, while Millikan, Siekert and Whisnant (1958) found "intermittent insufficiency of a carotid artery" in 85 out of 317 patients studied, or about 26 per cent. Gurdjian *et al.* (1960) thought that 30 per cent of the patients studied had occlusion in the arteries of the neck, and Groch, Hurwitz, Wright and McDowell (1960) found carotid occlusion in 16 per cent. Fisher (1952) found many cases of occlusion of the internal carotid. Newton, Adams and Wylie (1964) found some obstruction in 35 per cent.

Of late, a number of men have been warning against the indiscriminate making of angiographic studies, especially in those cases in which little is likely to be learned that will help the physician in deciding as to treatment, and will make the treatment better and more likely to work a cure. See Sir Francis Walshe (1963); John Agate (1963); and Denny-Brown (1960 and 1961).

The dangers of angiography were well described by Newton, Adams and Wylie (1964). Moniz (1924) told of his early difficulties with spasm produced by the injection of the contrast material. See the discussion of this by Raynor and Ross (1960). Some men, like Newton, Adams and

Wylie (1964) said thcy had performed hundreds of arteriographies without disaster.

BEDSIDE DIAGNOSIS CAN OFTEN BE GOOD. A number of men have written to say that by taking a good history and carefully examining the patient a neurologist can usually make a good diagnosis at the bedside. There he can do a good job of localizing the lesion in the brain, in perhaps 8 in 10 cases. See S. N. Groch, L. J. Hurwitz, I. S. Wright, and F. McDowell (1960), A. B. Baker, Millikan (1958, p. 434), and O'Doherty (1963).

In 1958, Millikan said he was not much in favor of using angiography in cases of cerebral infarction. Fisher (1961) said that he did not use arteriography routinely; but said—doubtless with a twinkle in his eye— "I am always glad to look at other persons' films."

Wright and McDevitt (1954) were not much in favor of angiography because "It is of little or no value in the study of hemorrhage, thrombosis, or embolism, and is not without risk." Sir Charles Symonds (1959) said that in cases of hemiplegia, angiography has little value, and it has dangers. Other men have felt that with modern methods, and when using a small dose of the contrast chemical, there is but little danger, especially when the patients are well chosen. (See Van der Drift, 1961.)

Is IT HEMORRHAGE OR THROMBOSIS? Aring and Merritt (1935) wrote an excellent article on the differential diagnosis between cerebral hemorrhage and cerebral thrombosis. They studied 245 cases of patients who came to necropsy, and thought that the diagnosis could nearly always be made from the history. They found hemorrhage in from 40 to 50 per cent. There was immediate unconsciousness in 51 per cent with hemorrhage, but in only 32 per cent with thrombosis. Coma on admission was seen in 68 per cent of patients with hemorrhage and in 39 per cent of patients with thrombosis. Stiffness of the neck was seen in 55 per cent of patients with hemorrhages and 7 per cent of those with thromboses. Some 50 per cent of the patients with hemorrhage died in 4 days as did 28 per cent of the patients with big thromboses.

Merritt and Aring (1938) reported finding convulsions at onset in 14 per cent of patients with hemorrhages, but in only 8 per cent of patients with thromboses, and in 9 per cent of patients with embolism. Sir Charles Symonds (1959) said that an immediate loss of consciousness is twice as common with hemorrhage as with thrombosis. As was to be expected, hypertension was twice as common in cases of hemorrhage. More common in cases of hemorrhage were vomiting, Kernig's sign, dilation of the pupil opposite the lesion, conjugate deviation of the eyes, bilateral Babinski, leukocytosis, and bilateral absence of the light reflex.

Adams and Cohen (1947, p.268) wrote well on the differential diagnosis, and the correlating of symptoms with the site of the lesion. Groedel and Hubert (1925) thought that the diagnosis of hemorrhage is usually easy. They spoke of episodes—possibly of little strokes—in which the commonest symptom is dizziness. On p. 1024, they described a brief stroke.

Symptoms of different types of strokes. Excellent summaries of information in regard to the symptoms observed with different types of strokes were supplied by Critchley (1930) who studied especially the strokes due to obstruction of the anterior cerebral artery; see also, Adams and Van der Eecken (1958), C. M. Fisher (1955 and 1958), and Holtzman, Panin and Ebel (1959).

The symptoms of involvement of the middle cerebral artery may be headache, numbness, paralysis or paresis of the contralateral side, difficulty in speaking, hemianopia, and confusion. Hemiparetic signs occurring repeatedly on the same side of the body suggest a hemispheral deficit. Difficulty in talking is a hemispheral sign; numbness of the face, diplopia, vertigo, deafness, nystagmus, dysarthria, and dysphagia indicate brain stem dysfunction. Bilateral tract signs suggest brain stem localization with a non-hemorrhagic stroke. Hemianopsia suggests impedance in the internal carotid artery, or in a branch distal to the ophthalmic artery, or in one posterior cerebral artery. Complete blindness suggests that the impairment is in the flow via the basilar artery to both posterior cerebrals.

Millikan said he tended to diagnose thrombosis in the brain when he learned of prodromal episodes with recovery or improvement; also when consciousness was not lost, or when there was quick improvement.

OBSTRUCTION OF THE BASILAR ARTERY OR THE VERTEBRALS. Kubik and Adams (1946) found that when the basilar artery is obstructed, common symptoms are confusion, coma, headache, dysarthria, dysphagia, pupillary abnormalities, ocular palsy, facial palsy, hemiplegia, quadriplegia, and a bilateral Babinski. See also Duffy and Jacobs (1958) and Millikan and Siekert (1955), Van der Drift (1961), and an excellent paper by O'Doherty (1963). He said that aphasia is never present with an uncomplicated basilar obstruction. Transient blindness is common. See Sir Charles Symonds & Mackenzie (1957) The mortality rate is from 60 to 75 per cent.

Denny-Brown (1960) said that with occlusion of a vertebral artery, "There may be periodic visual blackouts, and spells of mental confusion, dizziness, weakness of limbs, and loss of consciousness.

Critchley (1931, Lancet) wrote a splendid article on the "cerebellar syndrome."

RUPTURED ANEURYSMS. A good article on ruptured aneurysms affecting the brain is by Schneck (1964), who studied 105 cases. He quoted extensive work by G. W. Pickering (1961). See Denny-Brown (1960).

INFLUENCE OF THE CAROTID SINUS. Ferris, Capps and Weiss (1937) published an excellent summary of what was then known about the effect of the carotid sinus on blood pressure, and on the physiology of the body. They said that permanent changes in blood pressure cannot be produced by denervating the sinus.

Kety (1950) found that a highly sensitive carotid sinus can cause syncope, perhaps by intense vasoconstriction. According to a very interesting paper by Engel, Romano and McLin (1944) an overly sensitive carotid sinus can cause syncope with vasodepression.

In 1946, J. M. Askey reported 7 instances in which a contralateral hemiplegia followed pressure made by the examiner on a carotid sinus. Engel (1950) in his book on "Fainting," spoke of the sometimes hypersensitivity of a carotid sinus. A splendid article is by Soma Weiss and J. P. Baker (1933). They felt that disease in the sinus does not produce hypertension, but it can cause a dizziness and fainting. They supplied a big bibliography. An exhaustive study of the carotid sinus was made by Ask-Upmark (1935). Foster Kennedy, S. B. Wortis and Herman Wortis (1938, p. 672) saw a young man who was having syncopal spells. He was cured with the removal of an old TB lymph node just over his carotid sinus. See Bouckaert and Heymans (1933) on carotid sinus reflexes.

There has appeared of late much literature on the operative removal of the carotid sinus for the cure of asthma. This has been done in thousands of cases. A number of men in the United States greatly question the value of the operation. The craze started in Japan, and one Japanese author has said that the craze is over in his country.

Daniel Silverman discussed the use of "serial electroencephalography" in distinguishing brain tumors from cerebrovascular accidents, and concluded that the difference is not always easy to show. Some men say one can often learn much from a scout film of the brain; some use "scanning," and some use ultrasound.

4

Many Names for Little, Brief, Silent, and Prodromal Strokes

This chapter is, in some ways, the most important in the book; but I suggest that it be only glanced at long enough so that the reader can be a bit horrified, and so that he will say, "How silly we were to pile up some 170 names for the little strokes. How wonderful if now we could all agree on a few simple—and preferably English—terms, and then use these in library indexes."

One big objection to the present-day jargon and Tower of Babel is that patients hate to be given a name for their disease that means nothing to them. Hundreds of letters from patients tell me that this makes for bad public relations. A patient is so much happier when his physician talks to him in simple English which he can understand. Imagine the bafflement of a German patient who has been told that he is suffering from "Pseudoapoplektische und pseudoembolische cerebrale Zirculationstörungen auf ischämischer Basis!" (as advocated by Groedel and Huber, 1925). One man has designed some very ingenious names, such as "transient ischemia with stable residual—brief neurologic dysfunction with persistence of minor subjective or objective neurologic deficits!"

Here are some of the terms used in the past, and some that are used today:

Shocks
Little shocks
Transient intermittent focal attacks of cerebral insufficiency and ischemia (Donald Macrae)
C. V. A. (cerebro-vascular accident)
Minor C. V. A.'s
C. B. S. (chronic brain syndrome)
T. I. A. (transient ischemic attack) (John Marshall, 1964, and C. Miller Fisher, 1965)

Short periods of weakness
Small blackouts
Episodes
Ischemic spells, or temporary ischemias, or ischemic anoxias
Chronic brain syndrome associated with cerebral arteriosclerosis
Brain damage
Transient attacks (Osler)
Transient attacks of aphasia in states of high blood pressure and arteriosclerosis
(Osler)
Transient aphasias of hypertensive people (Osler and Vaquez)
Transient cerebral strokes (Rothenberg and Corday, 1957)
Transient cerebral ischemia (De Bakey)
Transient strokes (Corday, Rothenberg and Wiener)
An ischemic episode due to cerebral vasospasm of sympathetic nerve origin
Recurrent ischemic cerebral attacks (Adams, 1956)
Transient cerebral ischemic episodes (Soderman, 1961)
Transient cerebral paralyses (George Parker, 1909)
Transient arterial spasms
Transient dysphasias or dysarthrias
Transient aphasias
Transient hemiparesis
Transient encephalopathy (J. Marshall and D. A. Shaw, 1959)
Transient cerebral crises and seizures (Heard, 1910)
Transient cerebral syndromes (Editorial writer in Annals of Internal Med.,
1952)
Intravascular cranial syndromes (J. A. Resch, 1964)
Acute cerebral ischemia (J. F. Fazekas, 1964)
Ischemic cerebral deterioration (J. F. Fazekas, 1964)
Transitory ischemia (J. F. Fazekas, 1964)
Infarct with progressive improvement—acute (J. F. Fazekas, 1964)
Infarct with progressive improvement—acute severe neurologic deficits with
appreciable continuing recovery
Infarct with progressive deterioration—increasing neurologic dysfunction after
severe ischemic episode
Infarct with stable residual—severe ischemic cerebral dysfunction with some
subsequent return of function, but with persisting neurologic deficits.
Diffuse ischemic cerebral deterioration—progressive intellectual impairment or
behavioral disturbance
Transitory ischemia with progressive deterioration—increasing disability after
each repeated episode of acute cerebral dysfunction
Transitory ischemic attacks (C. M. Fisher)
Transitory cerebral attacks (Fisher and Cameron, 1953)
Transitory cerebral paralyses (Sir G. W. Pickering, 1948)
Transitory phenomena preceding the onset of a stroke (Miller Fisher and
D. G. Cameron, 1953)
Transitory hemiplegias (H. W. Fleming, and H. C. Naffziger, 1927)
Transitory and larval forms of cerebral episodes (T. Clifford Allbutt, 1915)

Transitory paralyses (H. Jackson, 1880)
Transitory apoplectic phenomena (Trousseau, 1885)
Little apoplexies
Minor apoplexies
Capillary apoplexies (Charcot, 1868)
Attaques apoplectiformes (Charcot, 1886)
Apoplectiform spells
Apoplectiform attacks
Phénoménones apoplectiques subits et transitoires (Trousseau, 1885)
Multiple little apoplexies
Ictus apoplectique
Spells of transient congestive apoplexy (Maclachlan, 1863)
Congestive apoplexy (Maclachlan, 1863)
Mild apoplexies (Westphal, 1926)
Leichte Apoplexia (K. Westphal, 1926)
Pseudoapoplexia (Groedel and Hubert, 1925)
Apoplectic accidents, sudden and momentary (Trousseau, 1885)
Apoplectic Insults (Krehl, 1907; also Pal, 1931)
Irregular apoplectic attacks due not to hemorrhage or embolism (Griswold, 1884)
Congestion cerebrale apoplectiforme (Trousseau, 1885)
Intermittent insufficiency of the cerebral arterial circulation (Kinnier Wilson, 1941; P. W. Clough, 1958)
Common intermittent cerebral ischemias (W. R. Brain)
Acute intermittent insufficiency of cerebral vessels (C. H. Millikan, *et al.*, 1955)
Intermittent insufficiency in the vertebral-basilar system (Millikan, Siekert and Whisnant, 1958)
The syndrome of intermittent insufficiency of the carotid arterial system (Millikan and Siekert, 1955)
Intermittent claudication of the psychic apparatus (J. Grasset, 1906)
Intermittent arterial spasm (Priestly Smith, 1909)
Intermittent ischemic episodes (McDevitt, Carter, Gatje, Foley and Wright, 1958)
Intermittent narrowing of the internal carotid artery
Intermittent closing of a cerebral artery (Osler, 1909; also Moorhead, 1909; Wm. Russell, 1909; also Priestley Smith)
Intermittent cerebral insufficiency (Arnold Lieberman)
Cerebral intermittent claudication of the brain (Leri)
Arteries that broke (A. G. Ellis, 1909)
Silent strokes (W. M. Johnson, 1961)
Vascular crises (James Collier; also Pal, 1905)
Spells of confusion
Spells of bewilderment (Stengel, 1908)
Recurrent focal cerebral ischemias
Prodromes (H. H. Tooth, 1911)
Cerebral shocks (J. Hughlings Jackson, 1880)

"Repeated mental storms"
Fleeting cerebral accidents
Brain accidents
Pip-strokes (a British layman's ancient term)
Cerebral surprises (Trousseau, 1885)
Sudden cerebral lesions (Gowers, 1907)
Recurrent focal cerebral ischemic attacks (Van der Drift, 1961)
Momentary blockings in the brain
Minor episodes in the course of a cerebral arteriosclerosis
A small brain shock
Thromboses of cerebral arterioles
Multiple thromboses
Lacunar infarcts (M. Fisher)
Temporary angiospasms
Inadequacy of the cerebral circulation
Prolonged extreme contraction of cerebral arteries
Hypertensive encephalopathy
Multiple and transient strokes
Hirnerschütterung
Schlaganfall
"Stuttering onset" (Miller Fisher, 1951)
Thorem, a term coined for use when the differential diagnosis cannot be made
    between thrombosis and embolism
Syndrome of malignant hypertension
Subacute cerebral infarctions
Minor epilepsies (Trousseau)
Incipient thrombosis (Lundie, 1906)
Cerebral crises (Osler; also Ed. Rosenberg, 1940)
Hemodynamic crises which precede infarction (Denny-Brown, 1951)
Recurrent cerebrovascular episodes (Denny-Brown, 1960)
Vascular insufficiency (Denny-Brown, 1960)
Cerebral vascular insufficiency (Corday, Rothenberg, and Putnam)
Thromboses in evolution (C. M. Fisher)
Periodic transient episodes of vasospasm (Fisher and Cameron, 1953)
Accidents fugitifs (Leri, 1906)
Accidents cérébraux fugaces (F. Bremer, 1928)
Les petits signes de l'arteriosclerose (Josué, 1907)
Fleeting pareses (Westphal, 1926)
Regionären Gefasskrisen (D. Westphal)
Progressive arteriosclerotic psychoses (J. H. W. Rhein, Winkelman and Patten,
    1928)
Mental storms (J. H. W. Rhein *et al.*)
Arteriopathic neurasthenia (Kinnier Wilson, 1941)
Hypertonic contraction of cerebral blood vessels (W. Russell)
Severe little strokes (Sir G. W. Pickering, 1948)
Les spasmes vasculaires (Riser, Meriel and Planques, 1931)
Commotio cerebri (Krehl, 1907)

Cerebral insults (Krehl, 1907; also Pal, 1931)
Contusio cerebri (M. Staemmler)
Episodes of insufficiency (McDevitt, Carter, Gatje, Foley, and Wright, 1958)
Strokes in evolution (Millikan, Siekert and Whisnant, (1958)
Hemodynamic crises (Foley, 1956)
Prodromal episodes (C. H. Millikan, 1958)
Recurrent cerebral ischemic attacks (C. H. Millikan, 1958)
Vascular spasms (F. Bremer, 1928)
Vertiginous attacks (Jelliffe and White)
Recurrent symptoms of cerebral dysfunction (K. W. Sheldon)
Temporary arterial spasm (Langwill, 1906)
Acute cerebral episodes (B. S. Oppenheimer and A. M. Fishberg, 1928)
Pseudo-uremia (Volhard and Farr)
Angiospastic disturbance of circulation (Volhard)
Thrombo-embolic episodes (McDevitt, Carter, Gatje, Foley and Wright, 1958)
Rapidly regressive motor or sensory attacks in cerebral atherosclerosis (T. Alajouanine *et al.* 1960)
Acute localized brain anemia (George Parker, 1909)
Recurrent ischemic cerebral attacks (R. D. Adams, 1956)
Slight focal vascular disturbance of the brain (Adams and Cohen, 1947)
Hysterical (?) hemiplegia (Grossmann, 1902)
Progressive arteriosclerotic dementia (Rhein, Winkelman and Patten, 1928)
Brain damage (Lowenthal and Maringer, 1957)
Multiple and transient strokes (Marshall and Shaw, 1959)
Minor cerebral thrombotic episodes (D. C. Wallace, 1964)
Completed strokes (Shenkin, Heft and Somach, 1965)
Incipient stroke (Whisnat)
R I N D (reversible ischemic neurological deficit) (Louis Boshes, 1965)

5

The Symptoms of Little Strokes

A SUDDEN ONSET. A sudden onset is one of the commonest happenings and often the most diagnostic symptom. If this history is not obtained the diagnosis will probably be missed.

CONFUSION. During a few small strokes the person is so confused he may, for some minutes, be unable to move. If he is crossing a busy street he will stand out in the stream of traffic until someone leads him to safety on the sidewalk.

DIZZINESS, OR A SUPPOSED MENIÈRE SYNDROME. As I must keep saying, a dizzy spell which comes to a person past 50 is not likely to be due to Menière's disease: it is surely not Menière's disease when the hearing is normal in both ears, and it is still more surely not Menière's when, with the dizzy spell, there came a brief spell of aphasia, or diplopia, or numbness of an arm.

With some little strokes there can come, of course, some deafness, and there can come much ear noise. One man told me that "suddenly a boiler factory started up in my head."

In 1906 Emil Amberg wrote a splendid article on all the many causes for pseudo-Menière's disease. Every physician ought to read Amberg occasionally: also, Dr. Henry Williams' translation of Menière's book.

An important point is that in most cases of little strokes the world is not spinning around—the distress is more a feeling of a loss of good balance, or of equilibrium, or of position in space. It is a very frightening feeling that the person is going to be flung about. In my own case, it is often a vivid feeling that my bed or chair is going to turn upside down and throw me either on the floor, or up against the ceiling. If I had ever had such a spell while on the street I am almost certain I would have fallen flat.

SPELLS OF VOMITING OR NAUSEA. Many a person who suffers a little stroke vomits with it. Rarely, he will keep vomiting for a few hours or even two or three days. Neurologists have located a certain place in the back of the brain-stem where a vascular injury can produce vomiting. I knew a woman who, for six years, kept having little strokes with vomiting. At necropsy, her brain was full of black spots. Some people, after a little stroke, suffer much from nausea.

A LITTLE STROKE OFTEN INJURES THE PERSON'S MEMORY. What often puzzles me greatly is how a little stroke, which caused the man neither numbness nor paralysis, nor even a slight "neurologic deficit," could have left him with a brain so damaged that "much of his memory left him." I remember well the eminent college president who used to pride himself on being able to recognize and name on sight most of his old students. One morning, on waking from sleep, he soon realized that so much of his memory was gone that he could not recall the name even of his housekeeper! I had him examined by an eminent neurologist who, refusing to believe what the man said, reported "nothing wrong." He outraged the patient by telling him he had just become too fussy about his health! In this case the area of brain destroyed would seem to have been small, and yet the damaging effect on the man's storage of memory was very distressing to him, and it did not show signs of clearing up.

Some weeks later, while at dinner, the man felt a "slap" on his left cheek and soon found that he could not feel his cigar when it was in the left corner of his mouth. Interestingly, because the neurologist could now detect this area of anesthesia with his pin, this time he accepted the evidence, and agreed with the patient and with me that there had been a little stroke! But the doctor still refused to accept the man's statement that, with his first stroke, his memory was so badly damaged that he was going to have to quit work.

The strange feature about the loss of memory after a little stroke is that while the patient cannot quickly remember the name of the old friend he would like to introduce to someone, he may be able to remember easily and quickly a hundred thousand scientific facts, and the meaning of thousands of words in several languages besides his own.

INABILITY TO WORK. Quite a few persons who suffer a little stroke are so disabled mentally that they either stop going to work or they go to their office and there get nothing done.

INCREASED IRRITABILITY. A common change noticed in persons who have had a little stroke is an increase in irritability; perhaps an abnormal irascibility, and a great impatience with annoyances.

I can remember one man—the owner of a business—who, after a little stroke, said he was distressed over his irascibility. He said that by unjustly bawling out his old and faithful employees, he was driving some of them out of the business, and this was worrying him.

CHANGES IN CHARACTER. A few hundred times a wife has told me that on a certain day she "lost" her old husband and lover, and got, in his place, a stranger who was "ornery" and difficult, and a sore trial to her. In a few cases the wife had to leave the man. Often, the fellow disgusted her with his strange new ways, as by his not bathing, not changing his clothes, not keeping clean, and perhaps by his changing for the worse in some of his sexual habits.

I remember a distinguished banker who was the leading layman in his big church. One day, after a bad dizzy spell in which he nearly fell down, he disappeared, and detectives had to go out and hunt for him. They found him in a distant city living with a prostitute. His stroke would seem to have changed him completely.

President Wilson's changes in character. My old and very interesting friend, Dr. Thewlis once told me of a day when he was in Paris, and had dropped in to visit President Wilson. It turned out to be the sad day when the President had wakened with a little stroke so destructive that it had made of him a changeling with a very different personality, and a markedly lessened ability. Dr. Thewlis said Dr. Wilson told him that that morning when he got up, his hand was so shaky he could not shave himself. At the time the doctors were reporting that he had a cold, but recently I received a letter from Gene Smith, who wrote a splendid Life of Wilson (*When the Cheering Stopped,* Morrow, 1964), in which he told me that Dr. Grayson said he knew that the President had had several little strokes—some of them before he left for Paris. Incidentally, Gene Smith's book should be read by every physician who would like to understand what little and big strokes can do to a man.

In Paris, Ike Hoover, the White House butler, immediately saw that, after the bad morning, his Chief was a very different man. As Hoover wrote later, the President, who before that had always been kind and thoughtful of the comfort of those around him, suddenly became crabbed, difficult, unreasonable, and fussy. He immediately fired his closest friend, Col. House—thinking him a spy. Wilson thought the Embassy was filled with spies.

As we all know, in the few years that followed, Wilson died slowly with one little stroke after another. One fairly big one hit him one day as he was giving an important speech. At the moment, I happened to be listening over the radio, and immediately, with the change in the man's voice, and with his hesitation, I sensed what had happened.

My old and always well-informed friend, Dr. Alonzo Taylor, once told me that some time before the little strokes began to hit Wilson, Dr. De Schweinitz, the famous ophthalmologist, told Taylor that he was worried over the serious changes he had seen in the retinas of the then-president of Princeton, showing that his arteries were beginning to go bad.

I sometimes felt sure that President Franklin Roosevelt had just had some little strokes, and one day when he was giving a speech, some physicians who were with me felt as I did, that a little artery had plugged up in his brain. Certainly, the picture taken of the gaunt President with a sweater around his shoulders, as he sat between Stalin and Churchill, suggested an arteriosclerotic man close to death.

We all know that President Eisenhower, one day, had a brief mild aphasia—a typical little stroke, which, fortunately, did not leave a bad residue.

Loss of Good Judgment. Many people, after a little stroke, lose their good judgment about many things. I remember a patient of mine—president of a big Life Insurance Company—who had quickly to be retired when, after a little stroke, he wanted to lend large sums of money without adequate security. I have seen many cases like this in which the man should have been declared incompetent, but wasn't, because his family could not bear to take so unpleasant a step.

An example of the loss of judgment a man may suffer after a little brain injury was that of an able realtor who, after 3 little strokes outraged his partner by selling a house for half of what it was worth. The brain-injured man said that, on religious principles, he had sold it for exactly what it had cost him many years before!

Mental and moral degenerations. One of the most remarkable stories about little strokes was told me by a young woman who said that after two or three bad dizzy spells, her father, at 50, had become more or less of an idiot. In the big business which he had built, his sons could no longer trust him to do anything. Formerly, a cultured gentleman, he began to spit all over his house; he ate like a pig, and he would urinate in the back yard where the neighbors could see him. In many ways he was like a decerebrate animal. The only thing he could do that required any intelligence was to play cribbage. He lived on in this way for 30 years, making a nervous wreck of the daughter who took care of him. A wealthy old man I knew, a bachelor, some months before his death disinherited his siblings and married his disgusting scrub-woman.

Loss of All Interest in Life and in Loved Ones. Anyone who will read some of the histories recorded in this book will note that in case after case one of the most striking features about the illness was the patient's sudden loss of all of his old interests and loves and joys. Commonly, after a little stroke, a woman will not even ask about her formerly adored grandchildren. A formerly sociable person will not want to see old friends and cronies. Certainly, no physician should ever disregard this highly significant symptom.

SUDDEN AGING. Often a wife, when asked about her husband's aging, will say, "That's right; after that peculiar spell of his, he very quickly changed—mentally and physically and sexually—into an old man."

AN INABILITY TO THINK CLEARLY. Many people, after a little stroke, if they are asked about their thinking, will say that they have trouble thinking clearly, and organizing their thoughts. They are easily confused, and puzzled and flustered.

FEELINGS OF GREAT FATIGUE. Many persons, after one or more little strokes, complain mainly of feelings of great fatigue. This may come in spells.

A TENDENCY TO WRITE ERRATICALLY. As I have said, after many a stroke, an intelligent person will complain that when he writes a letter long-hand, he must check it carefully, because words will be left out, or he will find that here and there he wrote a word different from the one he intended to write, or thought he had written. In his book, "Episode," my friend Eric Hodgins remarked that after he had largely recovered from his big stroke, "It was disconserting to try to set down one word only to wind up with quite another." Also, Hodgins found he no longer could use his beloved typewriter. I tell in this book of another professional writer who, after a little stroke, could no longer use all her 10 fingers in typing.

With a severe injury to his brain, a man's writing will be so changed that the bank has to send for him to leave a new signature; and with another severe injury, the writing can become "jiggly," tremulous, or serrated, like that of an old man.

OVER-EMOTIONALISM. Often after a little stroke, the person is so overly-emotional that he will cry, much against his will. I remember a woman who, after a little stroke, felt outraged because every so often—much against her will—she cried, when she was not at all unhappy! Actually, many people who cry after a stroke should be depressed as they face the possibility that life for them will never be perfectly comfortable or desirable again.

FEAR OF BEING ALONE. I always suspect a little stroke when a person who formerly was fearless, after one or two peculiar spells, becomes fearful of being left alone. Perhaps the person is afraid of being suddenly so crippled by a stroke that he cannot reach the phone to summon help. Actually, I tell in this book of a man of 70, who spent a cold night on his bath-room floor, clad only in his pajamas. Another man got a little stroke while in the bath-tub, and could not get out. The mother of one of my patients (who insisted on living alone) spent two days and nights on the floor, until her daughter came to see why she did not answer the phone. One man in the tub turned on the hot water; then got a little stroke which made it impossible for him to turn it off. And so he nearly boiled until someone heard his screams and came to help him.

WAKING IN THE MORNING WITH MUCH ILLNESS. One would expect that with our blood pressure dropping markedly at night, most little strokes should come while we are asleep, and often this is the case. See Dickinson and Thomson (1960) and Denny-Brown. Occasionally, a man will tell me that he woke one morning with "a head on him," as if he had been drinking hard the night before. On reaching his office he found he had lost some of his memory and some of his old skills.

DIFFICULTIES IN SWALLOWING, WITH CHOKING AND VIOLENT COUGHING. Small and perhaps transient difficulties in swallowing are common after little strokes. Because of a poor control of the epiglottis, food will "go down the wrong way" to cause much choking and violent coughing at table. The patient may have trouble starting swallowing, unless he has water or food in his mouth.

Once I saw a friend—a distinguished physician—suddenly lose his ability to swallow. For the rest of his days (about 6 months) he had to live with a tube in his esophagus. Another friend who woke to find swallowing very difficult, lived only a week. Others who woke unable to swallow well recovered slowly.

POOR GROOMING: "SOUP ON THE COAT." As I have said, one of the most diagnostic symptoms of a severe little, or silent, stroke is poor grooming. A tendency to go out on the street, poorly shaved, dirty, and unkempt.

STICKY AND ROPY SALIVA IN THE THROAT. Ropiness of saliva should always suggest a bulbar injury.

BURNING TONGUE, AND OTHER DISTRESSES IN THE MOUTH. I must have seen 1,000 persons past middle age complaining of a burning tongue which had failed to yield to scores of injections of vitamin B. Often I could get the history of a little stroke, and occasionally that of a big stroke. I never saw such burning helped by vitamins or mouth washes. In some cases the burning is felt on only one side of the tongue.

Sometimes there are other distresses in the mouth. For instance; a retired secretary of 61, with a marked hypertension, said that three years before I saw her, she had wakened with a dry feeling on the end of her tongue, which then spread all over her mouth, until it became very distressing, and constant—day after day. She had trouble also in starting to swallow. The trouble was not due to a lack of saliva. Some of these people will say their mouth feels puckered as if they had eaten a green persimmon.

Others, after a little stroke, complain of a hot feeling in the palate, or a "sand-paper lining," or a "furry lining," to their mouth. Many say that for a day or two after a dizzy spell they kept biting their tongue so severely that big red ulcers formed. Evidently, a nervous center that normally keeps the tongue away from the teeth was not working well. Other persons, for a day or two, bite their upper lip.

VILE TASTE IN THE MOUTH. A stout man, aged 55, after what he thought were several little strokes, suffered much with a bad taste. This was so distressing that he used to get up several times a night to wash out his mouth. He had no trouble swallowing, but a feeling as if food was regurgitating from the upper third of his esophagus. At times he drooled from the right corner of his mouth.

Once, when driving his car, he suddenly felt a drawing in both arms and hands so disturbing that he had to go quickly to the side of the road and stop. Later, again while driving, he had another little shock. His hands went to sleep, and he got severe cramps in his abdomen. Another spell took away much of his memory. A while later he was found to have a thrombosis of a blood vessel in his eye.

A woman of 50 said that for 18 months, off and on, she had had a vile acid taste in her mouth. She woke one morning with it. It is interesting to note that in this case some men said it was due to the menopause; some, to a colonic diverticulosis; some, to abdominal adhesions; some, to a sinusitis; and some, to an allergy. A surgeon wanted to remove her gallbladder on general principles. Unusual in this woman's case was the fact that the bad taste tended to come and go, which is hard to explain. Her husband said he could always tell by glancing at her face when she had it. With it, she always looked as if she were in pain.

INABILITY TO WEAR DENTURES. A curious and rare story is that of a man who, right after a little stroke, could no longer wear his dentures. His hand-writing got so bad he had to get his sister to write his checks for him. One morning he woke with a terrible headache and the loss of some of his ability to hear. Later, he had a brief spell of semi-consciousness.

LOSS OF SMELL. A fairly common symptom of a little stroke is a sudden loss of the sense of smell, perhaps with a loss of the sense of taste. According to Ferrier (1880) this loss of the sense of smell can be in one side of the nose. I cannot remember ever having heard of this, but I doubt if I ever asked about such a unilateral loss. In one of Ferrier's cases, the sense of taste was lost on one side of the tongue, and hearing became defective in the ear on that side. Grasset (1906) described little strokes followed by a loss of taste and smell.

ANNOYING SMELL; WOMEN WHO THINK THEY SMELL BAD. C. M. Fisher (1958) saw a person with a thrombosis of the basilar artery which brought a complaint of smelling a pungent odor. I saw a woman who complained bitterly that after a little stroke the odor of her perspiration distressed her terribly.

Occasionally, elderly women (practically always unmarried) will complain of smelling bad. No one else around them will be able to smell anything wrong. All of these women I have seen were probably psychotic. One who came with her husband was a paranoiac, as were her two sisters.

THICKNESS, OR SLURRING, OR HESITATION, OF SPEECH. Occasionally, for a few days or months after a little stroke, the person's speech will be thick, "mushy," slurring, or hesitant. Sometimes a secretary will say that one day, at a certain moment, she knew that her boss had had a little stroke because his voice changed in quality, or his dictation did not make sense.

One day a woman of 52, whom I had known for years, came in talking squeakily like a boy of 14 whose voice was changing. At the same time that her voice changed, she had much trouble swallowing. A few months later she died, and an autopsy showed lesions in her bulb.

SUDDEN LOSS OF WEIGHT. Commonly, after a little stroke, a new homeostatic setting seems to be made somewhere in the brain; and with this, the person rapidly loses from 20 to 90 pounds, *and then goes on at the new level.*

I remember well the previously stout mother-in-law of a physician friend of mine who, at the age of 57, suddenly lost 60 pounds. The significant thing was that she still looked and felt well, and had no distress anywhere. She had not changed her dietary habits. I knew this woman for several years after that, and her weight remained at the new level.

In these cases, the patient does not look cachectic, and hence the physician should suspect a stroke, and not a cancer. Also, the person may have no indigestion or abdominal pain; and the red blood sedimentation rate may remain low. I have seen this sort of sudden loss of weight also in the cases of many persons who had a big stroke. For instance; my over-weight mother-in-law, after a brief attack of aphasia and hemiplegia, with no change in diet, quickly lost 90 pounds. In the next 6 years in which she lived, her weight remained stabilized at the new level.

SHARP SUDDEN DROP IN BLOOD PRESSURE. A remarkable sign that strongly suggests that the person has had a little stroke is a sharp drop in a previously high blood pressure. I have seen a high pressure drop to normal and stay there. This phenomenon with little strokes has been described by several writers. It occurs also with big strokes.

SUDDEN BRIEF SPELL OF WEAKNESS IN A LEG, OR A TEMPORARY LIMP. I have seen persons whose little stroke produced an hour-long numbness, or a ten-minute weakness in an arm or hand or leg. Certain muscles will be weak—but not paralyzed.

ATAXIA. Some persons for a while after a little stroke will be somewhat ataxic—reeling like a drunken person.

INABILITY TO WALK STRAIGHT. An able and once athletic physician, when in his eighties, thought that he must have had a little stroke because, suddenly, as he was walking rapidly on the street, he felt compelled to walk to the right; then he had to walk to the left. After 30 seconds he was able to walk straight again.

CLUMSINESS OF ARMS OR LEGS, OR A LOSS OF A GOOD SENSE OF BALANCE. Often, with a series of little strokes, men and women become a bit tottery or tipsy, so that occasionally they will have to grab a bit of furniture to keep from falling. A man who, in his youth, may have been a football star, whom few could trip up, may in his seventies be annoyed when he sees how poor his sense of balance is. He may say, "Now, if I trip on an uneven place on a sidewalk, I may fall on my face."

THE OLD PERSON WHO FALLS AND BREAKS A HIP. I suspect that some of the elderly women who fall down so heavily as to break a hip, fall because of a very brief and later unremembered black-out. I remember well the very honest old lady who fell down a flight of steps and broke her hip. Her husband wanted to collect some insurance, but she refused to let him, because, as she kept saying, she remembered that just before she fell, she "blacked-out."

FALLING TO THE FLOOR. Quite a few little strokes cause the person to fall to the floor. A former football coach, aged 60, said he had been wonderfully well and strong until shortly before I saw him. Then, one night, he fell to the floor. He picked himself up and fell again. He got up, and this time was able to stand, but he was weak. After that he did not feel right, his hands trembled; he could not work any more, and he aged much. He said he knew he had had a little stroke!

A station-master, about 50, while standing, watching a train come in, suddenly collapsed onto the floor. He picked himself up, and fortunately, was left with only a few discomforts.

FALLING OUT OF A CHAIR. Many a time a man whose usefulness on this earth was suddenly ended with a little stroke began his troubles by falling out of a chair, or off of a toilet seat. On getting up the person maintains he is all right, but he isn't.

SHORT STEPS. Every physician, and every intelligent layman, should be able to tell what has happened to the man who shuffles along with short steps, sometimes 6 inches long—steps in which his feet do not rise above the ground. The French, for many years, have called this type of walk "la marche à petit pas" (the walk with the small steps). Petrén refused credit for first describing this syndrome. He ascribed priority to Charcot (1888) and to Blocq, who wrote on Astasie-Abasie. Other French neurologists gave the credit to Dejerine. Petrén spoke of Trepidanter Abasie. He added to his article a splendid "Bib."

RUBBERY LEGS. The first case of rubbery legs (some call it pseudoparaplegia, but I will use here the term my patients have all used) I can remember is that of a production manager in a big manufacturing company. He, naturally, had been a very able man; but then, one day, he fell out of his chair. He picked himself right up, and said he was all right, but after that his associates saw that he was unable to get anything done. Soon he lost control of his legs, and had to get around on crutches. Obviously, in a moment he had suffered severe damage to his brain, and soon he had to be retired.

Very interesting and instructive to me was the case of a dear friend—a fine physician, aged 66, who during a couple of weeks had three very brief spells of complete aphasia. The cause was assumed then to be vasospasm, but, as Osler used to say, an "obviously transient vasospasm" has a bad habit of leaving a permanent injury, and this is what happened to my friend. Shortly after the aphasias he developed a bad case of rubbery legs, which after a few years put him into a wheel chair. Fortunately, he remained for the next 10 years or more, well-dressed, well-groomed, and his old, highly intelligent, good-natured and friendly self.

A similar case was that of another physician who, one day, had a spell of aphasia which lasted an hour. At the time he became a bit disoriented, and for a few hours, he could not hold his urine. Next day he was all right, but for some time afterwards he felt tired. He soon developed rubbery legs, and unfortunately, a Parkinsonian syndrome.

Another dear friend, one of my favorite professors in medical school, in his sixties developed such a mild case of rubbery legs that he could walk along the street and even down hill only so long as he could rest one hand heavily on my shoulder. Like other men with rubbery legs, for many years he remained his fine, brainy, kindly, and well-groomed self. But then he became so ataxic he had to employ a man to help him get bathed and dressed. Then he went into a wheel-chair, and eventually, in his late eighties, his ability to recognize old friends and to chat with them failed and he had to go into a hospital. A few years and he died.

Another physician friend with rubbery legs, said that with the coming of the weakness, his memory had become severely impaired. With his first little stroke, he promptly lost 20 pounds.

A woman physician of 71 suddenly lost 25 pounds, and then began to have rubbery legs. The remarkable fact about her syndrome was that, from time to time, she got better. This series of cases makes me wonder if, for some unknown reason, rubbery legs is a disease of physicians! On searching the literature, I found a few references to rubbery legs—usually called "cerebral paraplegia," or "ataxic paraplegia." See J. Mitchell Clarke (1915) and M. Critchley (1931 in Lancet).

SIMULTANEOUS HEART ATTACK AND STROKE. Many a patient says that pain shot down from his brain into his thorax. Many a time it was so severe that, with the first glance, able internists thought it was arising in the heart. But the proper diagnosis became apparent when the patient said that when his chest pain came, for a few minutes he saw double, or he had some difficulty in talking, or he lost his sense of balance.

Often, of course, as I shall show in Chapter 9 (see notes there) thrombosis comes at about the same time in the heart and the brain. The injury to the brain could well have followed the injury to the heart, which for a short time, so lowered the blood pressure that blood could not get through a narrowed place in a cerebral artery. This sort of thing I have found described by several men. In many cases, unless the heart specialist takes such a good history from the patient's relatives that he learns of symptoms that point clearly to a brain injury, he will recognize only the coronary attack. But if he is observant, he will note that the patient's disability is due, not to a heart injury, but to a brain injury.

Although there may be a small abnormality in the electrocardiograms, if the patient's chest pain is constant and not influenced by exertion or excitement, it is not likely to be anginal in origin. Another important point is that the patient's "cardiac reserve" is good; and as he sits in the doctor's office, he is breathing quietly and comfortably. His wife, if asked, may say that with his "heart attack" he changed greatly in personality. In some cases the pain, when it shot into the man's chest, went on down into his abdomen, where it still is.

A woman of 68 complained of *constant* pain at the lower end of her sternum which some men feared was due to heart disease. Her husband said she had had several "spells" which had left her with twitching of the right side of her face; a coarse tremor in both hands; weakness of both legs; some uncertainty in walking; and some deafness.

BURNING PAIN OR "MISERY" THAT SHOT INTO THE ABDOMEN. As I must keep emphasizing here, early in my career as a gastroenterologist I learned that a widespread "burning misery" in the abdomen which never lets up for a minute, for months or years, is probably arising in the brain. In 1935, I. S. Wechsler wrote on abdominal pain as a symptom of disease of the brain, and told where in the brain the pain-producing disease can be located. Ernest Sachs and Lloyd Ziegler, as they discussed Wechsler's paper, told of lesions in the brain that they had seen, causing abdominal pain. As a number of writers on little strokes have said, many of these patients are operated on to no purpose. (See J. Pal, 1905.)

A big, sad-looking woman-physician of 72 had been going from one clinic to another for over a year, complaining of much abdominal discomfort and a tremendous hyperesthesia of the skin of her torso, such as is typical of little strokes. I learned from her daughter that the woman, who had always been very active and social, had one evening felt a very distressing hot flush run down over her abdomen. She thought she was dying, and in a few minutes she went into a brief coma. When she woke, she said that that evening on her way home, she had driven her car into a road-scraper, which showed her that her brain was not working right.

She suffered from such difficulty in swallowing, and such distress in her throat that for months she spent much time in the offices of laryngologists. Her right hand soon cramped up so that it had the typical appearance of a hand that has been involved in a big stroke. She lost all of her old interests, and never again had a comfortable minute. She became a recluse, and lived on, miserably, for 5 years. She soon lost the ability to read well enough to get pleasure from a magazine or a book.

Another middle-aged woman-physician suddenly had a fairly severe little stroke, with dizziness and wooziness and apathy. With this came a terrible rending distress in her abdomen. If she had not protested vigorously, her surgeon would immediately have explored her abdomen. He could have made the correct diagnosis in a minute if he had noticed the poliolike weakness of the muscles of her neck and trunk which, for many days, made it impossible for her to sit up or to hold her head up. Months later she had a second similar stroke which, again, filled her abdomen with pain. Thorough studies in her home city showed nothing wrong in her digestive tract.

CONSTANT ABDOMINAL "BURNING MISERY." An arteriosclerotic, but strong, rancher's wife of 58 was seen by me because of her great and constant abdominal distress. All my assistant could find was a gallstone. I would not consider an operation for this because the woman had never had a colic, and besides, a gallstone does not produce the constant burning all over the torso—such as this woman had. That is seen often with severe little strokes.

From relatives, I learned that she had been wonderfully well and strong all her life until two weeks before I saw her, when one morning she woke feeling terribly ill, and with the room spinning around. When she tried to get up, one leg was so weak she could not stand. After this, she never again could do any work—she was so miserable and weak and full of pain. She had lost much of her memory, and all of her interest and joy in life. Her once high blood pressure had dropped suddenly to normal. In a few weeks she lost 45 pounds!

VIOLENT INTESTINAL PERISTALSIS. A woman of 70, after suffering a little stroke with a brief hemiplegia, complained of severe cramping abdominal pain. With this, violent peristalsis of the bowel could be seen through her thin abdominal wall.

CONSTANT ABDOMINAL PAIN. An intelligent woman of 40 said that 10 years before, "*something blew up in her head,*" and left her dizzy for an hour or two. Curiously, her right ear had become so sensitive to sound that never again could she stand the noise of a typewriter near her. Formerly friendly and kindly, she became irritable and irascible. Following what appeared to be another small stroke, she got a *terrible "misery" in her abdomen* which remained constant for the next 12 years.

SUDDEN ABDOMINAL PAIN, AND 20 LITTLE STROKES. An able woman of 45, while walking along the street, suddenly got a *pain in her epigastrium,* so awful that she lost consciousness and fell to the ground. When she woke, she found half of her face convulsed, and one hand drawn into her groin. One of her feet felt wooden. She was taken to a hospital, but by the time she reached the place and could be seen by a neurologist, his examination "showed nothing." But during the next 25 years she had a series of some 20 little strokes. Some produced a little change in character with some loss of memory, and a lessened ability to get things done. Finally, after one bad spell, she could never work again.

SPASM-OF-THE-STOMACH TYPE OF LITTLE STROKE. An able physician I saw the first time when he was 48. After years of good health, suddenly he had become exhausted, irritable, and drowsy. Examinations showed nothing. He improved and was fairly well for five years. In January, 1935, he returned to say he had waked one night, restless, with great mental distress, and a bowel full of gas. Following this, for weeks, he had slept all day and all night. Soon he went into a manic spell in which he became highly irritable. Six weeks later he suddenly fainted, and when he woke, his stomach was so uncomfortable that for 5 months he took little besides milk. He was so irascible that his wife left him.

Examinations again showed nothing physically wrong. Later, as I chatted with him, he told me that on the night when he woke, he knew something terrible was hitting his brain. Immediately, his stomach became so hypersensitive that the swallowing of even a *glass of water would promptly bring pain. He said he could feel it hit his stomach.* Several other patients told me of this type of great sensitivity. Significant was the fact that after that midnight episode, the doctor lost all of his old interests and joys in life. Occasionally, he would have a short spell of mania and insomnia.

BALLOONING OF THE STOMACH. A man told me that one day it felt as if his stomach were being ballooned painfully. Interestingly, he sensed that at the time "something awful was happening" in his brain.

A PULLING SENSATION. A man of 54 complained of severe pain in his epigastrium. The minute he started eating, he would feel uncomfortably full. He had a constant "pulling sensation" in the lower right quadrant of his abdomen. Pulling sensations are commonly seen with strokes.

What impressed me most was the fact that the man was so dulled that he could no longer do much work. From his wife, I learned that 6 months before, his troubles had started when he had waked at 2 A.M. with a "terrible pain" in his epigastrium, with nausea, vomiting and diarrhea. He then aged markedly, and lost all interest in sex. Later, after four years of poor health, he suddenly had a big stroke, with a hemiplegia. E. Leyden (1882) wrote of "gastrische Krisen," some of which may have been due to little strokes. One of his patients wound up with a paraplegia.

SLOWNESS IN READING. As I have said, an inability to read, or to read with ease or pleasure, is an important sign—very helpful in showing that the brain has suffered much damage.

INABILITY TO LOOK AT TELEVISION. Habitual television watchers who can no longer look at television may have a severely injured brain.

FACIAL PAIN, OR PULLING SENSATION. With a little stroke many a person gets in his face a severe, constant, long-lasting and intractable pain of a rending or "pulling" type, which came suddenly, one day. In some of my cases of this type, the pain, although very different from tic douloureux, came and went much as tic does. Temple Fay (1932) wrote of an atypical facial neuralgia—a "syndrome of vascular pain."

In 1935, an able physician of 67—an unusual character—came complaining of a severe, painful distress in the left side of his face. This hit him when, at the age of 50, he was under terrible familial and financial strain. Then he had an attack of diplopia with strabismus and ptosis of the left upper eyelid. Strength in the lid muscle returned in 4 months, but vision in the left eye remained poor, and the diplopia bothered him for the next 12 years.

He described the sensation in his cheek as a very painful muscular spasm or "pulling," or "stretching," or a feeling as if there were a piece of rough rope between his teeth. Sometimes the distress was almost unbearable, strangely, it stopped when he lay down. As with tic douloureux, chewing or laughing aggravated it; and talking was so likely to bring it on that the doctor became a recluse.

Eighteen years before, when he was 49, his left arm had suddenly become paralyzed. After a while, it gradually regained its strength. At the age of 52, he woke one morning with this paralysis back again. After inheriting wealth, the man traveled the world over, seeing many neurologists. When, one after another, several men injected enough procaine into the left cheek and its nerves to produce good local anesthesia, the fact that the pulling distress was not relieved suggested that the cause was up in the brain.

I saw this man years later when he was 79, and he still had his old distress in his cheek, as bad as ever. He said that at 77, he had had an attack in which his tongue was pulled to the right, and made to feel uncomfortable. A little later he had another minor apoplexy which, for a short time, weakened his left arm and leg. His blood pressure was then 154/96. His arteries were hard, but otherwise he was young for his age; he was well-groomed, pleasant, intelligent, and mentally active. His left cheek was colder than the right, suggesting a poorer blood supply.

While he was at the Mayo Clinic, Dr. John Lundy injected with procaine the cervical sympathetic chain on the left side and produced for a while a warm cheek, but still the painful paresthesia remained. The doctor finally accepted my diagnosis of little strokes. He said he knew he had had many of these in his preceding 30 years.

PARESTHESIAS AND PAINS. Sometimes a little stroke will produce a feeling of a "flash of heat" in some part of the body. Heat in the palate, or in the bones of the leg bothered several patients.

TWISTED MOUTH. A hundred times I must have been given my hunch to ask about little strokes when I noted that in talking, the patient opened one side of his (her) mouth a little more than the other side. Time and again I have seen young doctors fail to notice this because they depended on asking the patient to show his teeth. Then the slight difference in strength of the muscles on the two sides of the face did not appear; it appeared only when the person was talking.

INABILITY TO THINK CONSTRUCTIVELY OR LOGICALLY. A few able physicians—friends of mine—after having had some little strokes, seemed to have recovered perfectly. When I chatted with them about ordinary matters of no great consequence, they seemed to be their old intelligent selves, but when they tried to tell me about some ideas they had for a medical paper they wanted to publish, they could not make sense, and wandered aimlessly in their speech. For a time I could not understand this, and then I gained the impression that their cerebral mechanism was adequate for a casual conversation, but not for a scientific discussion, or a bit of planning, based on much highly technical knowledge. Also, some men whose wives had had little strokes found that a woman who had a marvellous memory for unimportant matters, if repeatedly told how to attend to a bit of business at the bank, could not remember a single detail. Similarly, after a little stroke, a waiter might seem all right—chatting with fellow waiters in the kitchen—but he could no longer remember an order given him for food.

GREAT DISCOMFORT IN THE BRAIN. Some of the persons who have suffered a severe small stroke will keep complaining for years of a very distressing feeling in their brain—which they cannot describe. It can follow a big stroke.

LOSS OF APPETITE. After a little stroke many people, for some time, have no appetite.

LOSS OF LIBIDO AND POTENTIA. As one would expect, any man who has lost all interest in life, after a little stroke, is very likely to have lost interest in sex, and perhaps all ability to have sexual intercourse. Women similarly will lose all interest in sex.

LOSS OF SENSATION, AND NUMBNESS. Many persons, after a little stroke, complain of an area of numbness somewhere. Usually it goes away after a while.

BRIEF BLACKOUTS OR COMA. A few persons, during a little stroke, will black out for a brief time, and rarely, one will have a short spell of coma.

DISTRESSES IN THE SCALP AND THE TOP OF THE HEAD. Quite a few persons, after a little stroke, will feel as if something—like a "lump of dough"—was plastered down on the top of the head.

INSOMNIA. Some people, after a little stroke, suddenly develop a severe insomnia such as they never had before. Such insomnia can follow also a brief big stroke.

SOMNOLENCE. A patient, after a little stroke, may, for a while be somnolent.

BURNING AREA OF SKIN. Quite a few people after a little stroke complain of a distressing burning over perhaps a large area of skin. For instance: a nurse, aged 65, with a slight hypertension, some 16 years before I saw her, suddenly one day got a terrible burning from the neck down her back to her buttocks and then down both thighs. She said it felt like a boil. Otherwise she had remained healthy. She said she hadn't had a minute's let-up of the distress in the 16 years.

The worst case of burning I ever saw came to a man nearly 60 who, for two or three years, had been overworking terribly. Then came an awful sense of burning all over his body, so that he hated to sit down or lie down or even stand. I suspected a stroke because I had seen the same syndrome attack several persons who *I was sure* had had a stroke. A few years later, my friend quickly died with a big stroke.

HYPERSENSITIVITY OF THE SKIN. In some cases the skin—often that of the torso—is hypersensitive.

THALAMIC OR DEJERINE-ROUSSY SYNDROME. See Henry Head and Gordon Holmes (1911) who told of people with a weird subjective hypersensitivity of one-half of the body—on the right or the left. Some of the patients said they could hardly stand shaving one-half the face, or even getting their hair cut on that side. Women said they hated to wash their hair and their face on the sensitive side. Tickling on the affected side could be very unpleasant. Some people complained that emotion could distress the side. One man said he could not go to church because he could not stand the hymns on his bad side. I have had patients who could not stand the vibrations of big organ pipes on the side. In many persons there was a burning distress on the sensitive area. In some cases the distress followed a definite stroke. Head & Holmes described a number of cases in which the patient has had a little stroke. Jelliffe (1910) wrote about this syndrome.

Very important is the fact that a thalamic syndrome can be missed even by a neurologist if he relies only on his pin and cotton, because so much of the trouble of these people is subjective and not objective. One learns about it by asking the patient, and learning that his distress runs from the top of his head, on one side, to his toes on that side. Because in most of my patients with a typical thalamic syndrome, the complaint was of pain in one loin, they had been treated for months by urologists who kept dilating a "Hunner stricture." With one question, the urologist could have learned that the pain ran from the head to the toes.

A woman in her 70's, after years of good health, suddenly had what looked like a little stroke. Then she told me that she ached from her left cheek down to the toes of her left foot. Because most of her misery was in her *left loin,* one physician, who had not gotten the whole story, diagnosed diverticulitis of the colon; a urologist whose assistant had failed to get the story, kept searching for something wrong with the *left kidney,* while, later, another urologist spent months dilating a supposed stricture of the ureter. A surgeon wanted to explore the *left ovary.* If these men had only asked, they would have learned that the left half of her scalp was so sensitive that she dreaded shampooing her hair on that side.

A woman of 77, described a sudden little stroke which immediately left her with a distress all down her left side. At home she had been given three diagnoses; of something wrong with her descending colon; or her left kidney; or her left ovary.

A THALAMIC SYNDROME CAN COME WITH AN OPERATION. An able and always healthy nurse, aged 23, on waking from an appendectomy, found herself with a thalamic syndrome. Like some others of my women patients with this syndrome, on being questioned about sexual intercourse, she said, "Yes; I used to like it, but now, because of the great sensitiveness of one side of my vagina, I can hardly stand it." Evidently, during the operation, part of this woman's brain did not get enough oxygen.

I have seen several people like that who had a little stroke during an operation. For instance; a woman of 35 had a brief pelvic operation of some kind—as I remember, under gas anesthesia. She woke with a typical thalamic syndrome which made one side of her vagina painfully sensitive. This woman may have been like Sir Edmund Hillary who got a stroke high up on Lhotse, in the Himalayas, where the air was deficient in oxygen. The early balloonists used to get into similar difficulties when, without an oxygen tank, they rose to great heights.

A middle-aged woman had her gallbladder removed seven weeks before I saw her. On the second day after surgery she wakened with her mouth so dry that when she moved her tongue back and forth "it felt like two pieces of sand paper being drawn together." The roof of her mouth felt raw, and she had lost her sense of taste and much of her sense of smell.

A 50-year-old woman, on waking from an operation, felt a shock and, with it, lost some of her memory, so that ever afterward it was hard to carry out the orders of her boss at her place of work.

Several anesthetists have written about the dangers of producing a little stroke by giving the patient too little oxygen. C. B. Courville (1938) wrote an excellent paper on this, with a fine bibliography. He was concerned mainly with nitrous oxide anesthesias. Rankin (1957), who wrote on cerebral thrombosis during an operation, thought there might be a fall in blood pressure. Kety (1950) said that during pentothal anesthesia there is a 40 per cent decrease in the brain's utilization of oxygen. This occurs even when the cerebral blood flow and the arterial contents of oxygen and glucose are adequate. A. Behrend and H. Riggs (1941) wrote on this subject, and F. H. Lewy discussed the paper. Death can follow even a spinal anesthesia. Often necropsy on the patients who die while under anesthesia shows that they had come to the operation with serious arterial injury to the brain and heart. A few had a fatty liver. A. T. Steegman (1939) found necroses in the brain. John Denst (1953) supplied a good bibliography. (See also R. Leriche and R. Fontaine, 1936). R. C. Connolly (1961) feared cerebral ischemia during an operation.

PARKINSONISM AFTER A LITTLE STROKE. I have seen so many patients develop Parkinsonism after one or several little strokes that I am sure cerebral arteriosclerosis must often be a cause, and several authorities have had the same idea. Thus, Critchley (1929) wrote on "Arteriosclerotic Parkinsonism," and said that arteriosclerosis can give rise to either the complete syndrome or part of it. He said the symptoms can come suddenly, and dementia can follow. Kinnier Wilson (1941) said that Parkinsonism can follow little strokes.

AGITATED DEPRESSION. One day my secretary came into my consulting room to whisper to me that there was an insane woman outside, upsetting other patients, and would I please take her in quickly. Dismissing the patient who was with me, I went out and brought in a wild-looking woman of 65 with two handsome businessmen, her sons. Her clothes were dirty; her mop of gray hair tousled, and she was in such an agony of nervousness that she could not sit down, but kept walking up and down my room, saying that her suffering was more than she could bear. Her sons said that all night she roamed through their big house turning on the lights.

Obviously, she was in an agitated depression, which had come suddenly after a little stroke. Much of the woman's distress was centered in her abdomen, and, as sometimes happens in these cases, the skin of her whole torso was so sensitive that she screamed if I tried to palpate any part of it.

APHASIA. On rare occasions I have seen a person with a little stroke who was left speechless, and I have known a number who, for a few hours, had difficulty saying what they wanted to say. Some, for a while, mumbled or talked thickly or hesitantly. Some could no longer read, or read easily. A few had a little trouble writing either long-hand or on a typewriter.

There is another type of trouble after a little stroke in which the person knows what he wants to say, but has great trouble enunciating the words.

One of my dear friends, a physician about 70, had worked very hard all his life, with a huge practice. One day, while talking to a patient, he suddenly found himself unable to say a word. Soon he could talk again, but following this, he went down hill and soon died.

DANGERS IN DRIVING A CAR. A fine physician, who in his eighties looked 55, had always been very well. Then, one day, while driving on a highway he had a momentary blackout, and woke to find himself over in the left lane. Fortunately, the oncoming cars all managed to dodge him. Although much frightened by this episode, he kept on driving. This was wrong because a few days later he again had a blackout, and woke with his car in the ditch on the left side of the road. He felt all right, and drove home, but after this, he agreed that he should no longer drive.

Some other elderly patients of mine, when they lost consciousness at the wheel, hit cars and had their licenses to drive taken away.

TREMOR. A few people, after a little stroke, will get a tremor in one hand or a shaking of the head.

LOSS OF SIGHT. I have seen an occasional person who suddenly lost the sight of one eye due to the thrombosis of an artery in the brain, or the optic nerve. There is a whole literature on little or brief strokes associated with some blindness due to a spasm in arteries, usually in one retina or in the visual center of the brain. See Chapter 10 on spasm, and on blindness due to little strokes.

Some years ago a business man of 60, as he was crossing a street, fell to the ground for a moment. On rising, he found that he had lost vision in one eye. In the next few days he lost vision in the other eye. When I saw him a year later, he was working in a factory for the blind, and did not show any sign of injury to his brain.

SPASM OF RETINAL VESSELS. In a few cases of little strokes an ophthalmologist will report that occasionally he can see a spasm in some blood vessel of the retina—spasm which can cause a dimming of sight. In 1891, George Peabody reported (p. 166) that arteriosclerosis can be diagnosed in its early stages with the help of an ophthalmoscope. He also mentioned (p. 173) spasm in arteries of the retina, and sudden attacks of transitory blindness in one or both eyes, associated with aortic stenosis.

SEEING DOUBLE. Occasionally I see a patient with a little stroke who says that for an hour or so after his episode, or for a few days, he saw double. The symptom, when it is described, is very important because this happening strongly suggests that the trouble was not just "nerves" or hysteria, or Menière's disease, as some physicians had thought.

CHOKED DISC. One day, around 1940, one of my patients, a woman aged 65, previously well, suddenly lost vision in one eye. Able ophthalmologists and neurologists who found a choked disc, concluded—and correctly—that she must have had a hemorrhage into her brain. Like so many persons who suffer a stroke, at the moment of the injury, she felt no shock or pain. During the next several years she petered out with a series of little strokes. She never showed signs of a brain tumor. Today, a woman with this type of trouble might well be saved with an operation on the carotid artery.

PTOSIS OF AN EYELID. A man of 50, who looked old beyond his years, apparently because of a series of little strokes, once had a spell in which his left eye-lid drooped for a while. His physician diagnosed a little stroke, and later the man petered out with more such strokes.

Another man suddenly suffered ptosis of both upper eye-lids when he was in his twenties, and the power to lift the lids never returned. Then he had another little stroke which left him unable to work for the rest of his days. In his fifties he had a remarkable brief stroke with, for only a day, aphasia and hemiplegia. He finally succumbed to yet another stroke.

BLINDNESS AFTER A CONFINEMENT. I have read that K. Fink (1924) collected 130 cases of transitory post-partum blindness. Some of these spells may well have been hysterical in nature, but those that left some residue were probably due to a little stroke.

SCOTOMAS. Occasionally, a person who has had little strokes will tell of peculiar and transitory scotomas. Some are due to an injury in the visual center, while some are due to an injury to the retina. Aring (1945, p.31) found electroencephalographic changes in the occipital lobes of 3 men on his staff who *suffered migraine* during a decompression syndrome. He thought these changes indicated spasm of blood vessels, like those of Raynaud's disease. The work of Harold Wolff showed that during the scotoma of a migraine there is spasm of an artery, while during the headache, there is dilation. If ergotamine contracts the artery, the patient is relieved.

FLASHES OF LIGHT ON THE EXTREME EDGE OF THE FIELD OF VISION. For months, years ago, I saw flashes of light on the extreme left edge of my field of vision. Then they left. One day years later, I saw far to my left, for a second, a bright zig-zag figure, not migrainous in its behavior. Such flashes were mentioned by Maclachlan (1863). Once I saw a man of 60 whose little stroke not only brought the flashes, but also took away his sense of smell.

MIGRAINE AND LITTLE STROKES. At times a little stroke can influence the course of a migraine. For instance, a woman in her 50's who had never had migraines, had a little stroke. A while later, while driving her car, she suddenly had another little stroke so severe that if her sister had not been there to grab the wheel, they would have had an accident. For some time after this, she had frequent migraines. Later, she had another little stroke which did a remarkable thing: it wiped out her tendency to get the headaches.

DIARRHEA. Some people have told me of repeated episodes of what they called "a sudden emptying-out of the bowel." One such man—one of America's great industrialists—while having what looked like little strokes that affected his spinal cord, lost 50 pounds in weight, and developed rubbery legs. With his "spells" he suffered brief but violent attacks of diarrhea. Arteriosclerotic injuries to the cords of these people have been described by pathologists. Broadbent, in 1909, spoke of a little stroke with diarrhea.

A man with a systolic blood pressure over 250 mm. Hg. got a sudden attack of diarrhea, in which his bowels seemed to empty out completely. He had no pain, but he perspired tremendously, and became very pale. Some men have told me that one day they were terribly embarrassed when suddenly the bowels emptied out without any warning. One unhappy man had this happen to him in a crowded elevator.

CONSTIPATION. Occasionally, after a little stroke, a person will suffer from a constipation such as he never had before. This happened to a man of 64.

PAIN IN THE RECTUM OR COCCYX. Occasionally, after a little stroke, the person will complain of a constant pain in his rectum, and nothing can ever be found locally to account for it. One man of 65 with such a pain, at the same time had a bad burning feeling in his left thumb, a "clutching feeling" in his chest, some slurring of his speech, a slight aphasia, and a slight weakening of the muscles of the right side of his face. Later, he developed a Parkinson's syndrome.

I have seen many such persons with a severe and constant type of pain in a normal-appearing rectum. Often the nature of the pain can be suspected instantly because of its constancy; also because moving the bowels or passing gas has no effect on it.

LOW BACK PAIN. I have wondered how often a little stroke can produce, for a month or two, a severe backache. An able business man some years ago had a brief big stroke from which he recovered well. Later, he had two brief little strokes that nearly dropped him to the floor. One of these left him for a few weeks with a severe backache—which suddenly, one day, left him.

QUESTIONABLE PAIN. When, after a stroke, an old person complains of severe pain and his or her grown children refuse to believe that it *is* pain, the physician must ask if, before the stroke, the person was at all inclined to complain. If he never was a complainer, then he is almost certainly suffering pain, and he ought to be given a pain-reliever. Unfortunately, pain arising in the brain can be very resistant even to morphine.

URINARY INCONTINENCE. A few patients with little strokes tell of occasionally waking to find their bed wet, or of occasionally wetting themselves when "hit by a spell" while out on the street. I remember some men who, after several little strokes, kept dribbling so much urine that they smelled of ammonia. Grasset (1906) spoke of a rare case of this type.

SLIGHT FEVER. I have seen a few persons who, for a while after a little stroke, ran a low fever. This may have been due to some defect in homeostasis.

BELL'S PALSY. I have seen a few persons with a Bell's type of facial paralysis, who I suspected had had a little stroke, because when the paralysis of their face came, they had some symptoms such as temporary double vision and mental confusion, which pointed to an injury to the brain. A physician, formerly good natured—after the paralysis of one side of his face, became for a while, irritable, irascible, and cantankerous. When the paralysis came, he had a brief spell of diplopia and mental confusion, which made him feel that he was having a little stroke. After some months, he got back most of his old good nature, but was left with some weakness of the muscles in half of his face.

A man told me that after a dizzy spell, he had a feeling as if a hot wire had been run under one side of his tongue, and someone was pulling on it. This sensation lasted for a few weeks.

According to Smith Ely Jelliffe and Wm. A. White (1935, p.404), there is a cortical type of Bell's palsy recognizable by the particular distribution of the weakness of the muscles of the face. Dr. Benjamin Boshes (1958) put it the other way, and said that what sometimes looked like a little stroke could be a Bell's palsy.

A LITTLE STROKE DURING SEXUAL INTERCOURSE. A migrainous, sometimes depressed, and always poorly adjusted woman, with some "crazy relatives," complained that some years before, while having sexual intercourse, she had had a little stroke. Her hand and leg on one side had suddenly become numb and weak.

UNILATERAL RAISED EYE-BROW. Occasionally, as a woman who has had a little stroke talks to me, with considerable emotion, she will raise one eye-brow unusually high, while she does not similarly raise the other one.

STUTTERING. A most unusual little stroke was one which for the first time in a man's life, made him stutter badly. Curiously, later, another little stroke cured him! As I say elsewhere, in a very few cases I have seen a little stroke cure a severe migraine. An able woman told me that a little stroke once made her formerly lovable father unpleasant and irascible. Later, came another little stroke which made him kindly and affectionate again!

SNEEZING SPELLS. Very rarely a little stroke can produce spells of sneezing. A man of 60, six months before I saw him, had a definite little stroke, which brought on frequent spells of violent sneezing. Sometimes he would sneeze 10 times a minute until he was exhausted. Once he kept it up for seven hours.

A CHARCOT JOINT. I remember well a man with a typical Charcot type of injury, centering in his right wrist. There it produced a red hamlike swelling. Noticing dullness in his face, I asked if he had had anything like a little stroke, when the swelling had appeared, and he said, "Yes; this came shortly after the day, when at the office I fell out of my chair. My hand first became clumsy; I was nauseated and a pain shot into my abdomen. Later, came this swelling." Fortunately, with good physiotherapy, the hand and wrist soon became almost normal.

A woman of 58, never before arthritic, soon after a big stroke with a right hemiplegia, suffered some destruction of her right hip-joint. I suspected that the injury to the joint was trophic in origin.

CONVULSION. Only rarely have I seen a person who had a convulsion with a little stroke. Naturally, in such cases EEG's should be obtained because conceivably the person might for all of his life have been a carrier of epilepsy.

SENESCENT PSYCHOSIS AFTER MANY LITTLE STROKES. As we all know, the end-result of many a series of severe little strokes is a senescent psychosis—a disease well known to every physician who works in a general hospital, a mental hospital, an old people's home, or a nursing home for the aged. Some of these people are confused, and some become paranoid.

Inability to recognize near relatives. Many confused old people will, at times, fail to recognize a son or daughter, or wife or husband.

Narcolepsy. An able lawyer who, for 15 years, had been having severe little strokes, eventually suffered from narcolepsy. This may have been coincidental.

Senile tremor of the mandible. I have seen a number of old men who kept constantly "chomping" or moving their toothless mandible up and down. Critchley (p.208) mentioned this rare symptom of a little stroke, and Demange (1882) spoke of such a patient as an "old rabbit-face."

ARTHRITIC SYNDROME ARISING IN THE BRAIN? Several times I have seen an elderly person suddenly develop what looked like a widespread arthritis with perhaps weak hands and feet. Only close observation and chats with the family then showed that, in addition to the pains all over the body, the patient was in a mental depression such as he or she had never had before—a depression which strongly suggested that the whole syndrome had arisen in the brain. My friend, Dr. Edward Rosenberg, an expert on arthritis, tells me he knows this syndrome, and that after a few months, the patient generally recovers.

This disease, in 1872, greatly interested de Mussy. He wrote of arthritis that goes with hemiplegia, and also of "arterial rheumatism." This syndrome seems to have been known also to Trousseau (1885, p.816) who wrote about "cerebral rheumatism."

THE SHOULDER–WRIST SYNDROME. Occasionally one sees a person who, after suffering a coronary attack, gets a very troublesome pain in the shoulder, wrist, and perhaps the whole arm. I have seen a few such cases in which I had reason to suspect that the patient had suffered a little stroke, together with his heart attack. For instance; I remember well two brothers—about 60 years of age, one a physician—who both suffered from, first, the residue of a coronary attack, and, second, an almost unbearable causalgic pain in the left arm, but mainly in the wrist and hand. The histories suggested that both men had had a series of small strokes that started their troubles. This idea was strengthened when the layman brother suffered a hemiplegia. The physician brother told me that for 6 years he had been suffering a series of brief mild depressions, each one of which, he thought, had been brought on by a little stroke. I was satisfied with his diagnosis because he spoke with the thick speech which is so typical of a stroke. Also, he had no hereditary tendency to depressions. My hunch then was that these brothers had had an arteriosclerotic injury in both their heart and their brain, such as I describe in Chapter 9. In some cases the pain could be due to atherosclerosis in a subclavian artery, as described by Dr. De Bakey.

SUDDEN PAIN IN A TEMPOROMANDIBULAR JOINT. One day suddenly I was seized with a severe pain in one temporo-mandibular joint. It was so severe I had visions of living for the rest of my days on liquids put into my mouth by way of a tube. And then, in a few minutes it was gone, and I wondered if it represented a little stroke. Then a teenage girl told me of a similar experience, but her early age made me doubt the idea of a stroke.

Rarely, I have seen a patient who, for a few weeks after a little stroke, could not chew.

RELAXATION OF THE CARDIA. A man of 54 had a series of little strokes which left him with such an open cardia that when he lay down, gastric juice ran out of his mouth. This has happened to others of my patients.

He could not feel the fork in his hand, and he had a "sour mouth." He was badly wrecked mentally. Half of his face was numb and his eyes watered.

HURRY CAUSING A FALL. In a few cases, after a little stroke, the person said that if he hurried or started to run, he fell on his face so suddenly he did not know how it happened.

6

The Literature of Little Strokes, Brief Strokes, Silent Strokes, Transient Ischemic Spells, Etc.

As I have said above, for 35 years I failed to find much on little strokes because information on them was not indexed. In 1964 and 1965 I succeeded in finding some 250 articles or paragraphs or chapters, largely by starting with Osler's 1911 article, and working backward with the help of his small bibliography. Also I searched widely through the literatures of angiology, pathology, neurology, psychiatry, brain surgery, cardiology, ophthalmology, anesthesiology, hypertension, arteriosclerosis, Raynaud's disease and geriatrics.

THE ANCIENTS KNEW ABOUT SMALL STROKES. Fortunately for my purposes, Edwin Clark (1963) had searched the books of Hippocrates and had found notes on apoplexy—a word which meant "being struck with violence." The Father of Medicine, or one of his associates, told of small prodromal spells—like little strokes—which sometimes can warn the victim that a big stroke is coming. The symptoms mentioned were headache, ear-noises, vertigo, slowing of the speech, numbness of the arms, loss of memory, distortions of the face, tingling in the skin, and disorders of intelligence—all very modern!

Ph. Schwartz (1930) told of a Dr. Cohn who, in 1860, published a book on the early literature on strokes, running back to the time of Galen. Schwartz doubted if Cohn had learned much of value to us today.

I have read that the Latin terms for a stroke were "atonitas" and "sideratio," which suggest thunder and lightning. Perhaps from this Latin we get our word thunderstruck. In the many-volumed New English Dictionary of Sir James Murray (Vol. 9, pp. 1131-1132) I read that not only can God strike down a man but a planet can. Falstaff in "Henry the Fourth" speaks of apoplexy.

Interestingly, Homer used the stem of the word apoplexia to denote not only giving a blow, but driving a person out of his wits. By the Fifth Century A.D., "apoplectic" could mean that a man was stupid, foolish, or out of his mind. In modern Greek the word can mean stupefied or thunderstruck.

Caelius Aurelianus* described little strokes. He tells of attacks of pain in the head, dizziness, ringing in the ears, *a sad face, words indistinctly pronounced,* and forgetfulness of what has just been said! He tells of paralysis of an upper eyelid, and of a loss of smell. Most of these symptoms are, of course, typical of little strokes.

I found several references stating that Boerhaave, around 1700, described little strokes. According to Edwin Clark it was Wepfer, in 1658, who first correlated the apoplectic syndrome with cerebral hemorrhage. Wepfer must have made some thorough necropsies.

Osler's Work. In 1894, in his funeral oration on Oliver Wendell Holmes, Osler congratulated Holmes' friends, saying that they "had been spared that most distressing of all human spectacles, those cold gradations of decay, in which a man takes nearly as long to die as he does to grow up, and lives a sort of death in life." This statement showed me that Osler knew much about the little strokes. He knew the most important fact about them, which is that often, without having produced or left any "neurologic residue," they can have destroyed much of the person's old ability, and perhaps can have left him a sad bit of human wreckage.

So far as I know, Osler never spoke of the disease as "little strokes." He wrote little on the subject in the first editions of his great textbook. Dr. Joseph Pratt told me that he had never seen Osler demonstrate a patient with this disease, and yet, Osler spoke of the "extraordinary frequency of the attacks." He expressed his admiration for papers on "intermittent closure of the cerebral arteries," written by George Peabody (1891), Langwill (1906), Edgeworth (1906), Lauder Brunton (1909), William Russell (1907 and 1909), Hobhouse (1909), and Janeway (1913).

As early as 1896, Osler wrote about the little strokes that are sometimes associated with the Raynaud type of spasm in the hands. In 1874, Raynaud told of the association between the spasm in the blood vessels of the hands and the spasm in the blood vessels of the eyes. Osler spoke of a transient aphasia suffered by one of his patients with Raynaud's disease. Sometimes, in such cases, he saw even transient hemiplegias and brief spells of unconsciousness. In his Case 2, the patient had what I would call little strokes, with transient dizziness, aphasia, and loss of power in the right hand and foot.

In 1910, Osler told of a friend who, before he was 45, had suffered

* Translated by I. E. Drabkin, pp.131, 161, 169, 329, 567, 569, and 591.

scores of attacks of transient paralysis and aphasia. As Osler said so truly, a person even with a normal blood pressure can have such attacks. He said that Peabody (1891) had called his attention to the disease, which is "much more common than indicated in the literature." Most of the early writers on little strokes described mainly brief strokes or severe little strokes—that left some "neurologic residual."

The best of Osler's articles on "transient attacks" or "cerebral crises" was published in Canada in 1911. In it he told of attacks of headache, vertigo, confusion of thought, brief aphasia, paralysis and mental injury. One day a man of 43 found he could not say a word. Next day he could talk, and in 3 or 4 days he was well. Another man, aged 62, who suddenly lost the power of speech, in 5 minutes had it back. An hour later, he was again aphasic, and again, in a day or two, he was well. These are typical *"brief strokes."*

One of Osler's patients, after a brief stroke, quickly lost 25 pounds, and his systolic blood pressure dropped from 200 to 135 mm. Hg. These two phenomena I have often seen with little strokes. Rarely, Osler saw persons who suffered a transitory hemianopsia, or perhaps a brief spasm of a blood vessel in the eye (or in the visual center of the brain). Osler saw (as I have seen many times) brief strokes which, as he said so truly, produced abdominal pain "resembling that of the gastric crises of tabes!" Also, Osler saw cases in which the pain of angina pectoris was felt, not in the heart, but in the head, in an arm, in the legs, the right pectoral muscle, or even in a testicle.

For a while Osler accepted the idea that little strokes are due to spasm, but then his thinking changed when he saw many persons who, after suffering perhaps a brief spell of aphasia, diplopia, or confusion, found themselves left with a permanent injury to some part of the brain—which suggested strongly that a small artery had become plugged up with a thrombus. This sort of thing I have seen many times. Also, what bothered Osler, as in 1937 it bothered A. B. Baker, was the fact that "The condition of the smaller arteries is not very favorable to this view" (of spasm). Osler (1911) said also that "In sclerosis of the cerebral arteries, small foci of softening (of the brain) are not rare, and some of these may produce symptoms." So truly he said, "The patients may live for years, and be very comfortable in the intervals."

How remarkable that so far, I have not found a single article in which an author commented on this fine work of Osler. In spite of his eminence, his teachings about the little strokes were ignored by everyone. Equally astounding is the fact that F. W. Mott's fine article on little strokes in Allbutt and Rolleston's great system, H. M. Thomas' excellent article in Osler and McCrae's System, and W.C.A.'s article in the Oxford system were also completely ignored. One or two men may have mentioned

Mott's work, but I never saw any mention of the other two articles. Even more remarkable: these articles and Osler's have been ignored by all but a very few makers of extensive bibliographies on cerebral atherosclerosis!

THE EARLIEST WRITERS ON STROKES THAT I HAVE FOUND. Excellent is the article published in 1836 by the great Richard Bright. He reported cases, some of them with symptoms typical of little strokes. Bright had the genius to note a number of important points, such as the dull appearance of the face of some of the patients. This was practically never noticed again in the 100 years that followed. Bright noted "much vacancy" in a patient's face. Also Bright was unique in having learned the essential point in taking the history, which is *to ask the family* what happened. He even knew the great value of *re-taking the history,* and thereby perhaps learning of an early and highly diagnostic little stroke that the patient had completely forgotten, perhaps because, after he had fallen senseless to the ground, he had wakened with no memory of the occurrence. In many a case, without this story the correct diagnosis could not be made, and a harmless gallstone got all the blame.

Perhaps most remarkable of all was Bright's suspicion that in some of his cases the cause of the trouble was either in an *internal carotid or a vertebral artery.* What is "new under the sun?" Also, Bright had much the idea I have had that perhaps sometimes when a small artery gives way, for a brief period, the brain is shocked, and then, as this shock passes off, the patient feels perfectly well again.

Marc Dax (1836, whose paper was translated in 1964 by Joynt and Benson) wrote about a woman who suffered brief spells of aphasia, and then recovered. John Abercrombie (1846) skilfully wrote up many little strokes—some causing indigestion. Daniel Maclachlan (1863, p.123) wrote of spells of transient "congestive apoplexy," with vertigo, tinnitus, transient deafness, obscurity of vision, temporary blindness, flashes of light, double vision, sudden abolition of the sense of smell, faltering speech, impaired perception, drowsiness, partial loss of verbal memory, use of the wrong word, numbness, weakness of an extremity, sometimes limited to one or more fingers, neuralgic pain in the limbs, and unequal pupils. The patient can be well in an hour or two, or sooner. What a typical story of little strokes!

Nothnagel (1867) wrote on the spasm of blood vessels in the skin which can come with angina pectoris. Osler later wrote about this. Nothnagel gave much of the literature on the subject. He called it "angina pectoris vasomotoria." In his Case 1, he tells of something like a little or brief stroke.

M. Raynaud (1874) saw a little stroke type of syndrome in the cases of two patients who were suffering from arterial spasm in their fingers.

Nettleship (1879) was one of the first men to note that transient blindness can come with heart disease.

That great neurologist, J. Hughlings Jackson (1880) noted slight paralysis following an epileptic spell, such as he said was mentioned by Bravais in 1824. Jackson said that one can see such transient focal paralyses also without convulsions—due perhaps to a small clot, or to softening of the brain—from thrombosis of a blood vessel. He wondered why these transitory paralyses were ignored by physicians. Jackson could not explain the repitition of the transitory spells. Sir David Ferrier (1880) saw some brief strokes. One patient lost the senses of taste and smell on only one side of the nose and mouth. Priestly Smith (1884) described some cases of little strokes, with failure of vision.

An excellent article on brief strokes is that of Gasper Griswold (1884). Although he wrote 81 years ago, his article is well worth studying today. He suspected that often little strokes are due to a "functional cause," like a sudden lowering of systemic blood pressure—due perhaps to a bleeding into the abdominal veins. He knew that often at necropsies on people who have died of a small stroke, nothing wrong is found in the brain. Griswold said that the elder Garrod had written about such cases, Griswold spoke of "irregular apoplectic attacks," and of those brief strokes in which the symptoms at first look alarming but soon clear up. They may be due to spasm of a blood-vessel. Griswold reported three remarkable cases of brief strokes.

In 1887, E. O. Daly described a case of brief recurrent strokes. He said that Bastian, in his book, had described such strokes which he thought were due to spasm. (I read the book but could not find the reference). W. R. Gowers (1888, p.530) noted that patients with slight strokes lose their former sense of propriety. Stevenson (1890) saw a woman with Raynaud's disease and temporary losses of vision due perhaps to spasm in arterioles in her retina or visual center.

An early and excellent writer on brief strokes was George Peabody (1891). He noted, as many men did later, that at necropsy on a man who had died of a stroke, nothing could be found. He said that years before his day, Delafield and Prudden, the able pathologists, had written about this type of disease. Also—and this is remarkable—Peabody noted what Baker pointed out so clearly in 1937, that in persons over 60, brain arteries have lost their muscular coat, and hence cannot go into spasm. Peabody knew, moreover, that in the heart and brain a brief period of ischemia may well put an end to the function of some tissue, and even kill the patient, before histologic changes have had time to appear. (See Soma Weiss, 1940, and see more on this in Chapter 9.) Peabody favored the idea of spasm after observing it in the arteries of the retina.

Huchard (1910, p.459) told of writing in 1893 of transient aphasias and other little and brief strokes. He saw a man of 58 who suffered 4 such strokelets. In 1894, an able medical student named Lucas collected and reported seven cases of brief strokes due to a narrowing of the *internal carotid arteries*. He also reported two cases of little strokes (quoted from Stengel, 1908). Sottas, about 1894, also wrote a thesis on brief strokes. J. Grasset and J. Rauzier (1894) mentioned a little-stroke-type of spell.

Fox, in a letter to the Editor of the British Medical Journal (1895) described a case of a minister with typical little strokes. Also, he knew an actor who suffered from them. Hitzig (1898)* described the cases of a number of persons who, after a blow on the head, suffered with symptoms suggesting a little stroke. Beevor and Gunn (1899) saw a man with what looked like little strokes that were causing blindness.

GOOD ARTICLES PUBLISHED IN THE YEARS 1900 TO 1915. Kocher (1901, p. 345) wrote of "brain shock"—with a little type of stroke. Windscheid (1902, p. 346) described well the symptoms of patients with little strokes —with loss of memory, dizziness, faintness, headache, an inability to take in new ideas; also unsteadiness on the feet, fatigue, and an inability to work. He was one of those rare people who could see that, after a spell or two, a formerly bright man had changed much, and perhaps had aged. Barrett (1902) told of a man who woke blind in one eye and was well in 3 hours. Revendron is said to have written a Paris Thesis on little strokes in 1902. Grossmann (1902) described the case of a woman with severe brief strokes. In 1903, Browning, Adolf Meyer, and De Lancey Rochester, spoke of little strokes. Knapp (1904) told of a patient who had little strokes, perhaps due to a carotid obstruction. Pal (1905) knew about thrombosis of the basilar artery, and wrote of crises. H. G. Langwill, in 1906, reported several cases of brief spells of aphasia and hemiplegia that cleared up before the doctor had left the patient's house. Obviously, they were "brief strokes." F. H. Edgeworth, in 1906, in two papers, wrote on transitory hemiplegia in elderly persons. He described four cases. Edgeworth thought these troubles were due to spasm of arteries in the brain.

Emil Amberg, in 1906, wrote a remarkable article which should be republished, on "The Advisability of Eliminating the Term Ménière's Disease from Otologic Nomenclature." On page 116, he spoke of what I suspect were little strokes. He described many possible causes for so-called Ménière's symptoms. He spoke of disease of the brain causing the trouble, but he made no definite mention of little strokes. The big point he made was that often what is called Ménière's disease is not that.

Lundie (1906) saw a man of 88 with transient blindness of the left

---

* Nothnagel's Spez. Path. u. Ther., p. 78.

eye which he thought could have been due to "incipient thrombosis" in the arteries of the brain. H. Wilbrand and A. Saenger (1906), in their magnificent book, told of little strokes that can affect vision; and Hans Curschmann (1906) told of some spells that were associated with angina pectoris and loss of sight.

Gowers (1907) described "sudden cerebral lesions," probably little strokes. He knew that strokes could come in young people. Krehl (1907, p. 538) spoke of what Kocher (1901) had described as Hirnershütterung, or commotio cerebri. He seemed to be speaking of a little stroke type of attack. He wrote of "cerebral insults": or sudden "apoplectic insults," perhaps with disturbance of the circulation of the brain. He knew that with these upsets, at necropsy little damage may be found in the brain.

According to Huchard (1910), Josué, in 1907, described little strokes, but although I have read many of Josué's writings, I have not yet found the exact reference.

William Russell (1907), in his book, *Arterial Hypertonus, Sclerosis and Blood Pressure,* described the largest series of cases of severe little strokes or brief strokes that I have found in the old literature. These case reports are so instructive that I abstract a number of them here. A young doctor suddenly lost the power of speech, and strength in his right arm. In an hour, he was well. A man in middle life, one morning felt numbness on the left side of his body, including his face. He could move his arm, and he could stand, but his limbs felt as if they did not belong to him. In a few minutes he was all right.

A man of 63 one morning became aphasic for an hour or two. The next morning he woke with his left side powerless. His strength quickly returned.

A man of 48, on a Saturday morning, felt as if pins and needles were sticking into his left ankle. This feeling spread up his leg to the left half of his trunk to his shoulder and down his left arm. He could move his arm, but he could not grip anything with his hand. In half an hour, his strength returned. The next morning he was aphasic for an hour and a half. His speech returned, but he stuttered all day. Next day he was well. Later, he had more transient spells.

A man of 70 was unusually somnolent after luncheon. His speech became a little thick. On trying to write, he spelled words incorrectly. His walk was a bit unsteady.

A woman of 72, on a Sunday, vomited. Tuesday she became delirious, with delusions. Two days later she had an aphasia with hemiplegia. In a few days she was well. Months later, she had another attack of delirium, with a slight enfeeblement of the right side, and some aphasia. Next day she was well, except for slurred speech. Three months later, her right hand began to shake; she became dazed and unable to answer questions. The right arm and leg became paralyzed, but they jerked rhythmically. She later improved greatly.

A man of 72 suddenly got a weakness of the right side of his face, and slight impairment of speech. He quickly recovered the power in his arm and leg, but his speech continued slurred, and his face weak. Four months later, he had another attack of feebleness on the same side, with an increased difficulty in speaking. But soon he was almost well and mentally alert. Three months later he had a complete left hemiplegia and could not speak a word. This time he did not recover. He had *prodromal* little strokes.

Case 73 was very interesting as showing so clearly the relation between heart failure and the brain. A woman of 49 had angina pectoris, with a left hemiparesis. Her first anginal attack had come 7 years before, and with it her left arm had become paralyzed. It regained most of its strength in 24 hours, but every few weeks after that she would suffer from angina pectoris with a transient hemiplegia. (See A. Barnes and Fred Moersch).

Russell (p. 181) blamed his patients' spells on spasm of arteries. He knew that Raynaud's disease can accompany angina pectoris.

E. Schmoll (1907) reported the case of a woman with anginal pain and marked Raynaud's blanching of the fingers, which lasted several hours. Another woman with anginal pain would lose sensitivity on the inner side of her left arm, with formication and sometimes weakness of the arm. This would last either a few hours or one or two days. F. Parkes Weber and R. Grueber (1908) reviewed the interesting subject of those little strokes that cause transient blindness, and summarized the work of many men.

Alfred Stengel, in 1908, wrote very well about the possibility of partial thrombosis of some cerebral vessels. He said that Avicenna studied strokes in animals after tying their carotid arteries. Stengel reported having seen cases of carotid obstruction, such as Lucas had described in 1894. Stengel knew about those old people with cerebral arteriosclerosis who develop a psychosis, on their way to a final demented state.

William Russell, in 1909, again spoke of how common little strokes are. He wrote of "intermittent closing of the cerebral arteries," and the relation of this to temporary and permanent paralysis. Like the French, he thought of it as a claudication in the brain. He described brief strokes in the case of a farmer aged 50. Russell agreed with H. H. Tooth (1911) and Gowers (1875, 1877, 1888) that thrombosis is the commonest cause of hemiplegia.

Walter Broadbent (1909) spoke of the poor muscular supply of the cerebral arteries. He spoke of seeing a man with small strokes with diarrhea, and a transient hemiplegia. Six months later the man had a permanent hemiplegia. Lauder Brunton (1909), after noticing the marked spasms in his own temporal artery, with loss of pulsation—that ushered in his migrainous headaches—thought it probable that a branch of the internal carotid artery inside the cranium might go into the same type of spasm. He had a patient who, during a sick headache, would lose the senses of smell and taste—and get them back later. Edmund Hobhouse (1909) told of having seen patients with transient strokes which cleared in a day or two.

George Parker (1909) wrote well about "transient cerebral paralyses." He said we would never know much about small strokes until we knew "why the spasm"—granted that there is a spasm—which he much doubted. He said Cushing and Wiggers had produced some contraction of brain arteries. He had a patient who, so typically with a little stroke, fell out of his chair. Parker was aware of the fact that obstruction in the neck arteries could cause trouble. He doubted if edema of the brain could cause the symptoms because often they cleared up so suddenly. He knew that at many a necropsy little is found to explain the strokelike symptoms that were seen during life. In a few cases he found microscopic areas of destruction of the brain. Like Baker (1937) he knew that the muscular coat of the brain arteries is feeble compared with that of the systemic vessels. He was impressed by the fact that little stroke episodes are seen in some cases of Raynaud's disease.

Priestley Smith (1909) thought arterioles in the brain might cramp up, as he saw them do in the retina, sometimes producing transient blindness. He told of a man who sometimes would wake to find himself blind, and then he would recover the sight in one eye.

T. H. Moorhead (1909) wrote on transient spells of closing of the cerebral arteries. F. W. Mott (1910, pp. 608-614) wrote a splendid article on "transitory attacks of vaso-constriction," "pseudo-gastralgic attacks," and other forms of little strokes, with vertigo and "slight apoplectic or epileptiform seizures."

J. L. Miller (1910) ran into some trouble with little strokes when he was lowering high blood pressure in patients. He told of a patient who, when his pressure was quickly lowered, developed a left-sided transitory numbness, and later got repeated spells of hemiparesis, with numbness.

The great Leonard Hill, in 1910, described well the common little strokes with "cerebral anemia of slow onset." Hill wrote, "The cerebral circulation is controlled by a comparatively weak (if any) local vasomotor mechanism." In animals, he tied the carotid and other arteries. He knew much about what happens in different men when one or both carotid arteries are blocked. He knew that in animals the tying of four arteries in the neck can cause idiocy of a decerebrate type. Hill stated that the brain can function with a greatly reduced blood supply, as is shown by the absence of any marked cerebral symptoms in cases of advanced pernicious anemia (seen before the use of liver extract).

As I said, in an early chapter, J. D. Heard (1910) described well the brief strokes, and gave a fine bibliography. J. Mitchell Clarke, in 1910, wrote about severe types of little strokes in cases of migraine; and in 1915, he mentioned the distressing vertigo of many aged persons—a vertigo that can be due to cerebral arteriosclerosis.

George Allan (1910) described little strokes very well. He knew that they are likely to come when the heart has been weakened. He reported the case of a woman of 31 who had had spells of hemiparesis, lasting from 5 to 20 minutes. The trouble would begin with numbness. Once her speech was slowed; and once, for a time, her memory was badly impaired. She had had a bad heart for years. No permanent loss of function followed the episodes.

In Case 3, a woman of 26 had a mitral stenosis with angina. In the episodes of pain she would lose power in her left arm and leg and left side of her face. There were several occasions when there was aphasia, dragging of a leg, and a brief loss of memory.

H. H. Tooth (1911) mentioned little strokes under the term "prodromes," and C. W. Burr (1911) described some cases of this type. James Taylor (1911, p. 293) spoke of thrombosis in small arteries, which are often atheromatous. Edema can result, and later clear up. Taylor said (p. 300), in some of these cases, the mental peculiarity may be very slight, and may show itself only as emotional instability. He knew that the internal carotid artery can be blocked by atherosclerosis.

Oppenheim, in his great textbook (1911, pp. 813-824) spoke of "chronic progressive softening of the brain." Strangely, even with his great erudition, he apparently did not write much on little strokes.

Janeway (1913) wrote an excellent article on little strokes based on a study of 58 patients. He knew well the type of person whom I am constantly seeing—*without neurologic findings*. One man he saw had, typically, lost 35 pounds in weight and had had a decided drop in blood pressure. Some patients had a rubbery "giving out of the legs." Janeway knew the need for a physician's learning well the art of history-taking, and the "significance of symptoms." A doctor should know the need for digging out the story of the *"symptoms that the patient forgot."* Janeway told of spells of dizziness, transient aphasia, failure of vision, feelings of exhaustion, etc. So far as I know, he it was who coined the useful terms "brain death, heart death, and renal death."

Volhard and Farr (1914, p. 235) spoke of transitory hemiparesis and "functional brain troubles" and "pseudo-uremia" with psychic disturbances. They wrote of a bulbar ischemia, and "angina abdominalis." In the spells there can be disorientation, apathy, restlessness, fainting, or epileptiform crises. There may be edema of the brain. The heart can become infarcted, and perhaps there may be angina abdominalis, also dead fingers. They describe (p. 243) the case of a diabetic woman of 51 who had many sudden spells, some heart attacks, transitory aphasias and right facial paresis. Later she was mentally confused, and finally died. Necropsy showed much sclerosis of arteries of the brain and heart. According to Volhard and Farr, Vaquez wrote about transitory aphasia.

J. R. Hunt (1914, p. 712) wrote well on a little type of stroke. His study of the results of obstruction of the internal carotid is one of the best, and his list of early writers on carotid obstruction is probably the best.

Some of the Old French Literature on Little Strokes. In July, 1951, I received a kindly and very helpful letter from that wise neuro-psychiatrist, Dr. Percival Bailey. He said:

I had the good fortune to spend a couple of years as a student in the medical clinics in Paris. The syndrome (of little strokes) is well known to every French clinician, and you will find it described in any French system of medicine. Time after time Pierre Marie returned to this syndrome in his Tuesday clinics. The French literature concerning it goes back to his studies which he began to publish in 1901. You will find the fundamental articles in his collected works, Volume 1, page 71. See also his "Congestion et anemie cérébrale" in Traité de Méd. (Brouardel et Gilbert, Paris, 1901, 8: 531-551; 695-726); also, in "Lecons de Clinique Médicale" (8: 296, 1894-1895). I assure you that I agree with the importance of bringing this matter to the attention of American physicians.

I looked up these references and found that, as Dr. Bailey said, Marie knew well the little strokes. He noted that with the syndrome, the patient can have headache, somnolence, or insomnia, changes in character, loss of memory, difficulty in talking, transitory aphasia, also apoplectic attacks followed by hemiplegia.

In G. Roger, F. Vidal, and P. J. Tessier's *Nouveau Traité de Médecine*, (1920, vol. 19) under "cerveau sénile" (p. 430) I found the vascular lesions described. Miliary hemorrhages were mentioned.

In Pierre Marie's "La Pratique Neurologique" (1911, p. 170), I found described the syndrome of cerebral arteriosclerosis, which he said was written up by Mendel (1891) and Grasset (1906).

I read that J. M. Charcot (1858, p. 251) told of a woman of 35 who had perhaps a little stroke. In his Clinical Lectures (1868, p. 261, and 1886) Charcot discussed "capillary apoplexy." In his book (1886) he mentioned little strokes.

In Trousseau's book (1885, Chap. 40, p. 87) he discussed "*congestion cérébrale*," but doubted if congestion was producing the sudden and transitory apoplectic phenomena such as he kept observing. He called them "apoplectic accidents, sudden and momentary."

Later, Trousseau got the idea that little strokes are manifestations of epilepsy. He described a typical brief stroke. A man of 42 was found on his bed, unconscious, but in a short time he was all right. Trousseau talked to a valet who said that his master had been having a number of brief strokes; also, the doctor saw a man in his thirties who had had three short spells.

In Volume 3, Chapter 68, p. 1, Trousseau described spells, some of which could well have been little strokes; others may have been due to a severe form of Menière's disease, but he thought that at least some of them were of cerebral origin, or possibly due to *disease in the vertebral arteries.* He saw what I keep seeing—patients who, after a little stroke, get abdominal pain as soon as they eat.

In 1872, Noel G. de Mussy wrote well of vertigo with cerebral ischemias. He quoted Lecorché who, he said, wrote of such things in 1869.

Excellent is the huge *Traité de Médecine* of Charcot, Bouchard and Brissaud, published in 1894. In volume 6, Brissaud wrote well and at length on little strokes. He said that around 1700 Boerhaave had described "accidents cérébraux" ranging from vertigos to apoplexies. Brissaud said the Piorry (1826) told of troubles with the circulation of the brain in the Memoire on the influence of sadness on the flow of blood in the cerebral vessels.

Brissaud said that Rostan (1825) wrote about softening of the brain associated with anemia. Also, Bechelet (1868) wrote on cerebral anemia. Brissaud told of early workers, like Kussmaul, Dondernet, Callenfels, Nothnagel and Vulpian who stimulated the cervical sympathetic nerves. He said Vulpian studied the effects on the brain of tying all four arteries in the neck.

Brissaud told (p. 135) of the typical little strokes that can come to people who have just lost much blood. He told of chronic little strokes with much dizziness; also the injury done by cerebral anemia to old people. He advised (p. 137) the use of an ophthalmoscope in diagnosing obliteration of a carotid artery. He has more about little strokes on page 162, and on page 134, he told how disease of the heart can be associated with cerebral anemia!

Grasset (1906) said that in 1901 he described (in nephritics and the gouty) spells of forgetfulness, intellectual fatigue, dizziness, aphasia, and at times, slight hemiparesis, paraplegias, pains and numbness, which quickly cleared away. He said, so wisely, that there are mild and severe forms of little strokes. He spoke of intermittent claudication of the brain; also, the walk with the little steps—"la marche à petit pas." He said some physicians call this Petrén's (1900) gait, but it was described earlier by Dejerine. He said that Dejerine made brilliant contributions to the idea of little strokes around 1890, and later in 1906.

Leri (1906 and 1911) reported on what probably were little or brief strokes. On page 759 he told about the symptoms that are intermittent and paroxysmal. He spoke of vertigo, headache, ear noises, somnolence, and insomnia, character changes, a tendency to fatigue, a loss of memory, brief spells of transitory aphasia, hemiparesis, neurasthenia, *rubbery legs*, and senile epilepsy. In the discussion that followed, M. Anglade spoke of the common loss of smell, and Maurice Raymond spoke of pseudo-paraplegias ("rubbery legs").

I have read that in 1866 Proust wrote a thesis on little strokes. Huchard (1893, 1899, 1909, 1910) wrote extensively about arteriosclerosis, and described little strokes. He said (1910) that Josué (1907) described "les petits signes de l'arteriosclerose"; also, that J. Tessier (1908) wrote on the subject.

ENGLISH ARTICLES ON LITTLE STROKES FROM 1915 TO DATE. J. Gordon Sharpe (1915) told about seven persons, some of whom suffered from transient aphasia. A. Pelz (1916), O. K. Williamson (1918), G. Ricker (1919, p. 207), I. L. Nascher (1919) and Thomas Inman (1920) all described little strokes.

Henry Woltman (1921, 1922) described the commoner symptoms of the little strokes. Some 64 per cent of the patients had a normal blood pressure. *Neurologic residuals were seen in only 3 per cent of the cases.*

Foix and Nicolesco (1923) described episodes resembling little strokes. Fink (1924) reported 130 cases of transient loss of vision in women post-partum, perhaps after a big hemorrhage. Groedel and Hubert (1925) spoke of a *brief* stroke, and Josef Wilder (1926) quoted the work of several men who saw little strokes. K. Westphal and Baer (1926) and Westphal (1926) spoke of mild apoplexy due to spasm. Westphal (p. 33) wrote of the frequency with which little strokes come during the night. He spoke of "fleeting pareses," and gave a big bibliography. In 1926 Moniz was performing angiographies. He reported on this work in 1927.

G. W. B. James (1926) knew the need for getting the history from relatives of the patient. He spoke of the changes in character which cause a man "to be not like himself." He emphasized the fact that *commonly, a patient with a badly injured brain is without any neurologic residual.* How true! James' paper is one of the best.

H. W. Fleming and H. C. Naffziger (1927) spoke of transient hemi-plegias. Foix and Ley (1927) reported two cases of little strokes. M. S. Gregory (1928) told of a wealthy old man whose ability to make a will was challenged because he was so parsimonious he would not buy an automobile, or supply good food for his table; at times he failed to recognize friends; he kept repeating the same old stories; he gave orders and forgot he had done so; he went out badly dressed; his sphincters did not always hold; he might invite guests and not treat them properly; and he would tell vulgar stories in front of ladies.

Oppenheimer and Fishberg (1928) were impressed by spasm in both Raynaud fingers and in the retina. They studied the brief cerebral episodes in cases of malignant hypertension. Lhermitte (1928), Bremer (1928), and J. H. W. Rhein, N. W. Winkelman and C. A. Patten (1928) wrote of "repeated mental storms" in which *dementia progresses in steps, like going down a ladder.* The patient recovers a bit from a storm but each one "leaves [him] a little worse than before."

Barber (1928) described six cases of *brief strokes.* Some of them made him think of possible epilepsy. Keith, van Wagener and Kernohan (1928) described many cases of malignant hypertension with brief stroke-like spells. H. M. Thomas (1928) spoke so accurately of "insecurity of equilibrium." He knew that little strokes can come with angina pectoris. Riser, Meriel and Planques (1931) saw brief strokes, and quoted Pal and Barré. Alvarez (1932) wrote of the little stroke patient who complains of indigestion.

Gillespie (1933) saw patients with brief spells but no neurologic residues. He was one of the first to say that some badly changed patients do not see that they are changed. Sir R. Armstrong Jones (1933) was one of the first men to notice the abnormal personal habits and strange conduct of some persons who have had little strokes; also the tendency of some of these patients to disinherit their family, leaving all their money to a nurse or a housekeeper.

Wertham and Wertham (1934, p. 463) told of little strokes, also G. W. Pickering (1934). S. D. Jelliffe and W. A. White (1935, p. 740) wrote of those many vertiginous attacks which may be followed by mental enfeeblement and arteriosclerotic deterioration. Alvarez (1935) wrote two articles on unrecognized strokes. Cobb (1936) knew about little strokes. E. Krapf (1937) studied the mental disturbances of some persons with hypertension. Alvarez (1937) wrote 2 articles on little strokes and indigestion.

Foster Kennedy, S. B. Wortis, and H. Wortis (1937, pp. 672-674; also 1938) spoke of little strokes; also Stanley Cobb (1937, p. 741). Moniz, Almeida and de Lacerda (1937) reported angiographies on 537 persons, and found 4 with disease of *an internal carotid artery.* Putnam (1937) mentioned brief strokes. W. H. Chao, S. T. Kwan, R. S. Lyman and H. H. Loucks (1938) studied thrombosis of the internal carotid artery. They reported 2 cases, and listed a number of the very early papers on the subject.

Davison and Brill (1939) reported 7 cases of little strokes. E. F. Rosenberg (1940) made an excellent clinical and pathological study of the little strokes seen in many cases of malignant hypertension.

E. Moniz (1940) published—in German—a book on angiography. He started using this method in 1926. On page 284 he mentions strokelets. In 1927 he told of his first efforts at angiography.

Kinnier Wilson, on page 1099 of his magnificent textbook (1941), wrote of little strokes. He gathered a fine bibliography. On page 1104, he spoke of "arteriopathic neurasthenia," and told of the patient who becomes different; is "not himself"; is apathetic; with slow-thinking; poor judgment and an inability any longer to concentrate. Wilson went on to describe severe little strokes with much mental confusion, faulty personal habits, childishness, and a tendency to suspicion. Some such persons end up with a total disintegration of character, a shuffling gait, and a troubled speech. *He noticed the impassiveness of the features at rest.* As he said "brief apoplectiform attacks are very common," and *Parkinsonism can come.*

Alvarez (1941) wrote of little strokes that cause chronic fatigue. G. W. Robinson (1941) studied mild apoplexies in the aged. E. Moniz (1942, quoted by Ecker and Riemenschneider, 1953) saw the brief strokes, often due to disease in an internal carotid artery; C. D. Aring (1945, p. 39) described spells, focal and transient, with weakness, numbness, visual disturbances, unconsciousness, and convulsions. As he said (p. 42) "cerebral arteriosclerosis is just about as normal as death."

One of the very few men who noticed the *"untidiness of dress"* of many of the patients who have had little strokes was Rothschild, who in 1945 (p. 246) commented on this common symptom of a brain injury. Frovig (1946) wrote a splendid article on *carotid spells*. Alvarez (1946) wrote in Geriatrics a review of cerebral arteriosclerosis and little strokes. R. D. Adams and M. E. Cohen (1947, Part 3) wrote on hypertensive encephalopathy and described the transient cerebral disturbances of hypertensives with bad kidneys. As the authors say, even a slight focal vascular disturbance of the brain can be an event of serious importance. Alvarez (1947) wrote a chapter on little strokes for Oxford Medicine; also an article on little strokes in the American Journal of Nursing.

James Purves-Stewart (9th Edition, 1947, p. 455) mentioned intermittent cerebral claudication, spells of which can last perhaps for an hour. Sir George Pickering (1948) described transient paralyses in cases of hypertension and cerebral embolism. See also N. C. Gilbert and G. de Takats (1948), Russek and Zohman (1948), and Alvarez (1948). H. Woltman (1949) told of 200 patients with cerebral arteriosclerosis, and listed some of the common symptoms seen with little strokes. G. L. Engel (1950) wrote well on little strokes—a "common syndrome among elderly patients." He gave a big bibliography. See F. C. P. Cloake (1951); Wilson, Rupp, Riggs, and Wilson (1951); Denny-Brown (1951); and E. B. Allen (1951). Allen said these patients are "becoming the leading problem in psychiatry." K. S. Grimson, E. S. Orgain, C. R. Rowe, Jr. and H. M. Sieber (1952) wrote of thrombosis of cerebral arteries that can come when a high blood pressure is lowered too rapidly with the help of powerful drugs.

An Editorial writer in the New England Journal of Medicine (1952, pp. 154-155) wrote eloquently about the little strokes, and told of the havoc they can play with the brains of some people. Another Editorial writer (H. J. L. M., in the Annals of Internal Medicine, 1952) ably discussed little strokes. S. L. Cole and J. N. Sugarman (1952) wrote of the cerebral manifestations of acute myocardial infarction. E. Corday, S. F. Rothenberg and T. J. Putnam (1953) wrote much about spells of acute cerebral vascular insufficiency, and R. D. Adams and H. M. Vander Eecken (1953) wrote of the severe little strokes that assail some hypertensives.

Ecker and Riemenschneider (1953) studied brief strokes of the internal carotid type. M. Fisher and D. G. Cameron (1953), in an excellent article, said *they had the impression that transient phenomena preceding the onset of a big stroke are much more frequent than is commonly believed. The patient fails to tell about them, and the doctor fails to ask about them.* So true! Fisher and Cameron (1953) told of a woman of 70 with spells of great distress in her head.

I. S. Wright and Ellen McDevitt (1954) wrote, "*We see many patients who have a series of transient or 'little strokes'.*" H. G. Eastcott, G. W. Pickering and C. G. Rob (1954) told of a woman who had the brief strokes due to an internal carotid obstruction. R. D. Adams (1954) wrote a splendid discussion of the mechanisms of brief apoplexies, and reported a number of cases with necropsy reports. He studied the problem of sudden recovery. Alvarez (1955) published 2 articles on little strokes.

Millikan and Siekert (1955) told about 4 patients with brief spells. L. Berlin, B. Tumarkin and H. L. Martin (1955) reported 13 cases of odd strokes in young people from 18 to 34 years of age. Sir Russell Brain, in his book (1955) was one of the few men to mention the *importance of purely mental symptoms* after a little stroke. He spoke so truly of the patient's difficulty in remembering names; also, of his emotional instability, and his lack of patience with annoyances.

J. M. Foley (1956) spoke of the little stroke which can be due to a lacunar infarct (see Marie and others). Keith W. Sheldon (1956) in his book, spoke of pseudo-Menière attacks. He said that he knew about the little strokes—with short blackouts, short periods of weakness and changes in speech. In his Case No. 5, he tells how one morning a man of 67 could not feel the razor on his face, and he could not feel heat on his foot on that side. That was about all. Sheldon spoke of the *thalamic syndrome* that can follow a little stroke.

W. T. Foley and I. S. Wright (1956) wrote of the many patients they see with *a series of "little strokes"* which may range in severity from slight numbness or weakness of the side of the face or slight difficulty with speech to hemiplegia, and which may last for from a few minutes to several days, with complete recovery. E. Corday, S. F. Rothenberg and S. M. Wiener (1956) wrote on transient strokes, and S. F. Rothenberg and E. E. Corday (1957) studied angiospasm in monkeys. They discussed the mechanism of production of transient cerebral strokes. John Rankin (1957) wrote much and well on little strokes in people over 60. The necropsy often shows little. Alvarez (1957) wrote on the abdominal symptoms of little strokes. A remarkable article on the little strokes that produce blindness was written by Charles Symonds and Ian Mackenzie (1957). They quoted 33 papers by men who reported cases of little strokes with blindness. See end of Chapter 10 for more such references.

W. S. Fields, E. S. Crawford and M. E. De Bakey (1958) believed that the cause of occasional cerebral insufficiency is outside the skull in some 25 per cent of cases. They said that occlusion of neck vessels has been known since F. Penzoldt wrote in 1881, and Oppenheim and Goras wrote in 1900 and 1901.

In the *Classification and Outline of Cerebrovascular Diseases, the Report of the Committee of the Advisory Council for the National Institute of Neurological Diseases and Blindness* (1958, p. 419) there is some discussion of temporary ischemia. "Attacks may last 10 seconds, 10 minutes, or even an hour." Clough (1958), in an editorial in Annals of Internal Medicine, spoke of "Alvarez' little strokes." S. O. Lindgren (1958) wrote on disease of the internal carotid arteries.

That eminent neurologist, Dr. Benjamin Boshes (1958) described well the little and brief strokes. As he said, they are common and frequently misdiagnosed. Often the dizziness is interpreted as being part of a Menière syndrome, but the ears are normal. As Dr. Boshes said so wisely,

The reaction of the individual to the process of aging depends to a large extent on his previous personality. The well-adjusted, mature, adequate man can handle the sunset of his life well. He can give of himself, or his substance, and can share the pleasures of those about him.

The man who has always been insecure can easily go to pieces when age comes upon him.

McDevitt, Carter, Gatje, Foley and Wright (1958) spoke of intermittent ischemic syndromes, or thromboembolic episodes.

H. J. Roberts, in his book *Difficult Diagnosis of Obscure Illness* (1958, pp. 359 and 360) spoke of the very common small strokes. C. M. Fisher (1958, p. 325) spoke of the attacks of dizziness. Wisely he said that in such cases a physician may have to observe several spells before he sees one that is typically and definitely a little stroke. He knew that often the diagnosis of Menière's disease is wrong. In a fine big article (1958) he told of transient ischemic attacks. J. St. C. Elkington (1958, p. 276) told of some severe brief strokes.

J. Marshall and D. A. Shaw (1959) wrote on multiple and transient strokes and said the disease is common. Sir Charles Symonds (1959) spoke of ischemic episodes and carotid artery spells.

R. A. Kuhn (1960 and 1961) described brief strokes, mainly of carotid origin. Groch, Hurwitz, Wright and McDowell (1960) spoke of 15 patients with what looked like repeated transient ischemias. Alajouanine, Lhermitte, and Gautier (1960) reported 105 cases of brief strokes, with nothing found at necropsy. Gurdjian, Lindner, Hardy, and Webster (1960) mentioned "vague attacks" that looked like little strokes.

W. A. Soderman (1961, p. 377) wrote of people who fell out of chairs, and had other transient cerebral symptoms. Edward Weiss (1961) described well the mental changes that can come with little strokes. C. van Buskirk (1962), B. J. Alpers (1962), Noyes and Kolb (1963, p. 223) spoke of little strokes. T. P. Kearns and R. W. Hollenhorst (1963) reported a case of carotid occlusion. A while ago the U.S. Government put out a booklet on the Little Strokes. Lord Brain (1964, pp. 192-195) wrote on this subject.

It is interesting to note that about 1925 a dam burst or a tabu was broken, and after that a few men wrote each year about little strokes. Dams burst again about 1950 and 1960.

To the hundred and more men who, I am sure, have written, and written well, of little strokes, and whose papers I did not find and hence could not mention here, go my apologies.

7

Some Interesting Little Strokes*

A Diagnosis That Would Have Been Easy if the Significance of Certain Early Episodes Had Been Noted. A while ago, while going through an old file, I ran onto a case record that suddenly taught me much about little strokes and how easy the diagnosis can be if we will only get the history of the earliest episodes, and if then we will realize what these episodes meant. The record was that of a good friend whom I saw professionally for the first time in 1925. He was then about 50, and the head of a large business. He was a keen, alert and friendly man. One day he came in and said, "As you know, I have always been raring to go at my work. Then, one morning a few weeks ago, I woke to find myself so tired that I had to force myself to get up, get dressed, and go to the office. And when I got there, I found I couldn't do anything; I could not even answer my mail."

Today, if I were to hear such a story, I would not be puzzled; I would immediately recognize the story of a man who has had a severe silent stroke during the night, but in 1925 I had not yet learned enough about little strokes to be sure of what an atypical story meant. Hence I examined my friend from head to foot, and when I found nothing, I had to tell him I did not know what was wrong.

At that time I left San Francisco, and my friend went to a physician who promptly removed his "chronic appendix." When this did no good, my friend went to our leading heart consultant who, for the next few years, treated him without success for heart disease which probably was

---

* If here I fail to mention hypertension, diabetes, or other contributing factors, it is because no such factor was found. I regret that, in most cases, the patient came from a distance, hence I cannot tell what happened to him after his consultation with me.

not there because the man never had any symptoms of heart disease. His troubles were all those of an injured brain.

For the next 22 years, on my annual vacation to California, I would visit my old friend. He continued to be his old kindly and well-groomed self, and he continued to go to his office for part of each day, but all he could do was to sit at his desk. Then he became unsteady on his feet; later he became afraid to go out on the street alone, and later, he feared to be left alone in his apartment.

After some 15 years without improvement he showed signs of a Parkinson's syndrome, and in another 5 years he became so weak that it was hard for him to get about. In 1946, he became paralyzed and bedfast, and then he gradually petered out. Part of his brain died while the rest of his brain and all of his body were still in good shape.

Now, the remarkable fact is that recently, when I happened to run onto his old record and read it, I found something which, in 1925, should quickly have given me the diagnosis. I cannot understand now how I could have been so stupid as not to see the significance of two episodes. There, on the first page of my friend's history, was the key to his whole illness. One day in 1923, his right hand had suddenly become numb, partially paralyzed, and unwieldy. For several months it gave him trouble, and then it became normal again. The story was as typical of a little stroke as one could ask for, and yet the physician who then was taking care of him did not see its significance, and in 1925 I did not see instantly that it gave the clue to what happened one night.

In 1924, my friend thrust his right hand into the open gear-box of a pump on his farm, and lost several fingers. Again, his family physician did not do any thinking, and perhaps did not even ask how the accident had happened. I, too, in 1925, failed to wonder, and to ask the questions that I should have asked. It was only in 1955, when I reread the record—with the knowledge gained in 30 years of study of hundreds of patients with sclerosis of the brain arteries, that I was able to see that first, there had come a little stroke with injury to an arm, and later a little stroke that had caused the man to fall. In trying to save himself, he had apparently thrust his hand into the gear-box which he was oiling. Finally, there came the big silent stroke in the night.

As can happen in these cases, the man went for the next 20 years with no more recognizable strokes. What was remarkable was that with so much brain damage, he had no "neurologic residuals," and he showed no tendency to recover. I have often puzzled over this fact, that in many cases of severe little or silent strokes, there is no recovery, or no recovery from one or two symptoms such as a burning skin and a difficulty in writing. Many a man with an aphasia and a hemiplegia will soon learn to talk and walk again, while his arm may remain largely useless.

ANOTHER INTERESTING CASE. An able and still young-looking executive, aged 68, told me that he had been well until a year before, when at a stop-light he had crashed into the back of the car ahead of him. Since he had always been a good and safe driver, with never an accident, he concluded that something must have gone wrong with his brain, and this worried him. Then a few minutes later he side-swiped a car. This so frightened him that, when the police came, he asked one of them to drive him home. His physician soon came and found nothing wrong except a systolic blood pressure of 180 mm. Hg.

Then I got from the man the information that for a while something had been going wrong with his nervous system; his ophthalmologist said that his vision had been failing, without any sign of disease in his eyes. Also, for a while he had been having difficulty in reading, and in getting the meaning out of a legal document. He had had to read it over and over again—something that he had never had to do before.

He could not remember any little stroke, but this is so interesting—when I talked to his secretary, she said, "Why, of course; he had a little stroke four months ago. One afternoon, as he sat dictating to me, I saw a sudden and frightening change in him. Although he thought he was all right, he was talking gibberish, and so I insisted on taking him right home. His physician, on arrival, found him talking well, and apparently all right."

Ten days before I saw the man he had come home feeling well, but about bed-time he had suddenly noted a peculiar and very distressing feeling of tightness and distention in his abdomen. With this spell the man felt a very disturbing "hot feeling" in his palate. He had no trouble swallowing, and the food went down the right way, but soon he got pain in his cheeks and both forearms. Two days before I saw him, his flatulent abdominal distress was interfering with his sleep. He was swallowing air and belching by the hour—a nervous trick. He felt so much distress between his shoulder blades that he could not stand up straight. An examination showed nothing objectively wrong.

His palate continued to feel hot; and one wrist and hand still hurt so much in a causalgic way that, like a few other patients, he thought at times that he would be better off with the arm amputated. He was still able to go to his office every day. At times he had "an ugly feeling" in his face. Then he got spells in which he would feel terribly uncomfortable all over his body. Fortunately, he continued to remain well-groomed, and he still was able to play golf. His memory remained fairly good, and he wasn't particularly irritable or emotional.

One day he came in to tell me that he had recalled the fact that 10 years before, while out walking, suddenly he had felt the same distressing hot feeling in his palate that was bothering him again. It was so awful when it first came that he felt sure he was having a little stroke. This ability to remember a stroke that had occurred years before is typical of quite a few cases.

CASES IN WHICH THE FAMILY MAKES THE DIAGNOSIS. Often when I have been puzzled—suspecting a strokelet, but getting no history of one—all I have to do is to wait a while. As time passes, the man's wife, or his grown children will some to my aid, as they will keep remembering little strokes that hit the man, perhaps 10 or 15 years before. Suddenly, one of the grown sons will say, "Remember, Mother, he must have been having a stroke that time in 1950 because right after that curious spell he had, he became so irritable and unreasonable and unlike his old self."

In a case of this type, for a while I could not convince the man's doctor that the fellow had had some strokes, until the patient's wife and grown daughter got to remembering several occasions when he had behaved in so unreasonable and insane and unpleasant a way that the two women knew that his brain had been injured, and his formerly pleasant and affectionate character had been greatly changed. A few weeks after I last saw him, he had a big stroke, about which there could be no doubt. The literature on cerebral arteriosclerosis is full of stories of men who, before their final big stroke, had a dozen or more little prodromal ones. Hippocrates knew about them.

One must get the story from relatives. The following story is worth telling here to show how poorly a patient's troubles can be diagnosed even by able consultants—when they have not obtained the essential story from the family. A woman, aged 40, complained of "horrible nervousness." For years she had been very strong and well. She had cooked for a resort, where she had worked 15 hours a day.

Two years before I saw her, one evening, when she was well rested after a happy vacation, she suddenly felt dizzy, so dizzy that she lay down. Strongly indicative of a brain injury was the fact—told me by her husband—that for a while she had trouble talking, and she saw double. During this spell, when she wanted to urinate, someone had to almost carry her into the bathroom. Then she vomited, and the doctor who was called thought she had food poisoning. After sleeping awhile, she woke with a pain in the right side of her head. When she tried to walk, she reeled like a drunk, and could not follow a straight line.

Something that her physicians should never have ignored was the fact that, after that spell she was a changed person, unable to work; unhappy; not feeling right in her head; depressed; unable to think clearly; and without interest in anything. Her legs were "tingly," and she felt a vibration throughout her body. On some days she could not "write straight." She could no longer read because she could not concentrate; she would find herself reading over and over again the same sentence. She had only a few good days. She kept getting pain down her left arm, and around the left side of her chest—a pain that was not brought on by exertion. She had aches and pains all over. At times she slept poorly, but then she might sleep 15 hours a day. Her hearing and her vision failed a bit. Unable to remember words, she had difficulty saying what she wanted to say. She felt as if any minute her eyes would cross. She remained somewhat ataxic in her walk.

Her husband said that after the big spell her old good nature left, and she became so irritable she screamed at people. She became afraid of being in the house alone, and she rapidly lost 20 pounds.

She was well examined by neurologists who found her EEG's and spinal fluid normal. Tests for syphilis were negative. Apparently because their tests with pin and cotton showed nothing; because the woman always failed to give the essential points of her history; because the doctors failed to get the highly diagnostic history from the woman's husband, and because they ignored her difficulty in talking, they diagnosed "just nerves."

She was angry over this because, as she said so wisely, just nerves could not in a minute have changed an active, cheerful, strong and hardworking woman into a chronic invalid who felt utterly miserable, and could not work or even read comfortably. She had more medical good sense than had her physicians!

I agreed with the woman that she had had a stroke. As I expected, in the next 4 years in which I kept in touch with her husband, I learned that to a large extent she recovered. She even learned to drive her car again, and once she wrote me a letter.

ONE CANNOT CURE LITTLE STROKES WITH AN OPERATION. The following story interested me much because it showed so clearly that even a distinguished internist can miss a diagnosis completely if his assistants fail to get for him even a small part of the all-essential story.

A widow of 65, after a lifetime of perfect health, began to suffer severe abdominal distress. Most of it was "a constant burning" over her left hip. Puzzled, her able home physician sent her for an examination to a big university clinic. There, an intern took a brief and useless history. When the roentgenologist found some silent gallstones, the professor of medicine accepted this as the cause of all the distress, and got the professor of surgery to remove her gallbladder. Naturally, the operation had absolutely no influence on the woman's burning hip.

When I saw her and noted her dull face, I asked her about little strokes, but her memory was so poor and her mind so confused, that in a few minutes I knew I could not get much of a history out of her. Accordingly, I telephoned her son who came and gave me the all-important story. He said that some 3 years before, his mother, who had always been a strong, energetic, attractive and able woman, had had an attack in which she felt she was going to black out; she became confused, and for a while was stuporous. When she woke from this spell, she was full of fear of she knew not what. When she tried to eat, for a while she choked and coughed violently because food kept entering her larynx. She was so ill she was taken to a hospital where the diagnosis was "a toxic goiter." Apparently, soon the doctors changed their mind about this, because they just sent her home. This spell left her with much insomnia, much sweating, and much fear of being alone.

For the rest of that summer she was too weak to do her housework, and she was too tired even to talk much. More examinations with many tests showed nothing. Then someone found a small umbilical hernia and—how typical this is—a surgeon pounced on it as the cause of all her troubles. But a repair of the hernia did no good.

Her son said that 3 months after her first little stroke (He knew what her trouble was!), she had another one. She got up at night to urinate, and was seized with an awful pain, so severe that she lost consciousness; she fell to the floor, and hurt her nose. Later, she had another little stroke, which again caused her to pitch forward off of her toilet seat. This left her so utterly miserable that she wanted to die. Typical of such misery after a little stroke was the fact that no sedative or tranquilizer or pain-reliever ever gave her any relief.

Interesting was this woman's statement that when she entered one of the university hospitals to which she was sent, she suddenly remembered the 3 little strokes, and tried to tell the resident about them, but he would not listen to such a story; impatiently he told her just to answer the questions that were asked her, and this she then did.

Then came her fourth and last little stroke—a bad one. It came when she was half-way across an avenue. She almost blacked out, and became so confused that she could not move. She stood there with the cars whizzing past her until a man ran out and led her back to the sidewalk. With this, there came the constant burning misery over her left hip, also the feeling of much gas in her bowel—gas which she could not get up or down. Typical of a little stroke was a change in her handwriting so marked that the bank asked her to give them a new sample of her signature.

I have now known this fine old lady for perhaps 14 years; she has remained uncomfortable, but so far as I know, she has not had any more little strokes. One wonders why.

A DOCTOR'S TRAGEDY. To show that even a wise old doctor, when he had little strokes, could not "sell the idea" to his physician friends, I need tell only of the fine, able physician of 70 who told me that suddenly, after a lifetime of good health and overwork, he had had a few little strokes which had shaken him up so badly that he could no longer see many patients a day. He had to force himself to do what little work he was doing. When he told two able internists—friends of his—that he had had little strokes, they hooted at the idea, and told him that there were no such things. The doctors said he had become a "neuro" and a hypochondriac, and "he should snap out of it." They turned him over to a psychiatrist who, also, refused to accept the idea of little strokes. But, with all this, the fact remained that the unhappy doctor could hardly work; and he said he wanted to work more than he had ever wanted to work in his life before! How stupid it was to accuse a man like that of having suddenly become a hypochondriac.

ANOTHER DOCTOR WHO HAD A HORRIBLE DEATH. Back around 1935, I saw another physician, aged 65, who for long, in spite of our friendship, had resented my talking about little strokes because he was so sure such things did not exist. Then, one day, he suffered a severe little jolt, one which, in a moment, left him confused and slowed-up and unable even to read. Soon he had another severe spell, again, without any paralysis. This one destroyed so much of his brain that he was left lying in bed, diapered, and looking with vacant eyes at the ceiling. He showed no sign of recognizing anyone. He was worse off than a decerebrate animal. This was distressing enough, but what was worse was that he lived on for a number of years in this terrible condition.

LITTLE STROKES WHICH TERRIFIED THE MAN. A hypertensive man of 48 complained much of spells of abdominal *distress* (not pain), and marked distention of his abdomen. The first spell came suddenly one day, and made him think he was going to die. Next day he was all right. A month later he had another similar attack, and again he quickly recovered. Five months after that, he had a spell of retching which terrified him. With his first episode his blood pressure dropped suddenly from 190/100 to 105/75, which is typical of a little stroke.

Then, six months later, at 2 A.M., he woke with a feeling of great pressure over his heart, and again he felt he was dying. Following this, he had no symptoms or signs of a heart injury. A month later, while out walking, he suddenly felt so terrible he rushed to a hospital, where nothing wrong was found.

What interested me most about this fellow was that he was so sure, with his first big spell, that his brain had been terribly injured. At the time he was sure he was having a stroke. At the hospital, he told the intern this, but, as often happens, the young doctor refused to make any record of this *most important fact* on the history sheet. When I was called in consultation I found in the record much about laboratory and x-ray findings but nothing about his little strokes.

A SERIES OF UNUSUAL LITTLE STROKES. An eminent lawyer, 71, young for his age, in June, 1964, while working at high pressure, got dizzy on moving his head quickly. When he woke in the mornings, he had to get up from his bed slowly. Then one day, he found that for a while he could not walk straight. A few weeks later, while strolling, he fell down. After a while he got back enough strength to get up and walk some yards to his house. Three days later, he had a spell in which he was comatose for some minutes; later he blacked out briefly while sitting in a chair; and later again, while in his bed.

He had always had a low blood pressure. After his spells he could read too slowly for comfort. When I saw him he still was writing well, except for the fact that he left out words and letters. His interests remained strong. His face was still mobile and he was pleasant, attractive, friendly and well-groomed. He talked well without hesitation. His blood cholesterol level was 316 mg. A neurologic examination, including EEG's, showed no abnormality. Since his strokes, he had been carrying on with his big burden of business administration.

A MAN WITH MANY RATHER MINOR SYMPTOMS. A man aged 45 was well until 6 months before I saw him, when he suffered a series of spells of confusion with uncertainty of balance. He felt as if drunk and tipsy. His feeling of confusion lasted for 15 or 20 minutes, while the lack of balance remained for two or three hours. In these spells, *he felt that he was having a stroke*; he had a miserable feeling in his head, and some numbness on the inner sides of his thighs. His feet would get distressingly cold and clumsy, and his toes would cramp up. The left hand sometimes cramped, and at times it got a bit clumsy and numb. Occasionally, he got a feeling of "pulling" in the back of his left hand. Many people, after little strokes, have mentioned this feeling of pulling in muscles here and there in their body.

A little place on the outer side of his upper lip on the left side got numb. He used to have an excellent memory; but after the spells came it began to "have holes in it." His wife became annoyed when he kept asking her the same question over and over again. He could no longer stand crowds and cross-talk. At times he felt as if he might any moment fall off his chair. He developed some cardiospasm, and with this, his appetite went.

He had had perhaps 20 of the curious spells in the 6 months before I saw him. Occasionally he would bite his tongue painfully. When walking, his legs would tire, sometimes so much that he would wish he could lie down on the sidewalk! His libido remained but his potentia left. He had a few spells in which there came a small black scotoma, which soon went away. One day he found his legs so weak he could hardly walk. He had spells in which he was dizzy, nauseated, weak and tired; and he feared he was going to black out. Once he did fall against a row of lockers in his club. After this he became very irritable. He had to force himself to work, and he lost all interest in his hobbies. Electroencephalograms showed nothing abnormal.

An Unusual Amount of Ataxia. A physician, born in 1890, told me that in 1951, he had had a little stroke which immediately took away his libido and potentia, and left him with so much ataxia in his hands and legs that his wife had to help him to the bathroom. For a while he had trouble writing. He said that on January 13th, 1952, he had another little stroke, which caused a pain to come in his neck, and then run down his right arm into his wrist. Both of his shoulders hurt. Because the pain left him feeling very bad, and unable to think clearly, he realized that something had gone wrong with his brain. He could not drive his car because he was too weak to pull the wheel around, as when he wanted to park.

With one of the little strokes, his eyes felt distressed. He rapidly lost 20 pounds of weight. Later, something went wrong with one hand, and he got some atrophy of the muscles of his thumb. With this, he had trouble buttoning his clothes, and picking small objects off a table. Also, he got some twitching of the muscle under his right eye. For a year the muscles of his legs ached; also, he had a numbness in the right leg, which made it hard for him to control it.

A Woman Who After Little Strokes Failed To Recognize Her Husband. The mother of an eminent physician, after a series of little strokes, became a bit childish and confused, so that she could not seem to recognize her old husband. Although rational about many things, she kept wondering why "that strange man kept hanging around the place."

A Man Who Recovered Perfectly from an Unusually Severe Little Stroke. The experience of a fine-looking man of 70 interested me much. One evening, as he was about to retire, he dropped to the floor of his bathroom. He remained conscious but could not get up, and could not even call out to his daughter. In his pajamas, he had to spend a cold night on the floor. In the morning, his daughter found him, and helped him up onto his feet. A few hours later he was perfectly well. His son told me that in the two months before this episode, the old gentleman had had 4 little strokes, in each one of which he had fallen to the floor, and for a while afterward had been unable to stand.

To me, the remarkable fact about this case has always been that 10 years later, when I met the son, he told me his father was in good health and had had no more spells.

A Physician Who Held a Big Practice in Spite of his Marked Loss of Memory for Recent Events. One day I saw a kindly old doctor of 84, still practicing, who said he thought he had been having little strokes. One day he just could not count off eight one-dollar bills with which to pay a tradesman; he would forget the count before he got to eight. What was remarkable was that the old doctor was still well-groomed and pleasant; he could still make diagnoses, and he could start to prescribe, but then he would forget what he had wanted to write, and his secretary would have to remind him. Without her devoted help, he could not have continued in practice.

A LONG SERIES OF PECULIAR LITTLE STROKES. A man of 67 complained that he could no longer read well, and no glasses would help him. He said his head was "no damned good," also that he had "a kink in his left leg." One day, with a little stroke, his tongue got so dry that it almost stuck to the roof of his mouth. His wife said that a marked change in his temper caused her to quarrel with him for the first time in their lives together.

One day a little stroke came while he was sitting in a restaurant. It weakened him so that he had to remain there for two hours before he got strong enough to walk out. With this, he got such a numbness in his arms, that he could not write well. In a later spell his brain "wouldn't work right." In another spell he became so confused he drove his car through a red light. That evening he had to urinate constantly. Then, one morning, he was seized with a severe non-anginal pain under his sternum. He found he could not chew gum because he had no saliva. Another little stroke constipated him. There came an acute burning distress in his left cheek. A neurologic examination showed "nothing wrong."

THREE LITTLE STROKES. A hypertensive widow of 63, for a time around the age of 40, had a glycosuria. Later, on waking one morning, she found it so hard to open her mouth that for six weeks she was fed through a tube. She could not chew, and she had trouble swallowing. But her mind remained clear, and soon she was back at work. In the next spell she suddenly felt a distressing pulling and cramping feeling in the muscles on the right side of her neck. This remained with her for years. Then suddenly, while reading, she felt a great distress in the right side of her scalp and her right leg. She sensed that she was having a stroke, and was badly scared. For the next three days her right hand was clumsy and her right leg did not behave well in walking. These symptoms soon cleared away.

THREE CASES OF LITTLE STROKES IN THE NIGHT. A woman of 65 said that she had always been well and active until one morning when she woke terribly dizzy, badly nauseated, and vomiting. For the next three days she slept most of the time; she lost much of her memory, most of her interests, and all joy in life. Like some people who have had a big stroke, she kept saying that the distress in her head was almost unbearable.

A BANKER OF 61 WHO ONE DAY DID NOT GO TO WORK. The wife of a banker was much puzzled one day when her husband, after breakfast, didn't go to work. He never again went to work or showed any interest in his bank. The wife could not get him to explain his behavior, and she was much puzzled when doctors examined him and "found nothing wrong."

As she told me later, she soon saw that much of her husband's intelligence, and all of his charm, were gone. Over-night the once able and dynamic man had changed into a dull, taciturn, withdrawn and sexless person who made no decisions, did not read, and hardly looked at TV. Fortunately, his old gentleness and kindliness and willingness to stay clean and well-groomed remained.

One day his wife saw him, apparently unseeingly, walk into a wall. Another time he fell to the floor and seemed to be "out" for a minute. He was then, for a while so aphasic he could only mumble. His wife said he hadn't enough good brain left to realize what a terrible thing had happened to him; he never mentioned his inability to work, and he never complained about anything. He was easily confused, and sometimes had trouble shaving and dressing. He wound up walking with the short weak steps of an old man.

A Noise in the Night. A married woman, aged 61, who said she had always been healthy and cheerful, suddenly developed insomnia, a mental depression and great nervousness. Two years before, while sitting in a chair, she had suddenly pitched forward onto the floor. At that time she found she could not move her left arm and left leg, but her speech was not affected. In four days she was well. With this spell, her previously high systolic blood pressure of 180 mm. Hg. suddenly dropped to normal, and her formerly frequent headaches stopped coming.

Three months before I saw her, she went into an agitated depression. With this, her systolic blood pressure went back up to 180. She developed a Parkinsonian face and a monotonous voice. She could not do her housework. One night she suddenly got the fear that people were going to kill her. Curiously, another night she was wakened by what she said was so loud a noise that she thought the house was coming down. The people about her did not hear anything. Her home physician diagnosed a little stroke.

The Old Person Who Keeps Asking One Question Over and Over Again. Many a time the grown children of an elderly parent have told me that what impressed them most after their old mother's little stroke was that she kept asking, over and over again, "What happened? What happened?" She evidently did not grasp, or remember, what they said to her.

Diarrhea and a Sudden Drop in Blood Pressure and Weight. A hypersensitive widow of 67 said she had been remarkably well until 5 or 6 years before, when she began to have sudden attacks of unexplained diarrhea. With these spells, she lost 20 pounds; also, got so weak she could hardly walk. Studies of her digestive tract showed nothing wrong.

Two months before I saw her, she had waked, nauseated, mentally confused, weak, and with everything spinning around her. Later, she remembered that 4 years before, she had had another terrifying attack in which her systolic blood pressure, which had been running around 184, suddenly dropped to 100 mm. Hg. Also, she rapidly lost 43 pounds in weight: a typical little-stroke story.

Just before I saw her, she had had another spell, in which she got much distress in her abdomen. Her memory had failed so much that her husband had to give me most of the history. She often had trembling spells, when she was confused and upset. Her home physician kept looking for her disease in her sore abdomen.

STROKES THAT CAUSED VOMITING AND EMACIATION. One day, in came an emaciated, irritable, fidgety little old lady of 71, with an epileptic inheritance. She complained of attacks of vertigo, vomiting, and severe cramping abdominal pains, with diarrhea. The attacks of abdominal pain had come 7 months before, with a transient hemiplegia. With the stroke, there came some deafness with ear noises. She had had other little strokes *15 years before.* Curiously, her last stroke brought back in a severe form her old migraine.

LITTLE STROKES PLUS A SERIES OF BRIEF BIG STROKES. Interesting is the case of an able, hard-driving executive, whose progress I have been able to watch for 15 years. His case has shown how a man can have little strokes, then recover from a big one, and then live for years in good health. When I first saw him, he was 64, and had had some thrombosis of the blood-vessels of his legs. He had a markedly calcified aorta. Two years before I saw him, he suddenly got pain in his lower back so severe that for a few days he was thought to have a displaced disc, but then he suddenly recovered. Two weeks later, while standing in his office, he got a paralysis of his left cheek muscles and his right hand. He was a bit confused, and for a while could only mumble, but he managed to reach a chair without falling. In a few minutes these symptoms cleared away, and "under his own steam" he went to a hospital.

There, the doctors found that his systolic blood pressure, which had been running over 160 mm. Hg. had dropped to 120 mm. Hg. Fortunately, he soon recovered, and for two years he worked hard, and felt well.

Then he had a big stroke with an aphasia and a hemiparesis. But these symptoms quickly cleared up, and he went back to work. Ever since, his speech has remained hesitant on a few words. He has enjoyed pretty good health, and has kept going to his office. At times he has traveled to distant lands, sometimes alone. He has been on anticoagulant medication. He still is wide-awake and keen, and is a well-groomed, well-dressed, urbane gentleman.

AN ALCOHOLIC WHO HAD MANY UNUSUAL LITTLE STROKES. A brilliant but alcoholic lawyer of 76, told me of a little stroke which he had many years before I saw him. In 1951, he told me he was having what he called "pip-strokes" (one meaning of "pip" is small, as in "pip-squeak"), and he was probably right because, with them his apperance changed; he lost much weight, and he aged greatly.

In 1953, he suddenly lost much of the vision in his right eye, and for a while he weaved when he walked. He developed such a hand tremor that he could not drink a cup of coffee without spilling some of it. He could not sign his name. He had some aphasia, and he lost some of his memory. Then he got much better, and his sight cleared, but during the next year his right hand became ever more clumsy. In some ways he became senile, but he still kept himself clean and neat, and he kept going to his office.

A year later he apparently had another little stroke because he then walked into a half-open door as if he hadn't seen it. For two or three days after this he was not himself. Worse yet, when he got to his office, he found he could not read. He tried to talk to his daughter over the phone, but couldn't. Then he had a convulsion. After this, for a while, he could not walk. Then, he was much better until he had another little stroke which, for several months, left him with a slurred speech.

By October, 1954, he had recovered so remarkably well that he had gained back his weight. He had cut down on his drinking, but still he kept having some spells of mental confusion. Sometimes his aphasia would get worse, and his ideas of time and orientation would be vague. In 1957, his daughter found him sitting on the floor of his bathroom, pale, haggard and distraught. He said, "I have had another stroke." Later, on his way downtown, he suddenly felt ill, he sweated, he felt weak and hot, he wanted to vomit, and his bowels moved incontinently. Getting off the bus, he fell to the sidewalk several times, but finally managed to get home. Then, one day while trying to answer the phone, all he could get out of him was a squeak. After that he went rapidly down hill. Along the way, I consulted with an angiologist, but he felt the man was too bad a risk for any angiographic study.

A WOMAN WHO HAD HAD SPELLS FOR 25 YEARS, AND IN HER LATER LIFE OCCASIONALLY WET THE BED. A hard-driving and formerly very healthy unmarried woman of 49, a school-teacher, who looked wide-awake and well-adjusted, since the age of 24 had been having "queer spells." When I saw her, she was complaining of constant abdominal pain, spells of fatigue, and spasms in the muscles of her face. During the previous four years, in spells, the corners of her mouth had "pulled down." Then her head would feel as if it were being pulled backward. Occasionally, her face would "twist" painlessly for ten or fifteen minutes. At times she said she saw double "with one eye." On occasions, her speech was so slurred I had trouble understanding her. *She asked me if she could have had little strokes.*

At times she lost control of her right arm and right leg. Sometimes she could not write well. Also, at times she was a bit tipsy—with a poor sense of balance. On some occasions in the years before I saw her, *she had wet the bed.* At times her tongue had felt thick. Sometimes she had walked into a wall because she could not judge distances well. For a while she kept biting one lip, and her face "felt tight." Off and on, she had some numbness in her legs.

I had a neurologist examine her, but all he found was some lessening of sensitiveness in the right side of her face. He agreed that she probably had been having little strokes. I had already noted that when she wrinkled her forehead, the wrinkles were deeper on the left side than on the right. Trying to help her, one surgeon removed her stoneless and silent gallbladder, and another removed her uterus, but these operations did not help.

The neurologist and I thought of an epileptic component but we could not get any proof of this. There was no epilepsy in her family, and she did not have an epileptic temperament. We were unable at the time to get EEG's made.

A PRESSURE IN THE HEAD AND BURNING IN THE MOUTH. A hypertensive physician of 53 suddenly felt a pressure in his head and a feeling of heat. His ears began to ring. A few hours later he had another episode in which he "went to pieces nervously," and had a nervous chill. Then came a severe burning sensation in his tongue and mouth, and a tingling and burning and numbness in his feet and ankles. He said, probably correctly, that he had had a little stroke.

THE MAN WHO WANTED TO DIE PROPERLY IN HIS BED! A man of 65 said he had been well until a few weeks before I saw him, when one evening while reading, he suddenly lost all sense of balance, and felt he was dying. With it all, he managed to crawl upstairs so that he could "die properly" in his bed. Fortunately, after a few minutes he felt all right again, but later his memory became so defective he had to quit his work.

AN INTERESTING STORY. A woman of 70 just wrote to say that one day "I was sitting in a chair in my apartment and started to dress, and the whole world went out from under me. For a while I couldn't move or finish dressing. It was simply awful." That gives a good idea of how a persons feels when all his or her sense of balance goes.

TWO REMARKABLE CASES OF APPARENT LITTLE STROKE FOLLOWING A

GREAT FRIGHT. A big, stout, strong woman of 52, who had never been ill in her life, one day, a year before I saw her, while in a store, had a number of empty cartons fall off a shelf onto her head. They did not hurt her, but they greatly frightened her. That she hadn't been injured was indicated by the fact that she got on a bus and went home.

But next morning she woke to find herself utterly miserable, and with a constant severe pain in her epigastrium. The fact that this pain never let up for an hour or a day suggested to me that it was arising in her brain, and that she had had a silent stroke. The store people promptly gave her a generous settlement, so there was no problem of a suit for compensation.

Her gallbladder had already been removed, and a roetgenologic study of the stomach and bowel showed nothing wrong. In spite of this, her doctor explored her abdomen—and found nothing. Highly diagnostic of a little stroke was the fact that the woman quickly lost 60 pounds in weight, without any change in her diet, and then stabilized at the new level. Also very suggestive of a little stroke was the fact that she became utterly miserable with no interest in life and she could no longer do her housework. After a year the abdominal distress was still so constant and severe that she was thinking of suicide.

A physician who had a fright. A similar case was that of a pleasant, able and calm physician of 62 who told me that one day when he carelessly stepped off the sidewalk onto the street, he just touched with his thigh the fender of a passing car. It spun him around, but it did not throw him down, and it did not hurt him, but, for a moment, he was terribly frightened. Strangely, from that minute onward for the next year in which I knew him, he was miserable, unable to work, and suffering from the sort of constant abdominal misery that often follows a little stroke.

With time he got a little better, but that was all. He felt as I did, that, with the fright there must have come a little stroke. It did not seem possible that the disability was due to hysteria, and it certainly was not due to any desire for compensation. The man's lawyer had wanted him to sue, but the doctor would not permit this; as he said it was all his fault.

POSSIBLE MIGRAINE MADE WORSE BY LITTLE STROKES. A robust, previously healthy man—a top executive of 57—complained of strange spells in which he would suddenly feel terribly tired and weak. After a few hours he would just as suddenly come out of the spell. He had been studied by several eminent internists and neurologists, none of whom could make a diagnosis. At times he would get an "ice-pick stab" type of pain under the lower end of his sternum. I learned later that this suggests epilepsy, and I now regret I did not get EEG's made. This pain would come at any time, and might keep coming for hours. It had no relation to exertion, or the taking of food; and x-ray studies showed nothing wrong.

The two-year duration of the distress tended to rule out any serious disease in the abdomen, such as cancer of the pancreas. Because the story was somewhat like that of an abdominal migraine, I inquired and learned that in his early years he had suffered from severe sick headaches. As so often happens, the headaches quit coming when he was 30. The next question was, if at 55 he had begun to suffer with a severe equivalent of migraine, why had it come? The man said he had not been unhappy and had not been under any unusual strain. Then I asked about little strokes, and the man told me the typical story of one severe one and three smaller ones. With iodides and with time his condition improved.

A BRIEF STROKE. A stout, gouty, very able and pleasant executive—a man about 70, usually strong and well and energetic—while sitting at supper in a hotel, found his hand wouldn't work; then the leg on the same side became weak. There was no aphasia. He had to be taken upstairs in a wheel-chair; but by the time he reached his room, his attack was over.

8

Hints as to Diagnosis

As I have said, a physician will rarely make a diagnosis of little strokes if he does not quickly get a hunch from a glance at the patient's dull face, or from noting his poor answers to questions. Then he must get the highly diagnostic history from the man's wife or grown child, or a business associate. Also, the doctor must remember that an executive must look like an executive; he must talk like one; and he must be well dressed like one; and in the doctor's office, he must treat his wife or daughter as an executive and a gentleman should.

I remember the hunch I got one day when an aging vice-president of a big corporation spoke nastily to his beautiful young second wife. When she said to him, "I am sorry, darling: but that first big dizzy spell of yours came a year ago; not a month ago," the man snarled at her, saying, "Shut your damn mouth," I could not imagine a man in his position—and in his right mind—saying such an awful thing to a lovely woman; and soon I had plenty of evidence to show that the fellow *wasn't* in his right mind; a little stroke had ruined much of that.

Often the most diagnostic part of the history will be the fact that a marked change in the patient's health, ability, character, personality, judgment, and appearance came in a certain minute of a certain day, with perhaps a dizzy, woozy, vomiting, numb, aphasic, or weak spell. In some cases, the patient woke one morning feeling too dull, tired, and apathetic to go to his office.

THE DIAGNOSIS MUST USUALLY BE MADE FROM THE HISTORY. The clinician will rarely recognize a patient with a little stroke if he depends on (1) an assistant's brief history; (2) a neurological examination; and (3) laboratory and x-ray reports.

THE FIRST DIZZY SPELL CAN LEAVE DOUBT. I here emphasize the fact that in many a case one cannot call the first "dizzy spell" a stroke. One has to wait perhaps for months until the man has a little stroke which is so typical, and which leaves so diagnostic a neurologic residue, that the doubts one had are all cleared away.

DOES THE PATIENT THINK HE HAD A LITTLE STROKE? As I have said above, highly diagnostic is the fact that when a man is asked what he thought was happening to him when he had his queer spell, he answers, "I thought I was having a stroke, and thought I was going to die."

DIFFICULTY WITH THE PATIENT WHO COMES ALONE. As I have noted, if the patient *comes from a distance all by himself,* then the doctor may have to keep talking to him (her) for several half-hour sessions before an important and diagnostic part of the story is obtained. To illustrate: a stout, dull-looking woman of 63, who came to Rochester alone, complained of a painful quivering in her back. At the first interview she much wanted to spend all the time telling me about the color of the pills her doctor had given her. The only important point she could remember was that the severe distress had hit her on a certain day 6 months before. The next afternoon, she remembered to tell me that a year before, she had had a spell of the same distress in her back. Next day, she remembered that once, while out driving, she had blacked out, and her car had rolled over! Imagine her having forgotten that at the two first visits. Later, she remembered a little stroke that had left her, for some minutes, too weak to get up out of a chair. If only a sister or husband had been with her, I could probably have gotten the essential history at the first interview.

INABILITY TO READ. As I have said, very helpful in assessing the amount of injury suffered by a man's brain is information as to his ability to read, or look at TV, with any ease or pleasure.

CHEST PAIN. The following case report will show how, when a man suffers chest pain, a little observation—and answers to a few questions —will show that the cause was not a coronary attack, but a little stroke. On a Sunday morning, a man of 38 got a severe pain in his chest. His doctor told him to come to the office for an EKG. Because the elevator in the doctor's building was not running, the man walked quickly up two flights of stairs. Since this effort did not add to his pain, or make him short of breath; because his electrocardiograms and a Master two-step test showed nothing wrong; and because in the months that followed, his disability was obviously arising in his brain, I was sure the original spell had not been a heart attack.

THE GREAT FREQUENCY OF ABDOMINAL PAIN. In Chapter 5, I showed how often the main complaint of the patient with a little stroke is abdominal "pain"—either a widespread, constant "burning misery," or crises like those of tabes.

CONFUSION AS REGARDS MENIÈRE'S DISEASE. Elsewhere I have told how one can rule out Menière's disease, and diagnose a little stroke.

THE QUESTION OF EPILEPSY. A rare possibility is that a dizzy spell is a slight manifestation of epilepsy. Very seldom have I seen a case in which I had reason to suspect this. If I have any doubt, I inquire pertinaciously about epilepsy, or something like epilepsy, in the family; I have electroencephalograms made; and I may try giving phenobarbital or Dilantin.

A NEUROLOGIC EXAMINATION RARELY HELPS. Regretfully I have to keep saying that with *mild little strokes,* a neurologic examination does not help in the making of the diagnosis—because *no neurologic signs are found.*

THE POSSIBILITY OF A BRAIN TUMOR. Neurologists may wonder how often what looks like a little stroke turns out to be an early sign of a brain tumor. My experience makes me doubt if this often happens. In many a case the patient has suffered from "episodes" for so many years that if they had all been due to the growth of a tumor in the brain, the chances are that, long before, the victim would have been either operated on or would have died. That this is not always true was shown by Dr. Benjamin Boshes with his series of puzzling histories (1958). Actually, most of the histories he published would not have suggested to me a little stroke. If, as in many of Dr. Boshes' cases, there were severe pains here and there throughout a man's body, I would be inclined to suspect a fibrositis, a neuritis, or a metastatic cancer.

Always, whenever I have had a strong suspicion that a patient's symptoms were due to a brain tumor, I have asked my friends the neurologists to take over. I cannot remember having seen a patient with a typical series of little strokes who later was found definitely to have a tumor of the brain, but I have seen a few patients with what I thought were little strokes, but what a colleague thought could be symptoms of a brain tumor. Apparently, in every one of these few cases, my friend's first hunch was wrong because the patient refused operation, and he or she lived on without worsening symptoms for several years that I knew of. So far as I know, in only one case of mine, with rather typical little strokes, was the patient operated on. Unfortunately, she did not recover from the operation, and I never could learn from the surgeon if a tumor was found.

According to D. G. Freeman, M. A. Petrobelos and J. W. Henderson (1953), the commonest symptoms in 347 proved cases of *brain tumor* were: headache in 68; papilledema in 59; vomiting in 41; facial weakness in 34; convulsions in 32; a positive Babinski in 30; an intellectual slowing-up in 28; a hemiparesis in 27; an ataxic gait in 26; mental changes in 24; a general ataxia in 21; a disorientation in 16; a weakness in 15; an aphasia in 10; dizziness in 7; and psychic changes in 5. With the exception of vomiting and intellectual slowing, mental changes, weakness and dizziness, these are not the symptoms that usually come with mild little strokes.

THE DANGER OF ACCEPTING UNIMPORTANT FINDINGS AS THE DIAGNOSIS. As I must keep saying, the commonest diagnostic mistake young physicians make in cases of little strokes is to accept *unquestioningly* as the the cause of all of the patient's nervous and mental symptoms any finding, like a gallstone, that happened to be turned up during the examination.

MORE ON THE GREAT NEED FOR TALKING TO THE FAMILY OR FRIENDS. It is so important to talk to relatives, and sometimes friends, that I will emphasize this fact again. As I was writing this, in came a widow, aged 55, who said she was well until three years before. Then, one morning, she woke with a very painful right shoulder. Someone promptly removed her "chronic appendix." Next, a neurologist, wisely suspecting disease in her brain, checked her carefully and "found nothing."

Then she became so mentally confused that on going out she would get lost. It became hard for her to dress herself because the sense of touch in her fingers was so impaired she could not manage buttons. She lost all interest in life. She felt that her feet did not belong to her, and she became somewhat ataxic. This strongly suggested little strokes. Later, I got the diagnostic story from the woman's chum who had sat with her for some hours after the appendectomy. She told me that, after the operation, the woman had gone into a brief spell of coma, during which her mouth had fallen open on one side, and saliva had drooled out of that corner. A few weeks later, when the two women were at dinner, my patient had had another little stroke, during which she so lost consciousness that she let food run down out of her mouth onto her dress without noticing it. With a third little stroke, she had a brief coma, during which her mouth was pulled over to the right. The later course of this patient's illness suggested more a series of strokes than a brain tumor.

J. A. Resch (1964) wrote an article that is helpful because he told of the several types of little strokes that are produced by injuries to arteries in several parts of the brain. Drs. T. A. Lindstrom and K. R. Brizzee wrote (1962) that in the brain there are at least three small widely separated areas in which injury can cause vomiting. One is in the lower part of the fourth ventricle.

Drs. J. A. Jane, D. Yasbon, and D. Sugar (1965) told of the new technics for scanning the brain, also for using ultrasonics, but decided that angiography still appears to be the method of choice.

Dr. Michael De Bakey (1961) has shown that arm pain can be due to obstruction of the subclavian artery. He reported operations on 23 such patients.

9

The Pathology of Strokes

The literature on atherosclerosis is a bit disappointing because so little is definitely known. I should probably speak here not of one atherosclerosis, but of several types, as Foley (1956) has so wisely pointed out. Osler once (1909) summed things up briefly in his delightful way, saying that the cause of hardening of the arteries is "poor rubber and too much strain." One of my old professors used to say, "The contractor put in poor materials." One day in 1911 I suspected "poor materials" when I was called to see a man of 55, dying with calcified arteries. When his daughter of 28 asked me to x-ray her heart, I was astonished to find the most completely calcified thoracic aorta I had ever seen. I wondered if she had inherited some of her father's "poor rubber."

As early as 1872, Noel G. de Mussy summed up what was then known of arteriosclerosis. Other good summaries were made by Wm. Russell (1907), F. W. Mott (1909), Ernest Jones (1909), Clifford Allbutt (1915), Adams and Van der Eecken (1953), and Baker and Iannone (1961). The fine bibliography of the last two writers is very helpful. An excellent summary of our knowledge of strokes is in that unique book, "Strokes: How they occur and what can be done about them," by Irvine Page, with Millikan, Wright, Weiss, Crawford, De Bakey, and Rusk (1961, Dutton). As I wrote this, Dr. Page let me read a fine address he recently gave summing up beautifully the literature on atherosclerosis. At the end, he very wisely admitted that he was not very sure about anything.

OUR LACK OF EXACT KNOWLEDGE ABOUT THE CAUSATION OF STROKES. Why did a stroke come *when* it did, and why did it hit *where* it did in the brain? We do not know. There must be a local factor of extra strain on certain sections of arteries where the blood swirls and eddies, and strikes hard against the wall. Also, there are factors of poor metabolism,

95

as in cases of diabetes, gout, hyperlipemia, over-weight, and also hypertension. As Irvine Page says, we may be dealing with a "disease of regulation" (of various parts of the body chemistry). There can be factors of over-eating, over-drinking, or over-smoking.

Over-work, either mental or physical, does not seem always to be a factor. My father who, from the age of 34 to 84, was a very busy general practitioner—until the last few years on call 24 hours out of the 24—at necropsy had atherosclerosis only in his aorta. His other arteries were as soft as those of a child. He had a normal blood pressure. His immediate familial longevity was decidedly poor since both his parents died early, but this may mean little because they died from infections. My father was abstemious, neither drinking nor smoking, nor ever eating much; and he remained thin all his days. Two of his 6 children died young of infections, but the other 4 are mentally and physically young in their seventies and eighties.

Recently, some studies showed that the main cause of ulceration of the aorta is age. But the factor of age is not essential in producing generalized atherosclerosis, as is shown by the fact that many young people have hardened arteries. Also Resch and Baker, at 3,839 necropsies, found four per cent of persons in the ninth and tenth decades with no grossly visible atherosclerotic change. Before the age of 60, women had from 11 to 19 per cent less atherosclerosis than men, hence sex is a factor. After 60 the influence of sex fades out, and then the two sexes have about the same amount of arterial disease. Hypertension can be a factor, but that it is not an essential factor has been shown by many men. Woltman (1922) found that 64 per cent of the many atherosclerotics he studied had a normal blood pressure. Some writers, however, have found hypertension in 9 out of 10 cases of atherosclerosis. De Bakey found it in about half of his patients with atherosclerosis of the neck arteries.

Some statistics. Otto Saphir (1959, p. 1807) said that in necropsies made in a big city hospital, 25 per cent of the patients were found to have had "circulatory disturbances" in their brains, and William Boyd, in his book, mentioned the transient episodes (silent strokes) that tend to come during a person's sleep.

Van Buskirk (1962, p. 575) said that 40 per cent of vascular brain injuries are probably thromboses. Alpers (1959) examined 359 brains and found thrombosis in 30 per cent. Foley (1956) concluded that on performing necropsies on patients dying in a general hospital 1 in 4 is likely to show cerebrovascular disease. Baker, Refsum and Dahl (1960) and many others, have found that the arteries most often involved are the internal carotid and the first part of the middle cerebral. According to C. M. Fisher (1955), the *vertebral* arteries in the neck are very seldom diseased. He found only one such case during 130 necropsies. Some other men have found vertebral artery disease more frequently. Adams and Van der Eecken (1953) found atherosclerosis most frequently in the first part of the internal carotid artery, just above the bifurcation of the common carotid; also in the sigmoid portion; also in the first 3 or 4 cm. of the middle cerebral; in the anterior cerebral artery, and in the vertebral and basilar, and proximal parts of the posterior cerebral arteries.

EXPERIMENTAL ATHEROSCLEROSIS. I will not attempt here to review the big subject of experimental atherosclerosis. Early in 1909, a summary was made by Huchard, who said, probably wisely, that experimenters have made in animals the *lesions* of atherosclerosis but *not the disease*. Among those who have discussed animal experiments I will mention Timothy Leary (1934 and 1941). He concluded that often a high blood cholesterol is a factor. Duff and McMillan (1951), who worked with rabbits, said that "In the vast majority there is no defect in lipid metabolism, and no concentration of cholesterol." (See their big bibliography of 145 items.) They felt that there must be an unknown local factor to explain the patchiness of the lesion. Students of atherosclerosis in man have also felt much need for studying patchiness, and for learning why the disease attacks certain arteries and certain parts of those arteries.

THEORIES ABOUT ATHEROSCLEROSIS. Aring (1945) and others have felt that trouble in the circulation of the brain can start with stasis *in the veins*. (See Alpers, 1959, and Denny-Brown and Horenstein, 1956.) E. R. Clark, in discussing Chase's article (1938), said that his studies showed that in arteries, the endothelium is damaged first. Denny-Brown (1960, p. 209) spoke of the possibility of brief attacks being due to thrombi made up of blood platelets. This could conceivably cause short spells— spells which could quickly be recovered from. An excellent summary of our knowledge in regard to thrombosis was made by Liebow, Newill and Oseasohn (1964), by Carter in his fine book on infarction (1964), and by Campbell Moses' book *Atherosclerosis: Mechanisms as a Guide to Prevention* (Philadelphia, Lea & Febiger, 1963).

A splendid summary—up to 1958—of our knowledge in regard to the *Chemistry of Lipids as Related to Atherosclerosis* was compiled and edited by Irvine H. Page (1961).

Denny-Brown thought that metabolites in the brain might cause dilation of cerebral blood vessels, and Roy and Sherrington (1890) also had this idea. Rothschild (1945) thought there could be toxic changes in some brains, and Staemmler (1936) suggested that necrosis of a blood vessel might be due to a ferment.

Merritt (1963, p. 1612), thought that episodes might well be due to a failure of collateral circulation in the territory of the carotids or the basilar artery. Rook (1946) discussed unconscious spells that can follow much coughing, such as might lower the blood pressure. G. W. Pickering

(1948) wrote about edema as a cause of trouble in the brain. Knisely, Block, Eliot and Warner (1947); Harding and Knisely (1958); Knisely (1960); and Knisely, Warren, and Harding (1960) have done much to show that sludging of the blood as it passes through small arteries could cause partial obstruction. Knisely thought there can be leakage of plasma from the capillaries, with resultant thick blood, which will flow poorly.

Denny-Brown (1951) proposed the term "hemodynamic crisis" to signify the critical state which precedes or threatens infarction of the brain. Rothenberg and Putnam (1953) spoke of "cerebral vascular insufficiency," and Millikan and his co-workers (1955) used a similar term.

Dr. Irvine Page (1961) favored the filtration theory of atherogenesis which sees the blood pressure constantly forcing plasma through the blood vessel walls into the intracellular spaces. There seems to be a direct relation between the amount of lipid in the blood and the rate of atherogenesis. Actually, the rate is not governed by one factor alone. Hypertension is a factor.

A DROP IN BLOOD PRESSURE WITH A NARROW PLACE IN AN ARTERY SUPPLYING THE BRAIN. Many students of strokes have felt, as did Wilson, Rupp, Riggs and Wilson (1951), that highly important may be a sudden drop in the general blood pressure, combined with the presence of a narrow place in an artery in the brain. With this combination of factors, too little blood might get through. An area of cerebral anoxemia might then develop, and a stroke might follow. This idea is supported by many published case reports of persons who, when their blood pressure fell suddenly and markedly, had a slight or a big stroke. Such brain accidents have happened to people who, at a blood bank, gave a liter of blood too quickly. See Engel (1950); also Ebert, Stead, and Gibson (1941), who said that if from 15 to 20 per cent of a person's blood is rapidly removed, "circulatory collapse will usually follow."

Thompson and Smith (1951) showed in experiments on dogs and monkeys that if a clip is put on the middle cerebral artery so as partially to obstruct it, an injury to the brain is seen only if later the blood pressure is lowered to half its usual level. They said similar experiments had been performed by J. W. Watts. Thompson and Smith learned that different results in these experiments are obtained—depending also on the depth of anesthesia. Denny-Brown and J. S. Meyer (1957) made valuable studies in stroke production—also using monkeys. The simultaneous appearance of many small foci of stasis can produce an infarction. They watched the quick return of function in the brain when these little areas healed, and made a very informative study.

Corday, Rothenberg, and Wiener (1956) also studied the effects of a combination of a narrowed artery and a lowered blood pressure in monkeys and men. With good reason, they assumed that if this theory of a stroke formation is valid, then when a shock comes, the logical thing to do is quickly raise the systemic blood pressure. Actually, Corday *et al.* did this, with success. They had a man who once vomited so much blood that his systemic pressure dropped to 65/50, and he went into shock. A transfusion of blood raised the blood pressure to 160 systolic, and with this he promptly lost his paralysis and his "positive Babinski."

In discussing the paper of Corday *et al.*, De Takats said that a young wounded soldier might escape injury when his systolic blood pressure had been dropped to 80 mm. Hg, but a man past middle age with a cerebral arteriosclerosis might get a little stroke if his systolic blood pressure were to fall below 140 mm.

Kendell and Marshall (1965, p. 347) said they doubted if hypotension is the important cause. In 37 cases they quickly lowered the patient's blood pressure with hexamethonium, to (on the average) 42 per cent of the initial reading. In only one case did they produce an ischemic attack.

Fowler and De Takats (1949) met with 2 cases of transient hemiplegia following sympathectomy for hypertension. De Takats then urged that when a surgeon is operating, even under spinal anesthesia, he should see to it that the blood pressure is kept high. He said that Alan C. Burton (1953) showed that a lowering of the blood pressure by 20 mm. Hg can greatly decrease the flow of blood in the brain.

Other believers in the importance of a narrowed artery and a fall in blood pressure were Foix and Ley (1927); Alajouanine, Lhermitte, and Gautier (1960); Eastcott, Pickering and Rob (1954); Shanbrom and Levy (1957); Mogens Fog (1937, 1941); and Echlin (1942).

Denny-Brown (1960) doubted the importance always of a sudden episode of hypotension. He saw strokes following a drop in pressure but was impressed by the fact that he and his associates sometimes saw strokes come without any change in the person's blood pressure. Also, they saw falls of 40 mm. Hg or more with no stroke. However, in one case in which, using reserpine, they dropped the systolic pressure from 170 to 140 mm. Hg, the patient suffered many recurrent attacks. In the cases of some persons whom I have studied, a big fall in blood pressure did not produce a stroke. I remember a woman with a systolic pressure of over 200 mm. Hg who, when put to bed, in a few hours had a pressure of 130 mm.—and felt well. I remember a plethoric, red-faced woman in her fifties who, for some time had suffered much with a systolic pressure of over 220 mm. Hg. On two occasions she bled so copiously from her stomach that her systolic pressure dropped quickly to 130 mm; and she had no stroke. Instead, on both occasions, she lost all her old distresses and felt like a new woman.

In favor of the hypotension theory is the report of my old friend, Joe L. Miller (1910) who told of trouble with mild strokes when he quickly lowered the blood pressure of some hypertensives with hot baths. Similarly, Grimson, Orgain, Rowe and Sieber (1952), while using powerful drugs in the treatment of hypertension, occasionally had trouble with hemiparesis and hemianesthesia due to the hypotension they had produced. Their Case No. 1 was that of a 55-year-old man who had typical little strokes. In their Case 2, the patient collapsed with brain symptoms due apparently to the starting up of a ventricular tachycardia, with a sudden lowering of the blood pressure. In their Case 3, a man vomited much blood, and went into shock with mental symptoms. He was relieved of these when his blood pressure was raised to 160 systolic.

Crevasse, Logan and Hurst (1958) thought that a man needs at least 55 or 60 mm. Hg blood pressure to keep his brain functioning. Wahal and Riggs (1960) said that in those many cases of fatal stroke in which a necropsy shows no obstructive disease in the cerebral vessels, one possibility is that a marked drop in the systemic blood pressure caused the damage.

J. L. Murray (1957) studied 111 patients with apoplexy, and said he did not see any preliminary fall in blood pressure. Against the theory of a deficient supply of oxygen to the brain is Leonard Hill's (1910) comment on the fact that in the old days people with a severe pernicious anemia and a very low blood count could get by for months without a stroke. To show how well the brain can stand malnutrition, one need only look at young women with anorexia nervosa and a weight of 78 pounds, or the walking skeletons just freed from a war concentration camp.

RATE OF BLOOD FLOW. Another way of studying this problem of an occasional defect in circulation and function of part of the brain is to measure the flow of blood through the brain to see if changes in the flow are correlated with clinical signs of injury to the brain. Outstanding has been the work of F. Gibbs (1933), Lennox, Gibbs and Gibbs (1938), and of Kety (1950 and 1956), who devised methods for measuring the blood-flow through the brain. H. G. Wolff (1936) wrote a fine review article with a big bibliography. Since then, Kety and Schmidt (1948) found a falling-off in blood flow with age. Fazekas, Kleh and Finnerty (1955), and Heyman, Patterson, Duke and Battey (1953) found only a slight falling-off with age; also some falling-off with arterial changes in the brain.

Scheinberg (1950) found that persons with a poor mental status had a slightly lower amount of cerebral blood flow. Shenkin, Novak, Goluboff, Soffe, and Bortin (1953) studied the cerebral blood flow in 54 patients, and found no decrease in those with cerebrovascular disease. They could not duplicate the results that Freyhan, Woodford and Kety obtained in 1951. They could not see much decrease in flow with age.

Alman and Fazekas (1957) reported a lack of good correlation between a low cerebral blood flow and clinical signs of cerebral ischemia. They found a critical rate of cerebral blood flow of from 30 to 35 ml. of blood per 100 Gm. of brain per minute. Kety (1950) made a splendid study of the circulation of the brain, and found a positive correlation between mental function and cerebral metabolism. In coma, there can be a 40 per cent reduction in the *oxygen consumption of the brain* per minute and per 100 Gm. of tissue. The brain can go for only a few hours without an extra supply of glucose. The amount of oxygen in the brain can last only 10 seconds after the supply is shut off. A lessened consumption of oxygen can cause mental aberration. A big drop in blood pressure can leave the cerebral blood flow normal.

The adult human brain comprises but 2 per cent of the total body weight, yet it normally utilizes 20 per cent of the total oxygen, and 65 per cent of the total glucose consumed by the body; and it requires 15 to 20 per cent of the total blood circulation for the essential delivery of oxygen and glucose. This accounts for the fact that when supplies of oxygen or glucose are cut off, nerve function fails, with disastrous rapidity.

Schmidt, Kety, Strauss, Jr., Batson, Starr, Davies, Brink and Bronk (1944) summarized well the literature on cerebral blood flow and metabolism. Another splendid summary, with a big bibliography, is by A. C. Burton (1953).

WHY THE OFTEN QUICK RECOVERY AFTER A BRIEF STROKE? Pickering (1948, p. 1130) discussed several possibilities to explain the often quick recovery seen after a brief stroke. There isn't time for the absorption or canalization of a blood-clot in an artery, nor for absorption of a hemorrhage, nor for the clearing away of edema. But there may be a quick opening up of collateral channels. Quick recovery after a little stroke might be helped by a hypertension, which could keep forcing blood through the brain. Several men agreed with this. Aring, in a discussion of the article by Thompson and Smith (1951), said that he suspected that sometimes a quick recovery is due to a sudden return of a normal blood pressure. See also W. Spielmeyer (1928) and R. D. Adams (1954). Some men have wondered if perhaps a soft thrombus might be broken up, and the particles pushed on down the artery. Any theory to explain sudden recovery must tell us why, shortly after the symptoms of a little stroke have cleared away, a set of severe symptoms can return; also why, within a week after a person has had a brief stroke he may get a big one and die.

Evans and McEachern (1938), thought that restoration of function in the brain is due often to the quick opening-up of collateral channels. Similar conclusions were arrived at by Blumgart, Schlessinger and Davis

(1940) as they studied those thromboses in the heart which do not cause much trouble. Pickering (1951) was impressed with the fact that there is a type of Raynaud's disease in which small thrombi form suddenly in the arteries of the fingers. He and others were impressed with the fact that an infarction or embolus in a brain artery can produce a brief little stroke, with a syndrome strongly suggesting spasm.

AN INJURED BRAIN DOES NOT ALWAYS PRODUCE THE EXPECTED SYMPTOMS. Very interesting is the frequent finding by pathologists of injuries to the brain which, during life, did not produce symptoms. G. M. Humphrey, back in 1889, reported a study of the brains of 74 centenarians and of 900 persons who died when over 80 years of age. He found much atherosclerosis, but in spite of this, nearly all of the old people had been sane.

Many brain pathologists have been disturbed by the frequent lack of correlation between the symptoms experienced by the patient during life and the findings at necropsy. A number of these men have complained that in perhaps half of the cases in which the brain was examined nothing was found to explain a "stroke." Often, also, when a lesion is found, it is not in the place where it should be to explain the loss of function that had come in some part of the body.

Perhaps, in many cases, the pathologist would have found an accumulation of microscopic lesions if he could only have taken the time to make serial sections of parts of the brain and then to study them (See S. H. Birse and M. I. Tom (1960)).

Among the many pathologists who, years ago, complained of their inability to find the lesion they expected to see in or on a brain were George Peabody (1891), Jacobson (1893), George Allan (1910), C. G. McGaffin (1910), H. Oppenheim (1911, p. 822), Kashida (1924, quoted by James, 1926), Oppenheimer and Fishberg (1928), Spielmeyer (1928), G. W. Robinson, Jr. (1941), Rothschild (1942, 1945), Hicks and Shields Warren (1951), and Corday, Rothenberg and Wiener (1956).

Denny-Brown (1960, p. 200) said that "Cerebral infarction resulting from vascular occlusion is of two types: the one massive, complete, with very sharply defined edges; the other patchy, incomplete, and commonly hemorrhagic." The latter condition results in considerable disturbance of function.

Interesting, and doubtless significant, is the fact that pathologists have met with puzzles and disappointments also when looking for an anatomic explanation for a death due to *a coronary attack*. De Takats told of William Evans who, when he necropsied 2351 patients with a clinical diagnosis of coronary disease, in 57 per cent failed to find the expected thrombus in an artery. This agrees well with the 60 per cent figure for lack of a thrombosis in the brain given by Hicks and Shields Warren

(1951). Scheinberg, Peritz and Rice-Simons (1964) said that in 20 per cent of patients with recurrent ischemic spells no lesion could be found.

How Long Can Brain Cells Stand Anoxia? According to a statement attributed to Sir James Mackenzie, a man with Adams-Stokes disease, after a few seconds of heart stoppage, loses consciousness. But it will be from 5 to 10 minutes before the upper part of his brain is dead. The lower parts of the brain can stand a longer duration of anoxemia.

In 1937 I wrote up the results of much reading on the length of survival of different parts of the body. I read all I could find on what happens to the head of a guillotined man when it falls into the basket. Apparently there is never any sign of life in the man's face. Perhaps if someone were quickly to start transfusing the brain with oxygenated human blood, the head would come to life; the eyes would look around, and the lips would move (See Cobb, 1931, Schweigk, 1946, and Lambert and Wood, 1946). According to several workers, the cerebral cortex cannot be revived after 5 minutes of lack of oxygen. Cells in the mid-brain may last from 10 to 20 minutes, and cells in the medulla can last 30 minutes.

In view of the fact that cells of the cortex die after from 5 to 10 minutes of anoxia, it is a bit puzzling why people who have suffered a severe neurologic injury due to an obstructed internal carotid artery can sometimes recover so well after an operation performed to open up the artery. It would appear that, during the illness, the cells of the brain were only partly deprived of oxygen.

According to E. H. Lambert and E. H. Wood (1946) aviators "black out" and lose all of their vision within 4 or 6 seconds after being subjected to a centrifugal force that pulls the blood out of their brains. Apparently the retinal cells lose function within seconds after oxygen is withdrawn, and they regain it within seconds after the oxygen returns. Once, while terribly nauseated, I probably had a very low blood pressure because I "blacked out," and had no sight at all. Then a big "burp" came up; my nausea instantly stopped, and with this my vision promptly returned.

A Person May Die Before Histologic Changes Can Appear. George Peabody, back in 1891 (p. 173), said that a coronary artery can contract, and death of the patient can result before recognizable damage to the heart muscle can appear. See Ricker (1924, p. 560) and Nedzel (1943).

Actually, sudden death should take place before histologic changes can appear. Also, we should expect to see little strokes with recovery, if the blood returns, within 5 minutes, before the brain tissue can have died. Doubtless if, as probably often happens, some oxygen keeps getting through to the cells in the brain and the heart, these cells will not die. This could explain what happens in those cases in which a patient lies comatose for hours and then recovers.

Interesting is the observation that a man with Adams-Stokes disease will lose consciousness within seconds after his ventricles stop contracting. I remember seeing such a man apparently die for a minute or so, and then wake to go on and finish the story he had been telling!

According to Hannibal Hamlin (1964), with the help of the electroencephalograph one can tell when the brain has died. Similarly, when a man with a severe angina pectoris has a normal electrocardiogram (when at rest) he would appear to have a narrowed coronary with a partial anoxemia but as yet no infarct.

Many a time I have seen an able pathologist look up from a necropsy and say, "I haven't any idea why this man died. He must have died a 'physiologic death'." Perhaps his body got tired of making some essential chemical; or some essential part of his body did not get enough blood; or a toxic thyroid poisoned him for too long a time. And this has always sounded reasonable to me. I was delighted when I found Soma Weiss's fine paper (1940) on physiologic death—the physiologic changes that might cause sudden death. Excellent also is the paper by A. R. Montz on sudden death.

Cohen and Adams (1947) made what looks like a good suggestion when they said that the place that is producing symptoms may not be an infarcted area—but instead, a place near it. This would explain why sometimes there is a quick recovery from a small stroke. To make this clearer, I should say that in the heart a fairly harmless infarct near the bundle of His may, for a while, cause some heart blocking. Then, when the infarct heals, the patient can have a normal heart-beat again.

Interesting and suggestive is the statement of Van der Drift (1961) to the effect that "transient attacks occur when the oxygen tension in a specific brain area falls below a certain critical level." This could well explain the presence of symptoms in the absence of organic changes.

An excellent study of the mode of production of cerebral infarction by ischemic anoxia, and its reversibility in early stages is that of D., Denny-Brown and J. S. Meyer (1957) who, while working on monkeys, showed that "cortical ischemia can proceed to the point of failure of the electrocorticogram, with production of an 'injury potential'"; also, F. Gibbs (1949) showed that the EEG in an area of cerebral thrombosis shows only a flattening of the wavelets. Yet, the area can recover rapidly and apparently completely, without evidence of permanent damage to the local blood vessels.

Very interesting and logical and helpful is Dr. De Bakey's statement (1964, book, p. 337) that in the brain there is a distinction between viability and function. A certain degree of ischemia may inhibit normal function but permit the maintenance of viability for long periods of time.

This is why an operation which restores normal circulation can completely restore function of the brain.

As I have said, an increased severity of anoxic insult can increase the number of foci of "stasis"; also the extent of each focus, and a confluence of such (small) foci can lead to infarction.

THE FREQUENT CLOSE ASSOCIATION BETWEEN A CORONARY ATTACK AND A MILD STROKE. A number of men in the past have noted that when a man has a severe coronary attack he can have at the same time, a little stroke —which can easily go unrecognized until the patient comes to necropsy. One of the earliest writers to stress this was de Mussy (1872, p. 315).

The great J. B. Herrick, of Chicago (1912) spoke of the association of acute heart disease and a stroke. In 1915, J. Gordon Sharp wrote about seeing aphasia and other brain symptoms with angina pectoris. At the Mayo Clinic, in 1926, Arlie Barnes described the cerebral manifestations of paroxysmal tachycardia in which there can be a diminished output of the heart; and in 1930, Barnes' neurologic colleague, F. Moersch, wrote of the appearance of brain symptoms with paroxysmal tachycardia. Some patients became unconscious and a few had temporary blindness, convulsive seizures, paresthesias, pains, transitory aphasias, depression, exhaustion, hysterical symptoms, or a mild delirium.

Bodechtel (1932) wrote of brain changes with diseases of the heart. H. Stiirup (1952) studied 110 patients who had been treated for hemiplegia and apoplexy. At necropsy there were 6 with a fresh carotid thrombosis; 7 with cardiac decompensation, and 6 who, about the time of their stroke, had had a fall in blood pressure. Stürup gave a good bibliography. Scheinberg (1950) found in cases of heart failure the mean cerebral blood flow fell by 39 per cent, and the resistance was doubled.

Foley (1956, p. 178) said, "Arteriosclerotic heart disease was present in 83 per cent of 433 patients over 70, and in 92 per cent of 131 cases in which either infarct or hemorrhage was present in the brain." W. B. Bean (1938), Bean and C. T. Reed (1942), and Bean, Flamm and Sapadin (1949) discussed well the cases of central nervous system manifestations of acute myocardial infarction, and gave much literature on the subject.

D. L. Dozzi (1937) reported necropsies on 107 patients, 11.2 per cent of whom had a coronary thrombosis not diagnosed during life. Of the 41 persons with coronary thrombosis, 29 per cent had also a cerebral-vascural lesion. I have read that later (in 1940), Dozzi found complicating cerebral lesions in 33.8 per cent of 343 cases of heart disease.

G. W. Robinson (1941) also emphasized the frequency with which patients with heart disease can have mental changes. Scheinberg (1949) measured the cerebral circulation in 14 persons with heart failure and found it only 39 per cent of the average for normal people. Cole and Sugarman (1952) saw a patient with hemiplegia and a facial paralysis, who at necropsy was found to have only a fresh myocardial infarct. They could not find an obstructed cerebral artery. They thought that the cerebral anemia probably had not lasted long enough to produce histologic changes.

Sometimes the only symptoms of a coronary occlusion will suggest a brain injury. For instance, in Corday's Case 4, a man went into coma and died. The clinical diagnosis was obstruction of the basilar artery, but at necropsy all that was found was a coronary thrombosis. When the man went into coma he had a blood pressure of only 75/60, and this could not be raised in any way. Hicks and Shields Warren (1951) said that many a "coronary occlusion" is really a "cerebral event."

How Can a Vascular Injury that Left No Neurologic Residue Have so Terribly Wrecked the Patient? Often I puzzle over the fact that a feeble-minded, perhaps microcephalic woman, can be a useful maid in a home, able to read a bit; able to enjoy television; able to keep herself clean and neat; able to behave well; and to use all of her muscles well, while along comes a man who, after a brief stroke—which left no neurologic signs anywhere—has suddenly become pretty much an idiot, or even a comatose decerebrate animal. I wonder how this can happen.

Especially in view of the fact that after a surgeon has removed all of a hemisphere from the brain of a professional man, the man can go back to his highly technical type of work (F. A. Pickworth, 1934, p. 69), it is hard for me to understand why many a patient of mine who had what looked like a very mild little stroke, with no neurologic deficit, was left with much of his memory gone, or with all of his old ability gone.

Persons interested in this problem should read a fine paper by Klabanoff, Singer and Wilensky (1954). They studied the psychologic consequences of brain lesions and ablations. They added to their fine study a bibliography of 307 references.

In 1953, Drs. Adams and Van der Eecken (p. 235) said so wisely that the examinations of human beings whose brains have been suddenly disordered by occlusion of a blood vessel can give the neurologist a splendid opportunity to learn about the localization of the functions of the brain; because no other disease destroys certain areas with such precision, and at the same time leaves other parts of the nervous system undisturbed.

We Now Greatly Need Life-Long Studies of Patients with Cerebral Atherosclerosis. We physicians much need many life-long studies of persons who were seen perhaps in college with a hypertension. Later, a general practitioner may have seen a little stroke. Years later, perhaps a gastroenterologist saw the man with a burning pain in his abdomen. Still later, an internist may have examined him carefully, trying to learn why he had suddenly lost 30 pounds in weight. Then a cardiologist may have been called in when a pain shot into the man's thorax. A neurologist and an angiologist and a roentgenologist may have studied him when he had his first easily recognizable stroke; an ophthalmologist examined him one day when he saw double or complained of a scotoma; when he was 75, a psychiatrist talked to him when he became very restless and could not recognize his son; a professor of medicine saw him when he entered a university hospital to die, and a pathologist performed the necropsy. What is very much needed now is a gathering into one folder of copies of all of the case records made by all of the physicians who saw the one patient during the course of some 60 years. Perhaps when we get a few hundred such life-histories at Bethesda we will gain a better understanding of the disease. Also, we can use the life-long records made by good general practitioners of the type of a Sir James Mackenzie, and we can some day use many of the records made at Framingham, Massachusetts.

So commonly, when I was an internist in the Mayo Clinic, I would see a person with arteriosclerosis of the brain only once, and then perhaps just to make the diagnosis and suggest treatment. A hundred times I have felt as if I were looking at one frame of a reel of film, when I ought to be sitting for an hour, looking at the whole picture.

Obviously, different men must study the problem of little strokes with their several skills and technics; also they will see different types of cases in different places, such as private homes, "rest homes," huge city hospitals, university hospitals, "poor-houses," and state mental hospitals. Also, the general practitioner may hear of some mild little strokes; the Chief of Service in a big teaching hospital will see a more severe and disabling type of stroke, and the physician in a nursing home will see an even worse syndrome, perhaps of arteriosclerotic senescence.

BLACK SPOTS IN THE BRAIN

Around 1930, when I talked to my friend, Dr. James Kernohan—brain pathologist of the Mayo Clinic—about the patients with little strokes whom I was seeing all the time, he said, "I am so glad to hear you speak about those spells because, for years, I have been wishing that I could learn from some clinician what happened to those many patients who, at necropsy, I keep seeing with dozens or scores or hundreds of small or tiny hemorrhages (lacunae) in their brains. Surely, those serious injuries should have produced some symptoms—some of them temporary, and perhaps a few permanent." Dr. Kernohan showed me big sections of brains with many of the black spots scattered through them (see the illustrations in my paper in Geriatrics, for 1946). Some of these spots were as big as a small pea, while others were just visible to the naked eye. Others were visible only with the aid of a microscope. In some brains, arterioles and even capillaries were ruptured or thrombosed. In some places there were what looked to me like recent extravasations of blood.

As Dr. Kernohan said,

Years ago, when I first became fascinated with these spots—whenever at a necropsy I found a lot of them or some big ones—I would search through the patient's history to see if I could find mention of a little stroke such as I would expect to find when a part of the brain was destroyed, but almost always I failed to find what I was looking for; all the intern had recorded had been the story of some nervousness, headache, dizzy spells, or perhaps some unexplained pain in the patient's abdomen.

I agreed then that the black nodules must have produced some of the "little strokes" that I was seeing so frequently. I regret that Dr. Kernohan never found the time to write much about the spots. One of his students, Edward Rosenberg (1940) wrote an excellent article, much of it on the black spots seen in cases of malignant hypertension.

In only one case could I get a necropsy performed on a stroke patient *of mine.* She was a relative who lived in my home for 3 years before she died—having one little stroke after another. These spells commonly caused nausea, vomiting, shock, and a day or two of weakness. At necropsy, Dr. Kernohan found scores of black spots—all he needed to explain the many spells which slowly had pulled my relative down to her death.

Recently, when I asked Dr. Kernohan and Dr. Sayre, one of his associates, what percentage of the older patients with cerebral arteriosclerosis they thought had these black spots, they said perhaps 20 per cent.

This past year, as I have searched through the literature on cerebral arteriosclerosis and little strokes, I have found any number of illustrations of sections of brains—showing many of the black spots—but strange to say, few of the writers of the articles mentioned them; and this I have marvelled at. Perhaps the pathologists did not mention the spots because they thought they were too common to be worth talking about. We human beings often ignore what we see every day. Some men were probably speaking of the spots when they wrote of the petechial hemorrhages which are so common, especially in cases of hypertensive encephalopathy, or of carbon monoxide poisoning, or lead poisoning, or the encephalopathy of old "punch-drunk" prize-fighters.

Excellent is the description of the black spots by A. B. Baker (1935, Figs. 1, 15, and 16). He spoke of them as "ball hemorrhages," which is a fitting name, because many of the spots look like little balls. As Dr. Baker said, they are "solid accumulations of red cells." Also, so truly he said, as did Dr. Kernohan, "These, either single or fused, *are by far the most frequent type of hemorrhage observed in the brain.*"

Recently, C. Miller Fisher* wrote that during 1042 autopsies, cerebral lacunes were found in 114. The pictures on his p. 775 show spots like those I published in my article in Geriatrics.

A number of other pathologists have realized that petechial or "puncti-form" hemorrhages of all sizes are common. Some men have spoken of thrombi full of old blood pigment, or they have described arteries surrounded by remnants of red blood cells; some have spoken of ferruginous spots (full of old iron); several have written of "miliary" infarcts as the essential lesion of the encephalopathy of malignant hypertension; and Kubik and Adams (1946, p. 95) spoke of these lesions as explaining the "nervousness, forgetfulness, lack of initiative," and other symptoms of little strokes.

As I looked at Dr. Kernohan's microscopic sections of brain tissue, full of thrombosed capillaries or ruptured tiny arterioles I gained the impression that if enough of these lesions should appear in a small bit of brain its function could, at least for a time, be impaired. Also, when there was just an extravasation of blood, if in a few days or weeks this could be absorbed or cleared out, the person might regain the function of a weakened part of his body.

SOME OF THE LITERATURE ON THE BLACK SPOTS. Following are references to some of the many articles I have run onto in which there are descriptions and often pictures of sections of the brain, containing many black spots, "petechiae," or "tiny hemorrhages," or "scars of old hemorrhages," or "iron-containing Konkrementz," or lacunae.

Charcot (1868) spoke of "black nodules." Roy and Sherrington (1890, p. 107); also Wilbrand and Saenger (1906, p. 693), O. Fischer (1907) and Gustav Oppenheim (1909) described spots and "little knobs—Drusen." Allan (1910) and Mott (1910) spoke of small hemorrhages. H. Oppenheim (1911, p. 829) and A. Schonfeld (1914, pp. 376 and 377) gave much of the old literature on the black spots and "little nodules" or "Schwartz gefarbte Flecke." Ricker (1919, p. 207); Roger, Vidal, and Tessier (1920, pp. 430 and 452), and James (1926) said that in patients with transient aphasia, *if he studied the brain carefully enough,* he could find small hemorrhages. Staemmler (1927, see several pictures), McNally (1928), Tilney (1928, p. 1132), and Rhein, Winkelman, and Patten (1928) saw many microscopic miliary areas of softening all through the brain. Cobb and Hubbard (1929, p. 608) saw many spots with CO poisoning. P. Schwartz (1930, pp. 117, and 160 to 170), Spielmeyer (1930, p. 569, Fig. 26), Riser, Meriel, and Planques (1931, Fig. 3); Critchley

* Neurology 15:774-784, 1965.

(1930, p. 134, Figs. 9, 10 and 11; also 1931; fine bibliography), Gildea and Cobb (1930, Fig. 1), Cobb (1931), Pal (1931), A. Torkildsen and W. Penfield (1933, Figs. 4 and 8); Gellerstedt (1933, p. 371), H. S. Forbes, K. H. Finley, and G. I. Nason (1933); Cowdry (1933, p. 424, also good bibliography), Schaller, Tamaki and Newman (1937, p. 1063); Putnam (1937, p. 200); Arthur Ellis (1938, Fig. 13), Alexander and Putnam (1938, pp. 471 and 519), Davison and Brill (1939), and E. F. Rosenberg (1940) found capillary hemorrhages and miliary infarcts so widely scattered that they must have destroyed much brain tissue. Kinnier Wilson (1941, p. 1099) found microscopic lesions in the brain, and said that Achard, around 1920, and Evans, in 1924, had found microscopic hemorrhages. Rothschild (1945) found the brains of a third of senile persons with small hemorrhages (see his Fig. 11, p. 260). Aring (1945), Kubik and Adams (1946, p. 95), Cohen and Adams (1947, Fig. 2), Miller Fisher (1951, Fig. 6), Fisher and Cameron (1953), M. Y. Moore (1954), De Takats (1954); Byrom (1954), Foley (1956, pp. 180 and 181, Figs. 3, 4, and 12), Herbut's *Textbook of Pathology*, 2nd Edition (1956, pp. 1140 and 1426), Stephens (1957), Muir, *Textbook of Pathology*, 7th Edition (1958, p. 790), C. M. Fisher (1958, Fig. 6); Otto Saphir (1959, pp. 1806, 1807, 1814); all report black spots. R. A. Kuhn (1960, p. 27) said that a third of patients with strokes have blocked tiny arteries in the brain. Dickinson and Thomson (1960), W. A. D. Anderson (1961, p. 1380), and van Buskirk (1962, Figs. 10-18, p. 603) also wrote about the spots.

Foyers Lacunaires, PLAQUES, MILIARY NECROSES, ETC. Pierre Marie (1901) described what he called *foyers lacunaires* or little holes in the brain substance. He said that often a hemiplegia is due, not to any hemorrhage or softening, but to the lacunaires. Foley (1956) had the same idea. As he said, in this condition, "it looks as if the brain had been torn into holes that range from the size of a millet seed to that of a pea." He suspected they are due to infection after death, because the cavities seem to be filled with gas. He said (1956) "The true 'little stroke' is the symptom . . . that results when a patient has had a lacunar infarct." He spoke of showers of lacunar infarcts—showers which may be widespread throughout the brain. C. M. Fisher (1958, p. 420, also 1965) thought that "lacunes are probably the most common vascular lesion in the brain, and are the hallmark of hypertension." He felt they are produced when occlusion of certain "penetrating vessels leads to small circumscribed infarcts several millimeters in diameter which, in the healed stage, leave behind a lacune."

There is a big literature, especially in Germany, on the "miliary plaques" or "plaques jaunes" found in the brains of some aged persons. It is agreed that they are not always the cause of a senile psychosis; and not always associated with senility. Fuller (1911) said that their cause is not arteriosclerosis. He spoke of amyloid bodies which may have been something like the black spots. Tilney (1928) described again Pierre Marie's "l'état vermoulu"—or worm-eaten appearance of the brain.

W. R. Gowers (1888) and O. Fischer, in 1907, wrote of miliary "Nekrosen," or little nodules scattered through the brain, together with fine threads called Sphaerotrichia cerebri (See A. Schonfeld, 1914, and W. T. Moore, 1954). Some German pathologists wrote much about little "Drusen"—nodules that they found in the arteries of old brains.

Gellerstedt (1933) spoke of "clods" and commonly seen iron-containing "Konkrements"—possibly the black spots. Keith, Wagener and Kernohan (1928) found "small areas of rust-colored softening." Cobb and Hubbard (1929) said that petechial hemorrhages are more common than ordinarily supposed. Cobb made what looks to me like a good suggestion. He thought that sometimes blood goes through the wall of a brain artery—by diapedesis. This would explain why, in many cases, there is an injury to the brain without obvious injury to the near-by artery.

HYPERTENSIVE ENCEPHALOPATHY. The men who have studied hypertensive encephalopathy have emphasized the fact that in this disease the brain contains many petechial hemorrhages. "Acute cerebral episodes" were described in 1928 by Oppenheimer and Fishberg, who suggested the name for the disease. In 1928, Keith, van Wagener and Kernohan wrote their splendid paper on "The syndrome of malignant hypertension." Others who wrote well on this subject were Arthur Ellis (1938), Davison and Brill (1939), Rosenberg (1940), Adams and Cohen (1947), G. W. Pickering (1948), Byrom (1954), J. St. C. Elkington (1958), and Marshall and Shaw (1959). G. W. Pickering, A. D. Wright, and R. H. Heptinstall (1952) reported some cases in which, with an improvement in the malignant hypertension, the serious changes in the brain appeared to be reversed. F. A. Pickworth (1929) pointed out that people who have been poisoned with carbon monoxide and have many capillary hemorrhages in the brain, can become psychotic. Some of the men who were gassed during World War One later showed mental changes, much like those that can follow a number of little strokes.

CONCLUSION IN REGARD TO THE BLACK SPOTS. The black spots or nodules or lacunes have been seen by dozens of men, and I feel, as Drs. Kernohan and Baker do, that they deserve much more attention than they have so far received. If they were well studied in their stages of production and perhaps absorption, we might learn much more of what we want to know about why little and brief strokes come and go, and often—for some time—stay away. Certainly, when there are many black spots, they must injure some of the functions of the brain.

LITTLE OR UNUSUAL STROKES IN CHILDREN. As I have said elsewhere in this book, peculiar strokes can appear in children, where some can be due to rupture of tiny congenital aneurysms. Osler wrote up 135 cases of strokes in children. Berlin, Tumarkin and Martin (1955) reported 13 cases of severe early strokes, probably due to thrombosis of arteries.

HEREDITY AS A FACTOR IN PRODUCING ATHEROSCLEROSIS. For Cowdry's book (1933), G. D. William wrote a chapter on identical twins which suggested that a hereditary factor can produce arteriosclerosis and hypertension. Kallmann and Sander (1948), studied 237 monozygotic and 548 dizygotic twins, all of them over the age of 60, and found that the differences between the ages at death averaged 36.9 months in the cases of the monozygotics and 78.3 months in the cases of the dizygotics. One pair of monozygotics died—both of them—on the same day; another pair died 5 days apart, and another died 25 days apart. As Nöllenburg (1932), Dublin, and Pearl and Pearl (1934) showed, there is a definite tendency of long-lived people to have long-lived children (See Platt, 1947).

In a chapter in O. J. Kaplan's book (1956) Kallmann again told of his experience with twins, which strongly indicated a hereditary factor in aging, and perhaps in escaping from the deleterious influences of atherosclerosis and hypertension. G. W. Pickering (1955) also gathered much evidence suggesting a hereditary influence. See his bibliography. As long ago as 1872, Noel G. de Mussy studied the heredity of arteriosclerosis.

BRAIN INJURY DURING HEART SURGERY. Sid Gilman* found that during *open*-heart surgery, an injury can be done to the brain, with symptoms like those of a little stroke. Drs. D. S. Kornfeld, S. Zimberg and J. R. Malm† reported that in some cases of *closed*-heart surgery there came a temporary psychosis.

* New England J. Med. 272:489-498, 1965.
† New England J. Med. 273:287-292, 1965.

10

Vascular Spasm—Pro and Con

As we all know, many men have assumed that the strokelets are produced by a transient spasm in a blood-vessel—a spasm which produces probably a momentary ischemia of a small bit of the brain. In favor of such a view are (1) the transient nature of many spells; (2) the frequent sudden recovery; (3) the frequent discovery at necropsy of a brain infarct without any sign of obstruction in the blood-supplying artery; (4) the occasional association of Raynaud's disease with little strokes; and (5) the rare association of a little stroke with spasm in the arterioles in the retina or in the visual center of the brain.

Because the theory of spasm was early so attractive, anatomists soon set out to see if the arteries of the brain are supplied with vasomotor nerves; and then the physiologists, angiologists and brain surgeons looked to see if stimulation of the sympathetic nerves and ganglions in the neck can produce contractions of the arteries, and if section of the nerves or application of drugs will produce relaxation of the arteries.

ANATOMIC STUDIES. Among the men who early saw nerves on the arteries of the brain were E. Mendel (1891, who quoted Heubner, 1874), Obersteiner (1897), Gulland (1895 and 1898), G. C. Huber (1899), Muller and Siebeck (1907), P. Stohr, Jr. (1922 and 1928; see his huge bibliography), Hassin (1929), Bouckaert and Heymans (1935), Mc-Naughton (1938, excellent), and Dennis Williams (1938).

Beautiful photographs of nerves on pial blood vessels were published by Wilder Penfield (1932), Forbes and Cobb (1938), and others. Penfield reported that the innervation of arteries in the substance of the brain is similar to that in the pia. Important was the finding by E. Mendel (1891), Cobb (1931, p. 276) and others that the arteries in the brain are not endarteries, as was once taught. The connecting capillaries are numerous, and this collateral circulation appears now to be, at times, very important in preventing damage to the brain.

I have read that as early as 1811 Ravina, in order to study the behavior of the pial arteries put a window into the skull of a dog, and later (1850) Donders made good use of this technic. According to Ricker, an early study of this type was by Adolf Schramm (Strassburg Diss, 1824). Other early workers in this field were Callenfels (1855), Kussmaul and Tenner (1857), A. Schultz (1860), E. Leyden (1866), H. Nothnagel (1867), F. Riegel and F. Jolly (1871), and H. Cushing (1902).

Fine reviews of the literature were made by Karl Hürthle (1889), Wolff (1928), Forbes (1928), Forbes and Wolff (1928), Cobb (1937), Fog (1937), Forbes, Nason and Wortman (1937), Forbes and Cobb (1938), Echlin (1942), and C. F. Schmidt (1944). Any historian who wants an entrée to the old literature should read Hürthle's remarkable article. F. A. Echlin (1942) and others emphasized the fact that what happens to arteries when vasomotor nerves are stimulated in *animals* does not necessarily happen *in the case of man*. Man's vasomotor nerves running to arteries in the brain seem to be less reactive than are similar nerves in cats, dogs, and monkeys. Sir W. Bayliss (1895), Florey (1925), and Forbes and Wolff (1928) did not find much sign of a vasomotor control.

One reason for the uncertain results obtained by the earlier workers was that they did not realize that stimulation of nerves in the neck could cause changes in blood pressure which then could cause changes in the diameter of the arteries. Forbes, and Forbes and Wolff noted this in 1928. See also Forbes, Nason, and Wortman (1937).

Meagher and Ingraham (1929) saw slight effects of nerve stimulation in rabbits and cats, and E. D. Freis (1960) found that some constriction of arterioles followed stimulation of sympathetic nerves. De Vries (1931) and Putnam (1937) doubted if the cerebral arteries of man can ever contract enough to produce an infarct. Brain (1957) and others found little evidence that drugs in the usual doses have any effect on the lumen of cerebral blood vessels of man.

By 1932, W. Penfield could say that the extracerebral and intramedullary arteries are innervated in a manner similar to that of the blood vessels of the pia mater, and the two nerve plexuses are continuous. He said that intracerebral vasomotor reflexes are possible, and "a limited neurogenic control does exist." G. Chorobski and W. Penfield (1932) showed some parasympathetic control, and G. W. Pickering (1959) presented a good symposium on the subject.

Penfield (1933) reported that when a patient who was being operated on, with his skull opened, had an epileptic seizure, all that happened usually was that the pial arteries relaxed and stopped pulsating. Only occasionally did he see a constriction in the vessels, and that was *after* a seizure. He *never saw spasm before or during a seizure.* In 1938, he said he had observed 183 seizures at the operating table, and had never once seen blanching as a prelude. Once he saw marked constriction of arteries *following* a seizure which he had induced by electric stimulation of the brain. His impression was that the nervous control of the cerebral circulation is light, and probably affects mainly the pial and the larger cerebral vessels. He said also that the "arteries within the brain are not at all sensitive; only the arteries in close vicinity of the circle of Willis are sensitive." Some other men agreed as to this.

Everyone interested in the question of spasm in the cerebral arteries should study the splendid illustrations of Forbes and Wolff (1928) and Forbes and Cobb (1938, p. 210, and Figs. 93, 95, and 96), who showed how slight the amount of contraction there is—usually about a tenth of that obtainable in an artery below the neck. Forbes, Finlay and Nason (1933) showed how small the contraction is when epinephrin is applied to an artery. See also R. A. Lende (1938) who stimulated directly the arteries of cats and dogs—electrically and mechanically. Van Buskirk (1962) saw stimulation of cervical sympathetic ganglia produce a narrowing of only 8 per cent, compared with 80 per cent in skin arteries.

As years passed, more and more men reported having seen occasionally a slight spasm in arteries of the brain. J. L. Pool (1958) agreed that the smaller and more delicate arteries respond poorly, if at all, to stimuli, while the larger cerebral vessels can contract or dilate slightly. Pool, Bridges, Clark and Yahr (1958) saw vasoconstriction in blood vessels of the brains of men on stimulation of the upper cervical sympathetic ganglions, excluding the stellate. According to Van der Drift (1961) the nerve supply of the cerebral vessels comes from sympathetic, postganglionic fibers arising in the stellate and the superior cervical ganglia, but Carmichael, Doupe and Williams (1937) did not accept this.

Hürthle (1889) and others studied the effects of cutting the vagus and other nerves, and several men studied the effects of drugs painted on the arteries. Several angiographers have seen spasm in arteries appear the moment the contrast material entered. Denny-Brown (1960) said that too energetic an injection can cause a brain infarct. See Moniz (1927), and the story of his first efforts at angiography.

Kenk and Nall (1952) and Nall and Ferguson (1956) published excellent bibliographies on the physiology of the circulation of the brain, listing some 4,000 titles.

BECAUSE THE BRAIN ARTERIES OF MEN PAST 60 HAVE NO MUSCLE COAT LEFT, THEY CANNOT GO INTO SPASM. I have been much impressed by the—to me—unanswerable argument of A. B. Baker and his associates and others, against the idea of spasm. In 1937, Baker studied 70 apparently normal brains removed by a coroner because of an accidental death, and found that the media or muscle coat of the arteries was often gone. Brain arteries are different in this regard from most arteries throughout the body. In 1961, Baker and Iannone, and in 1963, A. B. Baker, E. Dahl, and B. Sandler confirmed the fact that in people past 60 the arteries of the brain have lost their muscle. Kameyama and Okinaka (1963) reported a study of the arteries in the brains and the necks of 400 persons aged 60 years or more, necropsied in the Geriatric Hospital in Tokyo. They concluded that in the internal carotid system, the cervical portion is rarely atherosclerotic, but in these aged people, in this lower segment of the artery *"the muscular layer has changed into fibrotic tissue."* The Japanese investigators felt, as Baker and his colleagues did, that in a person past 60 years of age, a little stroke—at least in an internal carotid artery—can hardly be due to spasm.

Among those who have noticed that the muscle in the artery walls in the brain is often atrophic, or gone, or replaced with fibrous or collagenous or hyalin tissue, were Charcot (1868, p. 268), Gull and Sutton (1872, quoted from Peabody, 1891), W. T. Councilman (1891), Triepel (1897, quoted from Curschmann), Wm. Russell (1907), Carmichael (quoted from Adams and vander Eecken (1953), F. W. Mott (1909), George Parker (1909), Walter Broadbent (1909), Thomas Inman (1920), Thoma (1922), Rolleston (1922), Rhein, Winkelman, and Patten (1928), Warthin (1929, p. 127), Neuberger (1930, quoted), Riser, Meriel, and Planques (1931), Cowdry (1933), Wolkoff (1933), Wertham and Wertham (1934, p. 171), Kinnier Wilson (1941), Aring (1945), G. W. Pickering (1948 and 1951), H. J. L. M. (1952), Putnam (1957), Meyer, Waltz, and Gotch (1960), Wahal and Riggs (1960, p. 15), Van der Drift (1961, p. 405), W. A. D. Anderson (1961), and Van Buskirk (1962).

As I said in Chapter 6, Osler lost faith in the idea of spasm (1) because of the great hardness of many sclerosed arteries and (2) because so often he saw that a man who had had a momentary aphasia had wound up with a permanent neurologic injury.

Florey (1925) and Fleming and Naffziger (1927) and others also argued that the walls of the arteries of the brain are often much too hard ever to go into spasm. William Hackel (1928) made an excellent study of the changes in brain arteries that come with age. Baker *et al.* studied the brains of 1,120 persons who had come to necropsy, and in a number of cases found decided sclerotic narrowing of arteries in the circle of Willis, and perhaps also in a middle cerebral artery. In 267 cases, one or more intracranial arteries were found to be decidedly narrowed or occluded, but here is the strange fact—there was no sign of any tissue change in the part of the brain supplied by the occluded artery.

LITTLE STROKES THAT ARE TRANSIENT CAN BE DUE TO AN ORGANIC

CHANGE IN AN ARTERY. A remarkable objection to the idea of spasm has now come from pathologists who, on finding thrombosis or embolism of an artery in the brain, have been surprised to learn that during the life of the patient *this rigid disease* caused the typical transient little or brief strokes with sudden recovery. These observations showed that the spasm theory is not needed. See the excellent Editorial by H. J. L. M. (1952), also an article by Millikan and Siekert (1955); also, very thoughtful articles by Pickering (1948 and 1951). Pickering (1948) saw 11 patients with emboli in their brain arteries but attacks exactly like those that might have been produced by hypertension.

MEN WHO FAVORED THE IDEA OF SPASM. Men who, at one time or another, mentioned favorably the idea of spasm were Kussmaul and Tenner (1857, quoted), Bastian (1887, quoted), George Peabody (1891), Huchard (1893, 1910), Grasset and Rauzier (1894), Pal (1903, 1905), Knapp (1904), Edgeworth (1906), Langwill (1906), W. Russell (1907), Krehl (1907), George Allan (1910), J. Gordon Sharpe (1915), O. K. Williamson (1918), Westphal (1926), K. Bremer (1928), Lhermitte (1928), Spielmeyer (1930), Riser, Meriel, and Planques (1931), Edwards and Biguria (1934), Wertham and Wertham (1934), Kinnier Wilson (1941), Moniz (1942), Arthur Ecker (1945), Purves Stewart (1947), Russek and Zohman (1948), B. J. Alpers (1950), Van der Eecken and Riemenschneider (1951), S. P. Hicks and Shields Warren (1951), Leriche (1952), M. Fisher and D. G. Cameron (1953), Charles Ecker (1953), I. S. Wright and McDevitt (1954), Foley (1956), Foley and Wright (1956), Rankin (1957), J. L. Pool (1958, big bibliography), J. L. Pool, S. Jacobson, and T. S. Fletcher (1958), E. D. Freis (1960), R. C. Connolly (1961), and Dukes and Vieth (1964).

MEN WHO WERE AGAINST SPASM OR WERE NOT SURE ABOUT IT. I have read that Weiss (1882) and Blaud (1899) were against spasm, as were W. Russell (1906, 1907), George Parker (1909), Clifford Allbutt (1915 and 1925), Norman (1916, quoted), Wells (1920), Thomas Inman (1920), J. Wilder (1926), James (1926), Fleming and Naffziger (1927), Bremer (1928, p. 304), deVries (1931), Forbes, Finlay, and Nason 1933), Merritt (1936), Baker (1937), Cobb (1937), W. Penfield (1937), M. Fog (1937), Putnam (1937), Carmichael, Doupe, and Williams (1938), Kinnier Wilson (1941), Cohen and Adams (1947), G. W. Pickering (1948), who said "Do not accept the idea of spasm unless you have no reasonable alternative," Carl F. Schmidt (1950), Kety (1950, p. 211), Wilson, Rupp, Riggs, and Wilson (1951), and Denny-Brown (1951 and 1955). James (1926) was much against the idea of spasm if only because whenever he could examine a brain carefully enough, he could find small hemorrhages.

An editorial writer (1952) said that spasm "is a glib device to explain what seems otherwise inexplicable."

Other doubters were Fisher and Cameron (1953), Corday, Rothenberg, and Putnam (1953), R. D. Adams (1954), Foley (1956), Rothenberg and Corday (1957), John Rankin (1957), W. R. Brain (1957), Clough (1958), Alajouanine, Lhermite, and Gautier (1960), Soderman (1961), Baker and Iannone (1961), Kameyama and Okinaka (1963), and Baker, Dahl and Sandler (1963).

Conclusion. Because of the demonstrations that the cerebral arteries of persons past 60 have no muscle fibers left, that constriction of the cerebral arteries is always slight, and that transient little strokes can be produced by thrombosis or embolism, I cannot accept the theory of spasm, especially in the cases of persons over 60. About the only use I see for the theory of spasm is that when a physician diagnoses spasm, this gives hope for recovery to a patient who has had a little stroke. His relatives will also be cheered. People are not so hopeful if they believe that an artery in the brain has plugged up and become permanently destroyed.

SPASM IN THE ARTERIES OF THE EYE AND THE VISUAL CENTER. In 1908, there was a great flare-up in interest in that type of arterial spasm—in one eye or perhaps in one visual center—that causes a blindness—usually transient. I here review a number of the papers published shortly after 1908 because studies of this type may eventually throw some light on the mechanism of spasm of arteries in the brain—granting that such spasm has something to do with producing little strokes. Josef Wilder (1926) described cases with transitory loss of vision and—this is important—later a defect in intelligence and a loss of memory.

In 1908 F. Parkes Weber and R. Grueber stirred up much interest by reporting many observations on the type of little stroke which can suddenly cause transient monocular blindness, usually with prompt recovery. Often, in the spell, an ophthalmologist will find one or more branches of the retinal artery contracted. In rare cases, at the same time, there can be a whitening of a Raynaud finger, a spell of giddiness, a feeling of swelling and numbness in the tongue, or a sudden failure in memory. These features will suggest a little stroke—due perhaps to spasm of an artery in the brain—like the spasm visible in the eye.

Weber and Grueber thought the angiospastic condition in the retina might be a manifestation of a disturbance which had its main seat in the cerebral cortex. Occasionally spasm in the retina will last too long, and then permanent blindness can result (much as possibly a change in the brain from spasm to thrombosis, can result in a hemiplegia). The authors told of a paper by Sulzer (1907) who saw a man of 63, with temporary blindness in the right eye due to an ischemia of the retina, which may have been due to the person's hypertension.

In 1894, A. H. Benson described the case of a man of 32 who got spasms in an artery of one eye, lasting from a few minutes to hours. Wagenmann (1897) told of a case—a man of 69. C. E. Beevor and R. M. Gunn (1899) told of a man of 34 with temporary amblyopia, especially in the right eye, with obliteration of a branch of the retinal artery. He had brief blind spells, some lasting only 5 minutes. Later he got a little stroke. G. W. Thompson (1902) described a similar case—that of a woman of 34. J. W. Barrett (1902) told of a man of 60 who woke blind in one eye. In 2 hours his vision began to come back, and in another hour he was well. In 1904, W. T. Shoemaker described the case of a lad of 17 who got partial blindness in the left eye due to ischemia of the retina. See Pal (1903, 1905). He spoke of a "blood-vessel crisis" in the retinas, and wrote much on spasm in arteries in the abdomen.

In 1957, Sir Charles Symonds and Ian Mackenzie made a splendid review of this literature on little strokes that involve the eyes, and abstracted the papers of 33 men. Anyone interested in this field must read the review articles by Parkes Weber, Symonds and Mackenzie, Priestley Smith, and Wilbrand and Saenger.

A. R. Lundie (1906) told of a man of 88 who had temporary blindness in the left eye with constriction of an artery. Lundie thought there might be spasm also in blood vessels in the visual center. H. Wilbrand and A. Saenger (1906), in their big book on the *Neurology of the Eyes,* described many cases of temporary blindness. They told of the different ways in which such blindness can be produced, as with hypotension due to much bleeding, or to thrombosis of a vessel.

In 1906, Hans Curschmann described angina pectoris associated with a cramping of arteries in the eyes. His Case 1 was that of a woman of 58 with angina pectoris who, with her chest pain, would get a transient blindness of the right eye, with paresthesias and cramps in her arms and legs: a sort of vasomotor storm. In his Case 2, there was angina pectoris, with dead fingers, and in Case 3, there was angina pectoris with blindness of the right eye, and spells that looked like little strokes.

In 1884 and 1909, Priestley Smith spoke of an "intermittent arterial spasm" as a cause of transient paralyses. He had seen changes in the retinal blood vessels, as in a middle-aged woman with many years of spells of complete blindness in one eye. Vision would return in half an hour. Finally, the eye became totally blind. Priestley Smith spoke of similar cases in which there was spasm, perhaps in one artery of the upper or lower half of the retina.

In 1924, Fink described the temporary loss of vision some women sustain just after having given birth to a child. In 1907, I saw a very stout woman of 40 who was purblind for a few days following an easy delivery. I have read that Fink collected 130 cases of such transitory postpartum blindness. Sometimes it came when the woman had a big hemorrhage and probably a big fall in blood pressure.

D. H. Noyes (1890) described two cases of temporary amblyopia, apparently due to spasm of retinal blood vessels. The giving of amyl nitrite cleared the vision in 20 minutes. Noyes saw a woman of 43 who said that every so often her sight would "go out" for 15 or 30 minutes. A man, in such spells, used to show great pallor of an optic disc, with narrowed arteries in the retina.

RAYNAUD'S DISEASE AND SPASM. Raynaud, in 1874, reported a case in which a man had spells of failure of vision, mainly in the left eye, together with asphyxia of some fingers. In another case, there was a narrowing of arteries in the retina. Edward Nettleship, in 1879, described the case of a woman of 26, with an intermittent blindness which later became permanent. His Case 2 was that of a man with severe aortic disease and attacks of transient blindness in the right eye. Julius Michel (1884) spoke of spasm in the retinal blood vessels.

In 1890, L. E. Stevenson described the case of a woman of 25 with severe Raynaud's disease, and temporary losses of vision.

In 1928, Bremer wrote of probable vascular spasm in the visual center such as can happen with Raynaud's disease. He spoke of "accidents cérébraux fugaces"; also "ictus apoplecticque." Oppenheimer and Fishberg (1928) were impressed by the close association between vasoconstriction in the retinas and in "white fingers." Osler mentioned this subject in 1898.

A thought-provoking article on vascular spasm is that of Sir George W. Pickering (1951). He said that Thomas Lewis (1929) did the first good research on Raynaud's type of spasm. The great Jonathan Hutchinson (1896) early saw that there are two types of Raynaud's disease, one in which there is pure spasm, and the other in which suddenly, in an apparently healthy person, a sort of atherosclerosis develops in the arteries of the fingers (see Lewis and Pickering, 1933-1934). No one knows why this arterial disease suddenly comes—even in summer. There may be some inherited hypersensitivity of the arteries.

Pickering (p. 848) said that commonly in the retinal arteries there come lasting obstructions. Similar obstructions come often in the small arteries of the heart (Blumgart, Gilligan, Zoll, Friedberg, and Schlesinger, 1940-1942).

Pickering emphasized the great value of the collateral vessels which open up when an artery becomes obstructed. He spoke of three theories to explain the obstruction of arteries in cases of hypertension: thrombosis; a tiny hemorrhage into the wall of the artery; or a necrosis of arterioles.

11

Puzzling Cases

In many cases the diagnosis of a little stroke would have been easy if only the episode had not come so early in the patient's life. The early age did not, however, rule out a stroke. Hippocrates told of seeing a stroke in a child, and Osler reported strokes in a series of 135 children. Also, a while ago a surprising number of young soldiers, when necropsied, were found to have much atherosclerotic change in their coronary arteries.

A Brief Stroke in a Woman in Her Twenties. One day I saw a frail, sickly young woman who, in her twenties, had a spell in which, for an hour, she was aphasic, and her mouth was pulled over to one side. She recovered in a day without obvious sequelae.

Several Strokelike Spells Early in Life. This is a remarkable case. A railroad flagman, when he was 5 years old, suffered so terribly with pain in his shins that he cried. Aside from this, he was well until he was 17, when suddenly he vomited and fell unconscious. He woke *after 40 hours of coma*, with a feeling of a heavy pressure in the back of his head, poor vision in his eyes, and weakness in both legs. His sense of smell was largely gone. In three days he was all right again, and back to work.

When he was 24, he had a curious spell in which he felt weak and numb all over. This time he remained conscious, and in an hour he was all right, but after that he could never again do any hard work. If he tried to work hard, he would get weak and despondent. He got a feeling of pressure in his head which he still had when I saw him. When he was 35, he had another bad spell in which suddenly he felt numb all over, and after that lost much weight. Also, he had a sudden, strokelike spell which left him with "a boiler factory in his head!" With this he had burning sensations all over his body.

When he was 53, he had another spell when his feet became numb. After that they remained that way. When he was 57, his feet became so sore that he could wear only bedroom slippers. He felt terribly heavy in his body. His teeth got so painful that he had them extracted. When I saw him, he could still read, but his vision was "foggy." He still had his "boiler factory" in his ears, and his sense of smell was poor.

I turned him over to some good neurologists who agreed that at intervals something had gone wrong in parts of his brain. As often happens with little strokes, each time what recovery he experienced came quickly —and the man was still in fair shape at the age of 62.

A Very Early Little Stroke. A man of 47 told me that 29 years before, *when he was 18,* he became very nervous, perhaps because every day he had to drive a truck over hazardous mountain roads. Then one morning, suddenly, he got a sharp pain in the right side of his head. Everything immediately seemed dim and unreal to him; and he had the feeling that he had lost some of his awareness of his surroundings. He would pick up a stone and try to see it as he would have seen it before, but it would seem to be at a distance, and unreal. Sent into a hospital, he had many studies made—but all showed nothing. His own diagnosis was a "small stroke." He knew that he had suffered permanent damage to his brain, because never again did he get back his old comfortable sense of awareness of his surroundings.

Possible Little Stroke in a Man of 18. A remarkable story which suggested an early stroke was that of a healthy-looking, pleasant, and well-adjusted young machinist (with sane relatives), who had always been well and happy, and without unusual strain until he was 18. Then he woke one morning to find he could not move his facial muscles. He could talk, but his lips burned, and his face swelled a bit. He was rushed to a hospital where he became too nervous to sleep. The physicians kept him in bed a month, making one examination after another. His family doctor removed his "chronic appendix," but naturally that did not help. The lad was so upset nervously and mentally that he did not go back to work for a year.

When I saw him, 5 years later, he was 23, and was working. He had not had any more spells, but he was still very uncomfortable. Although his facial muscles had regained their strength, they still did not "feel right."

Possible Stroke in a Young Man. Another mechanic, aged 33, suddenly felt a tingling back of his nose, and a little later he began to feel "peculiar." Then came another little spell in which his face tingled and he felt as if he had had a shock from an electric current. With this, he became much frightened because he was so sure he was having a stroke. Finding himself almost too ataxic to walk, he went to a hospital. There, the only abnormality found was a systolic blood pressure of 170 mm. Hg. The doctors told him to snap out of it. He was worried, but he had reason to be, because he had probably had a stroke, and it had left him uncomfortable. I do not know what happened to him later.

REMARKABLE SMALL STROKES THAT CAUSED MAINLY MENTAL DISTRESS. Another machinist, a stocky, unmarried, quiet and odd-appearing man of 36, said that his nervous heredity was good. He had always been well until 2 years before, when suddenly, while reading his paper at 7:30 A.M. he had almost blacked out. After 15 minutes he felt all right, so he went to work and had no trouble all day. A neurologic examination then showed nothing wrong.

Three months later he had another spell—almost certainly a little stroke—in which, again, he almost blacked out, and felt as if an electric shock had hit him on the right side of the top of his head. His eyes felt as if they were rolling, and *for a while he saw double*. He became terribly frightened because he thought he was dying of a stroke. Luckily, in 15 minutes he was all right. He was taken to a hospital, where his systolic blood pressure was found to be 85 mm. Hg. It soon went back up to normal. Nothing else wrong was found. His electroencephalograms were normal. He kept at work, but after the second spell, he kept feeling that there was something decidedly wrong with his brain. Every morning he woke feeling queer, dizzy, and tired. It was hard to get up and go to work. By four in the afternoon he felt better, and then two drinks after work made him feel well.

He still felt he was losing his mind. His walk was a bit ataxic; his memory had failed somewhat, and he had lost most of his libido and potentia. Fortunately, he still could handle his job as foreman of a shop. He said so wisely that if he were only 65 he *would be sure* he had had some strokes; as it was, he just *thought he had had them*. I agreed with him about one thing—one should not try to laugh off the suddenness of the coming of his illness, his double vision, and the loss of sex interest and power.

A SMALL STROKE AT AGE 25. A stout, pleasant woman of 51, with a systolic blood pressure of 260 mm. Hg, had had severe migraine since the age of 12. Four years before I saw her, she had become very nervous.

Two years before I saw her, at the age of 49, she was found lying on the floor, where she had lain unconscious for 4 or 5 hours. When she woke she was blind for an hour. Five months later she had another spell in which, for a while, she dragged her right foot. This foot and her right hand at times were numb. On occasions, her mind felt "muddled," and she was dizzy. With this, she became depressed and weepy.

Interestingly, one day as she talked with me, she remembered that 26 years before, *when she was 25*, and her son was just born, she had a spell in which, for a while, she could not remember anything. After that she had other spells in which her memory failed her badly—so badly that always thereafter she carried identification papers so that, if need be, she could find out who she was and where she lived. Roentgenographic examination of the skull showed signs suggesting a small aneurysm near the sella. Tests for syphilis were negative. I do not know what happened to her later.

A Long Series of Little Strokes—Beginning at Age 26. A doctor's daughter of 63, unmarried, a pleasant, highly intelligent ex-school-teacher and writer, when I first saw her was complaining of severe migraines. Her first little stroke came in 1917, when she was 26. It was an "odd spell" in which she lost consciousness. The next stroke that she could remember came at the age of 32, when, as she lay recovering from a hysterectomy, the room began to spin around violently. After this, for the first time in her life, she became over-emotional and weepy. Also, one side of her face and the arm and leg on that side suddenly seemed to be "drawn," and she began to talk oddly.

In 1927, another little stroke so changed her usually sweet nature that, for a while, she was quarrelsome. In 1935, she began to have sudden, unexplainable, but very distressing, attacks of fatigue. These kept coming for the next many years.

In 1936, while walking, she got an acute pain in the epigastrium; she lost consciousness for a short time, and on waking found her face and hand drawn to one side. Her feet felt as if they were made of wood. In 1944, she woke one night, sick to her stomach, and with her mouth "webbed together" with thick, sticky, saliva.

Then came years when she wasn't sure of herself; she was afraid to go out alone, and she could not make even small decisions. She realized that at times her brain was being affected by "little jolts." Occasionally, she got an attack of excruciating pain in her right armpit, which might last from twenty minutes to an hour. Sometimes, with this, there was abdominal pain.

I last heard from her in 1964, when she was 73. She said she could not then write a letter of any length without becoming painfully tired, but evidently her brain was clear. She could not do much housework.

Probable Little Strokes. The following history is puzzling, but it looked to me as if a big, powerfully-built, cheerful rancher of 35 had had a stroke. Eight months before I saw him, one morning after he had "snapped the necks" of some 70 minks, he felt that his right hand had become weak, and it felt peculiar. He also felt a sudden pain in the lower part of his back. That evening he went out to bowl, but he had to quit because of pain in his back. Also his right wrist felt too weak. Accordingly, he went home, and on getting out of his car, he staggered, but things did not spin around. He slept well, but next morning, when he got up, his right leg collapsed under him. He could walk only when leaning heavily on someone. If he stayed up a while too long he would get very tired, and he would start vomiting. He also got a "terrible pain" in the right side of his head. He felt as if his right cheek were weak and abnormal. His right eye did not see well, and his vision was blurred. He felt the head pain for a couple of days, during which time he remained in bed. Every time he would raise his head, he would get a severe pain in the right temple.

His home physician thought that he had had a stroke. Later, pain in his right leg moved over into the left one. For a while his left leg felt weak but gradually it regained strength. Eight months later, he was walking normally. Interestingly, when he got into a tub of hot water, with his left leg he couldn't tell the difference between hot and cold. Later, his legs became overly sensitive to cold. For a while he could not walk very far, but he could work all day around his mink ranch if he went at it slowly.

I thought of a beginning multiple sclerosis, and curiously, his two brothers had this disease, but a neurologic check-up showed "nothing wrong." He did not look like the sort of man likely to have hysteria, and I could learn of no reason for his getting nervous. The probability was that he had had little strokes.

A Remarkable Family With Early Strokes. An odd story was that of a woman who, at the age of 29, suffered an aphasia, with a hemiplegia, and almost complete blindness in one eye. A sister died at 39 with a stroke, and another sister, at the age of 41, was recovering from her third stroke. There was hypertension in the family.

Possible Little Stroke Postpartum. Another "early case" was that of a petite, brilliant woman with a psychotic inheritance, and a very severe migraine. At the age of 28, right after giving birth to a child, she had a hemiplegia, from which she recovered quickly and well.

A Series of Little Strokes Beginning at Age 31. A stout woman, aged 53, with a systolic blood pressure of 200 mm. Hg, complained of attacks of epigastric pain which had been coming for 20 years. They had become worse in the previous 2 years before I saw her. She had occasional 2- or 3-day spells of nausea, vomiting, and diarrhea. Her abdomen might get sore. Many roentgenographic studies had shown nothing abnormal in her abdomen. In the previous 18 months, she had lost 30 pounds.

After much questioning during several interviews, I learned that 22 years before, when she was 31, she had suddenly experienced a dead feeling in both hands and arms. This spell had left her for a time unable to carry anything, because she might drop it. Later, this situation largely cleared up, but the arms were left feeling dead and painful. A year before I saw her, she had had an attack in which her legs (perhaps rubbery) would not hold her up, and she collapsed to the floor. Then another spell left her without a good sense of balance. On one occasion, she nearly fainted, and was left weak and dizzy. After this she could no longer write clearly, and at times she could not talk clearly.

When she ate, the food felt as if it remained as a lump in her stomach. She fatigued easily. Twice, while driving a car, she lost consciousness and the person with her had to grab the wheel. After one of her apparent little strokes, her elevated blood pressure suddenly dropped to normal. Later it went back up to 175/100.

At one time she felt so queer she went to a psychiatrist, but he didn't think there was much wrong with her. She then began to get anginal distress on going upstairs. Later, she had a bad spell in which she fell down in her bathroom and was unconscious for the rest of the day. In another spell her face was pulled over to the left, and the right arm and leg were weakened. During this time she had to learn to use her left hand.

What interested me much about this case was that it was only after several sessions of pertinacious questioning that the woman began to remember several little strokes. She said, as other such patients have said, that one reason why she had gotten out of the habit of telling the story of her strokes, was that the physicians she had seen had refused to listen to her story, as she wanted to tell it; they always had said, "Just answer my questions," and that she had learned to do.

A Little Stroke Early in Life. A married man of 26, who had a poor nervous inheritance, complained of much pressure inside of his head. He said he had been well until 6 months before, when, suddenly he felt numb all over, and felt as if he was going under an anesthetic. He felt so exhausted he wanted to lie down on the street and go to sleep there, but he managed to walk out to his car. On the way he could not walk straight.

He and his wife were much frightened, as they thought he was having a heart attack. He went directly to a hospital where nothing wrong could be found. Later, he went back to work, and for a few days, felt all right. Then, again, he got a pressure in his head. At times he felt bad, but fortunately, at other times he felt well enough to work. My impression was that he had had little strokes.

One of Many Patients Who Knew the Little Stroke Syndrome Well Because He Had Seen Relatives Die Of It. In 1920, I saw an executive, aged 53, who complained of nervousness, depressions, spells of apprehension, heartburn, palpitation, and exhaustion after eating. This was vague enough; what impressed me much was that this man, who for all his days since childhood had read rapidly, said that one day, suddenly, something had gone so wrong in his brain that he could no longer read well; he could read only slowly, and then for only a few minutes. Surely his brain, in some way, had been damaged.

The first story I obtained from the man was that he had been strong, active, and well until 4 months before, when, after becoming very tired on a golf course, he had "collapsed." After this he hadn't felt well; he remained terribly tired; he couldn't put his mind to his business; he could not stand talking to people; he could not make decisions; and he could not even answer his mail. Several "complete examinations" showed nothing wrong except a slight hypertension. Interestingly, the man came to me complaining only of an abdominal discomfort. Later he told me that in the preceding 5 years, he had had several dizzy spells, each of which had pulled him down a bit.

Then, one day, as we chatted, he suddenly had one of those moments of lucidity that sometimes will come to a man who has been much dulled by a little stroke, and he remembered that, *beginning when he was 35,* he had had three sudden "nervous breakdowns." He said that these spells were small strokes. When I asked him how he could know that, he said —as a number of these patients have said—*he knew the disease well in all of its details because he had watched his father and his elder sister die slowly with a series of such strokes!*

PEOPLE WITH A POOR FAMILY HISTORY AND PROBABLE LITTLE STROKES

In the following series of cases there was a question in my mind whether the symptoms complained of were all due to little strokes, or whether a little stroke might have brought out a familial tendency to a mild psychosis; or perhaps the person's "nervous breakdown" was due purely to his or her poor nervous inheritance. In several such cases, a man's wife helped me much by saying, "Oh, no; this spell was not one of his old moody ones. This one came more suddenly, and was different. I am sure it was a stroke." In other cases the patient maintained that he (or she) had had a little stroke, and this statement greatly reenforced my impression.

WHEN A PERSON WITH LITTLE STROKES LETS GO OF HIS SANITY. Occasionally, I have seen a patient who said that he knew he had inherited a tendency to a psychosis; and so for all of his life, he had "clung to his sanity," and had fought off the occasional impulse to "let go"; but then, perhaps in his 60's, a little stroke came and weakened him so much that he lost control, and became depressed, paranoid, suspicious, unreasonable, "difficult," or childish.

The influence of heredity was probably shown in two cases I studied recently. In one, an old man suddenly had what looked like a little stroke, which left him acutely paranoid and accusing his relatives of trying to take his life so as to get his money. What interested me was that I knew that one of his daughters had always been decidedly paranoid. In another case, a man of 70 died screaming that his devoted daughter was trying to kill him for his money, and in this case, also, the relatives told me that the daughter had always been a very suspicious person.

I was much interested to find David Rothschild (1944) concluding, as I have done, that often a man who has been a bit odd by inheritance, but has for long "clung to his sanity," can be broken mentally by a little stroke which would not have much bothered a man with a better nervous inheritance.

PUZZLING SPELLS. Several women told me of a husband who had been having spells in which he would suddenly become slowed-up and oldish. Then, during the course of perhaps a couple of months, he would recover, and again behave like his old self. Then he would have another slump. In such cases one thinks, of course, of brief spells of depression, and this may have been what they were. But later, the coming of more spells with symptoms of focal brain damage satisfied me that the man had had little strokes.

A CASE IN WHICH THE WIFE WAS SURE OF A LITTLE STROKE. A case in which I was puzzled—but the wife was not—was that of a professional man of 51. He had always been moody and somewhat manic-depressive, like several of his siblings, and for 4 years he had been feeling nervous and worried and tired. Two years before I saw him, he had what was called a nervous breakdown, which followed what could have been a little stroke because, suddenly, he felt as if his head were about to burst open.

Some months after this episode, while driving his car across country, he quickly pulled over to the side of the road and stopped. For a few minutes he lay unconscious. His wife then took the wheel and drove to the nearest motel where, when the man got out, he found himself unsteady on his legs. His hands were too shaky to sign the register. He wept, and for 2 weeks he was weepy and inclined to sleep. He had no dizziness or vomiting or weakness of any muscles. An internist and a neurologist studied him and found "nothing wrong." The distresses soon cleared away, and years later, I heard that he was still well and at work.

Because of this man's past history of a cycloid temperament, I was slow to make the diagnosis of a little stroke, but the wife was satisfied that the spell represented a slight apoplexy. She maintained that it was very different from the ones that had ushered in the man's previous brief depressions.

A Curious Puzzle: a Young Woman With Perhaps Hysteria, or Perhaps Little Strokes. A migrainous divorcée, aged 25, had an alcoholic father. She bloated occasionally in a hysterical way. One day she had what looked like a little stroke, which left her with clumsiness of the fingers of both hands, but especially those of the right hand. The fact that this clumsiness lasted unchanged for several years was rather against hysteria.

Then, 10 days after the removal of a tooth in the floor of an antrum, she began to shake all over, and for months could not work. Her legs got weak and clumsy, and she had trouble walking. Her balance was so poor that if she tried to hurry, she would fall on her face. I have heard this story of falling down when hurrying from a number of persons—one a physician who had had a little stroke. Occasionally, the woman had some blurring of vision in her right eye. She would wake at night with pain in her right side and in her scalp and nucha. I had her studied by good neurologists who preferred not to make a diagnosis.

Strokes and a Bad Nervous Heredity. A married woman of 52 had always been nervous and migrainous, but always strong. Once she was in bed for a year with what the doctor called a heart attack, but she maintained it was "just nerves," and she probably was right, because her symptoms then were feelings of fatigue, apathy, refusal to see anyone, a pulling on the left side of her face, and much somnolence. Later, one evening, when she thought she was having a stroke, she suddenly began to perspire so that the water ran off of her. She felt too weak to get out of her chair, and felt that she was dying. She was terribly dizzy. Then came a chill; her right hand got stiff, and later she had trouble writing.

When I saw her, her right hand still felt queer. She had become so despondent that she cried easily. In a crowd she could not "see clearly." At times she could "hardly pull one leg after the other." *She often saw double.* Her blood pressure was low. Gradually she got better. For months she did not attempt to go upstairs because she was so weak and dizzy.

Her father tended to be despondent, and one of her brothers, for a while, drank so heavily that he wound up in a mental hospital. In this case it looked as if the woman's depression could have been due purely to her inheritance, but it is possible that she was correct in saying that she had had little strokes. One must not forget that sometimes she saw double.

12

My Personal Experience With Little Strokes

I am inserting here the description of a few tiny strokes I have had—most of them while in my seventies. Why do I describe them? Because the symptoms of the mildest and most fleeting of the little strokes are likely to be mentioned and described only by a scientifically trained old observer like me, who for 17 years lived largely in the world of physiologic research.

Certainly the average layman is not likely to go to a neurologist to complain that he had a transient scotoma, or perhaps flashes of light at the left edge of his field of vision, or that for a couple of days he kept biting his tongue severely, or kept biting his upper lip, or one corner of his mouth; or that on a half-dozen occasions, for a few seconds, he lost his normal and comfortable sense of position in space; or occasionally for a minute he had difficulty in swallowing, or rarely had a hemianopsia, or a feeling of slight ataxia while walking, or a brief spell of intention tremor, with failure of "feed-back" in his hand, or a coughing spell caused by the entrance of food or sticky mucus or saliva into his larynx.

The scientific observer may not be sure exactly how these symptoms were produced, or what they meant, but his training can cause him at least to make note of them in a diary, and later to report them. His thought will be that eventually, when several good observers report having noted these brief symptoms, such as some people experience in their seventies and eighties, we physicians will be better acquainted with the syndromes of the tiniest little strokes, produced perhaps by the plugging-up of a few arterioles. Some day, a clinician, when puzzled by the illness of an old person, will ask about showers of these minor symptoms, and if he learns that the patient has had them, this fact will help him in making the diagnosis. I wonder, also, if an observant and diary-keeping elderly man may not, as he sees an occasional scotoma, or experiences a brief severe pain in a toe or finger, start wondering if he is seeing signs of the steplike destruction of hundreds or thousands of neurones in his brain, such as we know is constantly taking place.

Another reason I have for mentioning my experiences with perhaps the tiniest of little strokes is to show that there probably is a world of minor symptoms which we physicians must some day learn about. Also, I have in mind what Plato said, to the effect that if a physician is to know a disease well, he should suffer from it some time in his life. I certainly understand little strokes much better for having had some slight ones myself. For instance; from my own experience, I know the great difference between the harmless and nonfrightening dizzy spells that are due to a postural hypotension (which I had occasionally, even in my boyhood), and the terrifying—seconds-long—"loss-of-position-in-space" spells which I occasionally experience today.

Very fortunately for me, all but one of my frightening spells came as I lay, semireclining, on my bed, reading. I would clutch quickly at the mattress, feeling sure that the bed was going to turn over and throw me out onto the floor. One spell—the most vivid and alarming one of all—came one day as I sat at my desk. I seized the desk and gripped it firmly because I felt so sure that in a moment I would be flung up against the ceiling. Fortunately, these spells lasted for only a few seconds, and then I was perfectly comfortable again. Many patients have told me that they had such frightening feelings.

I am happy to say that all but one of these little strokes were so mild that they left no serious or lasting residue that I could detect. I still walk rapidly and with usually a sure footing, and I feel about as well as I did when I was fifty, but I haven't the old splendid sense of balance that I used to have. I now understand perfectly why old people often fall and break a bone. Luckily, none of my severe dizzy spells came when I was on the street, because if one had come then, I probably would have had to fall flat.

I never had any true *vertigo*, with things spinning around; and my hearing has remained excellent, hence there has been no suggestion of the coming of Menière's disease. My systolic blood pressure is still normal (around 130 mm. Hg), and my retinal arterioles show almost no sclerosis. I can still read and "skim" as rapidly as ever I did, in four languages.

The only bad dizzy spell which left some lasting after-effects was one I had 26 years ago, when I was 55. It came at 10 P.M., one Sunday night after I had been reading all day. On getting up, I found my sense of balance so poor that in order to walk, I had to hold onto furniture. Again, my trouble was an uncertainty about my position in space. But, strangely, this time the sensation, which remained for several minutes, was not at all frightening. I cheerfully went to bed and to sleep, and had a good night. When I woke in the morning I was still a bit unsure of my position in space, but was able rapidly to walk a mile to work. Occasionally during the next ten days my desk would seem to move around as if on board a ship.

I was all the more sure that this spell had been a little stroke when I found that I had much more trouble in quickly remembering people's names than I had ever had before. This defect never has cleared away, but strangely, my memory for everything else has remained unusually good—perhaps as good as ever—a gift from my able father. Work on this book, which demanded many feats of memory, has been as easy as if I were still 20 or 30.

After the bad dizzy episode in 1939, I had a little trouble writing—such as I had never had before. Ever since, on reading what I have written long hand, I have found that every so often I have left out a word, or I have written a word other than the one I thought I had written. Curiously, this difficulty has never cleared up or even lessened; it is still with me. Interestingly, persons who have had a big stroke have told me they had this same slight difficulty in writing.

At times I am satisfied that something is happening to an arteriole in my visual center when, for a few minutes, I see a curious scotoma—perhaps a big orange area which soon turns to red, and then, in a few seconds, fades out. Another big transitory scotoma had a white center with a dark outer border. Such scotomas are different from the well-known scintillating migrainous scotomas which I have had for 50 years; also the strange scotomas disappear in a few seconds or minutes, while the migrainous ones always last from 20 to 25 minutes. Once, in 1964, I saw, for a second, a brilliant short zig-zag figure near the left edge of my field of vision. This suggested the plugging of an arteriole.

On several occasions I apparently had a little stroke during the night because, for a few days, food kept entering my larynx, causing me to cough violently; or, for a day or two, I kept biting my tongue, or I kept biting my upper lip, or perhaps I had a little trouble starting swallowing (unless I had plenty of water in my mouth); or some morning, for an hour or two, as I walked, I would keep stubbing the toes of one foot against the pavement—which is something I ordinarily never do. Once I suspected that I had had a little stroke during the night because for two days afterward, my ability to recall names quickly was unusually bad; and then it went back to its usual state—sometimes very good and sometimes very bad. Memory is such an astounding thing; sometimes I will remember in a second and use the Polynesian word for something—a word which I am pretty sure I have not thought of since 1903, when I left my old home in Honolulu.

I am satisfied that at times the tendency for our blood to coagulate in our arteries or veins must suddenly increase. How helpful it would be if we could learn why this happens, so that we could watch for it and keep it from happening. Some 8 years ago, for many weeks after I got an infarct in the big vein of my left leg and thigh, I kept seeing at brief intervals, day and night, little dark or bright spots which always disappeared in a second or two. I strongly suspected that sludged blood (Knisely) was going through a capillary either in my retina or in my visual center. Gradually these spots appeared less frequently, until after some months, weeks would pass and I would not see a single one. This last year I have rarely seen one of these spots. I feel sure it is more than a coincidence that I saw thousands of them shortly after I had a blood clot in a big vein.

I have not seen these momentary specks in the field of vision described in any of the few hundred articles on cerebrovascular disease I have read recently. I imagine they would be noted and described only by an observant physician.

One noon, many years ago, unwittingly, I ate a good-sized bowl of potato soup made very tasty by the addition of much chicken fat. Because chicken fat, all my life, has been for me a poison, that evening I developed such extreme nausea, that probably my systolic blood pressure fell from its then usual 110 or so down so low that while my brain functioned perfectly, apparently my retinal cells lost out. At any rate, I blacked out completely, and discovered that "blackout" is a good term, because for a few minutes, all I saw was blackness; then suddenly a big burp came up and, probably with the stoppage of reverse peristalsis, instantly my nausea left, and with this as instantly my vision came back. This experience reminded me of that of aviators who black out for seconds when they turn up and "pull out" of a fast dive. The centrifugal force must pull the blood out of their brains and their eyes.

In the past year I have had brief spells, fortunately lasting only seconds, in which I had severe pain on the under-surface of a toe—often the big toe, or in the tip of a finger. One suspects that an arteriole plugged up in the cortex in the area of the foot or hand. Some neurologists may feel that it is silly to comment on such transient phenomena, but perhaps now that I have commented on them here, many physicians will write to say, "In my late seventies, I had many of those tiny strokes you described, and I kept wondering why they came." As I said elsewhere in this book, a patient of mine—a banker aged 60 or so, who was having a number of severe little and even brief big strokes—one day suddenly got a severe lumbar backache. When it left as suddenly as it came, it looked as if it had been part of a shower of little strokes. I know these are hunches, but it is better to have a hunch than no idea at all. Many people tell me about momentary spells in which they feel as if, in a few seconds, a stroke would come. I know the feeling well, as I have had it many times.

Possibly a good observer can sense it when a few brain cells die. I have good reason to believe that in the past 10 years I have been sensing the coming, every so often, of injuries to a few neurones in my brain—injuries that commonly take place in my sleep, when my systolic blood pressure is probably below 100 mm. Hg.

I know two facts: one, that I am not as strong and steady on my feet as I used to be when, in half an hour, with giant strides, I could run down the steep side of a 13,600-foot extinct volcano—covered with black sand. My wind is certainly not what it used to be when I could run 2 miles rapidly every evening before I went to bed. Although I still enjoy walking about a mile in 15 minutes, my muscles and nerves and heart are certainly older than they used to be. Once, last year, I fell to the floor—due possibly to a momentary blackout too brief for me to recognize it. Once, for seconds, I had to walk to the right and then to the left, and I feared I would fall. One day, for a few minutes, I got such soreness of the sole of my left foot I could hardly walk on it. Once in a while, I suffer arterial hypotension with some unsteadiness on my feet. Fortunately, I still have a happy nature, and I still like to stay clean and neat. I still can work very hard 7 days a week from 8 A.M. till 9 P.M.

The essential fact is that in the last 10 years I have been recognizing many little happenings which I strongly suspect were each due to an injury to a tiny bit of brain. May it not be that the gradual accumulation of these many tiny injuries will, in another 10 years or so usher in old age? May it not be that a well-trained physiologist like me can recognize some of the hundreds of little injuries that slowly lead a man—tiny step by tiny step—to his final dissolution? Why should I not sense it many times when death takes a little bite of me? My impression is that in the last 9 months, I have had tiny strokes more often than ever before. Perhaps such tiny strokes occur now more often also at night.

13

Prognosis

I am sorry that I can say little about the ultimate prognosis of a particular individual who has had a little, a brief, or a silent stroke. I am cheered and made much more hopeful about a patient when I see that he is neat and clean, that he has expression in his face, and that he answers my questions well, also when he says that he can still enjoy reading. These facts show that the best parts of his brain are intact. I have very little hope for the man who is dirty and poorly groomed, with a dull face, and a dull mind; and yet I have seen a few such men recover; also I have seen some well-groomed and pleasant men who were unable ever to work again.

I knew a man, who by little strokes had been changed into an almost decerebrate animal, and yet he lived on for 30 years without getting more shocks. Another man, a neighbor and friend, who had a silent stroke in his twenties, lived comfortably into his fifties but could never do work of any kind. Still another man, whose story I told in a previous chapter, had 3 severe little strokes in his fifties, then never could work again, but lived in good shape for 20 years without more strokes that I could recognize. I was impressed much by the fact that another—a man of 70—after 3 severe little strokes could remain in excellent health for the next 10 years.

I have seen a woman get a fairly severe little stroke in her fifties; then recover only slowly from it, but yet be very active mentally and physically in her eighties. Many a time, when I have feared that more strokes would soon kill a frail little old lady, it was her strong-looking and able husband who died first.

Hence it is that I never want to hazard a guess as to what will happen to an individual who has had a stroke of any kind. As I say elsewhere in this book, I have seen a man of 81 have a big stroke with an aphasia and hemiplegia—in the morning—and recover so well by afternoon that that evening he took guests to dinner and to the theater.

After seeing many patients do very badly after falling out of a chair, I have gained the impression that such a fall carries with it a bad prognosis; but then again, I can remember several men who, more than once crashed to the floor, and then lived on happily, in good health, and able to work hard for 10 years or more. I have reason to be optimistic about the mental health of men who have rubbery legs. I have seen so many of them retain their old charm and ability for 15 or 20 years, after they had serious trouble walking. With all my close study of a few hundred persons with strokelets, I still know of no way in which to make a sure prognosis. The future is always a gamble.

Even a strong hereditary tendency may fail to bother the persons in the next generation. To illustrate: when two hypertensives—a man and his wife, both died with little strokes: he in his fifties and she in her sixties—I feared that they would pass on their troubles to their descendants, but today three of their four children are living in good health in their seventies. The one who is gone died in his sixties of a cancer of the pancreas.

I feel that we can honestly say to most persons who have recovered well from a little stroke that they must not go in daily fear of another one, because they may live for years in good health, and if they should have several more little episodes, these may all be mild and fairly harmless.

John Rankin (1957, second article) said that of 79 big-stroke patients who came to the hospital in coma, 78 died within 2 weeks, and usually they died within 5 days. The death rate for those in deep coma was 98 per cent. Of 47 who came in semicomatose, 33 died in two weeks, while of those who were conscious on arrival, only 25 per cent died quickly. All those with unequal pupils and positive Babinskis died. Abnormally functioning pupils, stertorous breathing and fever were bad signs.

Pincock (1957) said it is "remarkable how many [persons with cerebral thrombosis] can live happily for years." Twenty-four out of 117 who were followed for 8 years were found to be still functioning adequately. Twelve died a cerebral-vascular death, and 21 a cardiac death.

Millikan and Moersch (1953) studied factors, such as the age of the patient, that can influence the prognosis. S. O. Lindgren (1958) wrote on the prognosis of transient spells, mainly due to occlusion in the internal carotid and middle cerebral arteries. He found the prognosis poor in patients over 50.

David and Heyman (1960) wrote on factors influencing the prognosis of cerebral thrombosis and infarction due to atherosclerosis. In their group of patients, the mortality was heavy, and due usually to more infarctions.

Rothschild (1945) said that the people who become childish survive, on an average, 4.7 years. R. D. Currier, C. L. Giles and M. R. Westerberg (1958) studied the prognosis of patients with thrombosis of the cerebellar arteries, and found that half of them died in 5 years.

We all know that some of the persons who suffer a big stroke regain their speech, their ability to walk and their good intelligence, but not all of them get back the good use of their paralyzed hand.

In my experience, after a little stroke, the patient gets nearly all of whatever improvement he is to get in 6 months. After that he is not likely to improve much. As I have said I am apprehensive about the future of the man whose brain has been markedly injured; and yet I once saw an able physician, after he had become so changed that he would go on the street dirty, become well-groomed again and able to practice.

According to Herbert H. Marks (1961, p. 62), the little strokes so often are undetected that the true fatality rate in cerebrovascular accidents cannot be known with any certitude. He said that a patient in a hospital with cerebral thrombosis and a psychosis is likely to live for from 2 to 5 years. J. Marshall and D. A. Shaw (1959) found that of 305 persons in a hospital with a thrombotic episode, 22 promptly died, and 283 lived on for an *average* period of 5 years. During this time, 149, or 60 per cent, died. R. W. Robinson, Cohen, Higano, Meyer, Lubowsky, McLaughlin, and MacGilpin, Jr. (1959) studied 1018 patients for 10 years. The first shock was fatal in 21 per cent. Of the 737 persons who survived, 50 per cent died within 4.1 years. Only 18 per cent of a comparable sample of the general population, with the same age, died in 4.1 years. In the group with strokes 85 per cent of the deaths were due to vascular disease. The worst prognosis was seen in patients who developed congestive heart failure.

John Marshall, of London (1964), studied 180 cases of ischemic spells and concluded that the patient so affected is more than ordinarily likely to have a big stroke later, especially if his first attack is due to obstruction in the carotid area. Joan Acheson and E. C. Hutchinson, of Stoke on Trent (1964) studied 82 patients who had had repeated small strokes, and found that 42 got another stroke, on the average, about a year later.

14

Senile Psychoses

As we all know, some old people, and perhaps particularly old people who have had many little strokes, or who have suffered much from atherosclerosis, can slip into a sort of second childhood. Some can do this fairly early in life, while others never do it, even if they live into their nineties. As we shall see, many men have studied the factors which perhaps can determine what, in a given case, will happen.

One cannot attribute all of a person's mental aging to disease of his arteries. Some men, like C. M. Fisher (1955) thought that many more "second childhoods" are due to *atrophy* of the brain—perhaps of the Pick or Alzheimer type—than to arteriosclerosis. Some pathologists (See G. W. Robinson, Jr., 1941 and 1942.) have been impressed by the fact that at necropsy many old people who are found to have had marked cerebral atherosclerosis, during life were never mentally confused, while others who were mentally confused, at necropsy show little abnormality in their brains.

Some men have thought that a patient who has been mildly schizophrenic all his life is more than normally likely to wind up as a senile dement. A well-adjusted man can stay sane when he has one or more strokes, but a man who was always eccentric and poorly adjusted to life can become psychotic. Clow (1940) said that 61 of the 100 patients he saw with an arteriosclerotic psychosis, always throughout life, had had a narrow range of interests and a poor sexual adjustment. A third of them had suffered from sexual frigidity, or sexual promiscuity, or from some psychopathic behavior.

J. Rankin (1957) remarked that even after a necropsy on an old person it is hard to say how his brain disease began. Rothschild (1945, p. 246) wrote a fine description of mental aging, and spoke of the lack of tidiness

138

of some old persons. They lose the power of attention; they may become irritable, jealous, and often sleepless and restless; they may wander away and get lost; they may become paranoid; they can hallucinate, and get delusions; they can go into anxious and agitated states; they may become apathetic; many lose much of their memory, so that they fail to recognize a son or daughter; their speech can become rambling, and they may lose their moral standards. Later, for the new edition of Kaplan's book (1956), Rothschild wrote a splendid article on psychoses in the aged. Critchley (1931) and Rothschild felt that there is a decided difference between the type of psychosis that comes with cerebral arteriosclerosis and that which comes with senile brain changes. But there are mixtures of the two types. With other men, Critchley did not believe that brain troubles are due only to age. McGaffin (1910) wrote well on senile dementias.

E. B. Allen (1951) said that because of the lengthening life of our people, and perhaps because of the greater amount of cerebral arterio-sclerosis a longer life can produce, the number of persons with senescent psychoses is increasing, and these patients now *constitute the leading problem in psychiatry.* Allen spoke of the remarkable lucid moments these mixed-up persons sometimes have. He and others have pointed out that if a childish old man is given a job with a pay check, it may straighten him out mentally.

E. Krapf (1937) also noted what interested me in 1901, that under the pressure of an emergency, one of these senile persons, for a brief time, can act like his old self. Critchley, in *The Neurology of Old Age* (1931) wrote well, and gave a good bibliography (see also 1956). He devoted much space to describing the brains of very old people, like Thomas Parr. He made a big list of books on old people, and reviewed the literature on the brains of centenarians who came to necropsy. He described senile paraplegias (probably "rubbery legs") also the "cerebellar syndrome," and disorders of walking. In 1933 he discussed the mental and physical symptoms of the pre-senile dementias, and expressed the view that the disease is due usually to destructive changes in the brain. (See also G. W. Humphrey, 1889.)

R. D. Gillespie (1933), during the discussion of Critchley's work, spoke of the "Gradual failure of the intellectual functions with a progressive diminution of energy and initiative; various disorders of mood, and altera-tions in behavior." There may be "progressive failure of intellect and of interest"; also "false recognition." There are "affective disturbances, de-pression, apathy, irritability, suspicion, deterioration, agitation, childish behavior." These last two words of Gillespie's call to mind many state-ments of people who have written me about a parent's mental changes after a series of little strokes. The children may say something like this, "At times Mother now behaves like a naughty little girl."

In 1945, O. J. Kaplan wrote *Mental Disorders in Later Life*. Shock, in the second edition (1956) of his great statistical work, has a bibliography of 342 items. J. G. Pincock (1957) wrote an interesting article on the *Natural History of Cerebral Thrombosis*—in persons between the ages of 50 and 80 years.

Grünthal (1927) had a good bibliography on senile dementia, and a fine summary of the subject is that of J. M. Foley (1956). J. Mitchell Clarke (1915) wrote very well about the mental troubles of older people who complain much of vertigo. (See also Wahal and Riggs, 1960.) These men wondered why changes in the brain that seem to cause mental deterioration in the aged do not do so when they appear in the young. J. H. W. Rhein, N. W. Winkelman and C. A. Patten (1928) said that many old patients go into a second childhood after repeated "mental storms." Their dementia progresses by steps.

R. T. Monroe wrote a book entitled *Diseases in Old Age,* a clinical and pathologic study of 7941 persons over 61 years of age (1951). Nascher wrote a book on the aged in 1919. Still another book, on the subject, called *Problems of Aging* is by Albert I. Lansing and E. V. Cowdry (3rd ed., 1952).

Wartman (1933), after studying 500 consecutively-seen cadavers, said that although 9 out of 10 of the patients had atherosclerosis, 9 out of 10 during life, had remained sane. Robinson (1941) agreed with this.

Himmler (1951) spoke of the tendency of the psychopathic old person to neglect his personal appearance and to become rambling in his speech. George Savage (1920) wrote very well about the strange behavior of old people drifting into a senile dementia. Some hallucinate, and many become untidy. Some are restless and verbose. Good was the work of Howell (1949) who studied 200 healthy old pensioners, and found that 40 per cent had lost some sensation in the skin; 40 per cent could no longer feel much pain; 20 per cent could not feel even a light touch on the skin. Many lacked tendon reflexes and the normal vibration sense at the ankles. As Howell said, the doctor who does not know about these usual losses of sensation in old people might make a mistake and diagnose tabes in a normal man. Old men have told me that one reason why they had lost interest in sexual intercourse was because they had lost almost all feeling in the glans penis. Also, many old people leave a bit of food on their lips because they cannot feel it.

As I said in a previous chapter, the loss of good function in the brain in the aged can be associated with a slightly lowered metabolic rate—see Scheinberg, Blackburn, Rich and Saslaw (1953), Fazekas and Alman (1952), Fazekas, Kleh and Finnerty (1955), Himwich and Himwich (1956), and Heyman, Patterson and Duke (1953).

Dr. Benjamin Boshes wrote a fine description of the mental changes suffered by many aging persons who become "indifferent in habits of dress and toilet." The confused person may speak of dead parents and grandparents as if they were still living, he may wander away from home and get lost, and he may be so restless at night that he wanders up and down through the house. Dr. Boshes said that Pick's disease tends usually to show up in persons between the ages of 45 and 60; and usually the frontal and temporal lobes are atrophied. Within a year the person may be a senile dement, and perhaps aphasic.

Alzheimer's disease is often associated with senile plaques on the brain. It usually appears between the ages of 50 and 60 years. The patient becomes disoriented, with an impaired memory, and an impairment of general information and of proper emotional response. Pronunciation of words becomes so difficult that speech gradually becomes a jargon. The person's spoken language lacks comprehension, and he will make errors in both reading and writing. Epileptic attacks are common and there may be a parkinsonian disturbance in gait. In some cases it is difficult to differentiate Alzheimer's and Pick's diseases.

Dr. Boshes went on to say that with cerebral arteriosclerosis the patient is likely to feel fatigued. He may have headache, spells of dizziness, and a gradual or steplike impairment of physical and mental abilities. Later, there can come a loss of memory, garrulity, a clouding of consciousness, an incoherence of speech, a restlessness, great irritability, irascibility, a lack of patience, an aggressiveness, a meddlesomeness, much hostility, jealousy, and perhaps paranoid tendencies, delusions, sexual indiscretions, and strokes of various kinds.

A good description of Pick's disease was given by Carl Schneider (1927 and 1928). He said that there are 2 stages in Pick's disease: in the first, there is compulsive activity, restlessness and a lack of inhibition. The patients are constantly on the go, childish and silly. They joke and pun, and they are inattentive and hard to hold to a task. They may lie, steal, pile up debts, and misbehave sexually. Rarely, they get markedly depressed, but they can get dull and can lose interests. They have neither delusions nor hallucinations. In the second stage, there is progressive dementia; perhaps with aphasia. The person may keep repeating phrases or gestures or songs. The disease seems to be an entity.

One of the finest articles ever written on the presenile dementias is by George Jervis (1956). He spoke of Alzheimer's and Pick's disease as rare. He described other rare brain diseases of the aged, such as Jakob's (1921), Creutzfeldt's and Kraepelin's (See also Critchley, 1933, 1956.). A wise and kindly writer on the medical management of older patients was my old friend, Wingate M. Johnson (1961). Nils Gellerstedt's study of the cerebral changes in old age is said to be tremendous and thorough, and with a good bibliography. Noel de Mussy (1872) wrote well on mental changes in the aging. I hear that C. Canstatt (1939), on the diseases of the aged is good.

G. W. Robinson (1942) tells how he once used drug-convulsive treatment to shake people out of a senile syndrome. He says he succeeded with 35 out of 50 patients. I have seen a few senile patients who, in a depression, were able to stand electroshock treatments and to profit from them. Naturally, the treatment of such persons must be directed by able psychiatrists.

15

Treatment of Strokes

The treatment of strokes falls, of course, into several divisions: (1) that of protection from strokes; (2) stopping a series of strokes; (3) treatment of strokes that have just happened; and (4) the rehabilitation of persons who have recovered from the acute stages of a stroke.

In treating strokes the physician should be optimistic because it is remarkable how well many persons (not comatose) recover. Dr. Rusk tells in his article in the book, *Strokes* (p. 158), of a time when his skilled associates sent a woman home because they felt that with her confused mind there was no way in which she could be taught and rehabilitated. Six months later she walked in to show everyone how beautifully she had recovered. Even without any treatment it is remarkable how well many victims of severe little strokes can recover.

PEOPLE WITH MILD SMALL STROKES, OR BRIEF, OR SILENT, STROKES. People whose little stroke has left no residue, or only a slight one, obviously need little if any treatment. If they are stout, they will do well to reduce weight. If they have a marked hypertension, it may help to go for a while into a hospital to receive treatment with strong drugs like guanethedine and chlorothiazide.

Dr. Irvine Page and Dr. Harriet Dustan have found that in some cases, when the blood pressure has been decidedly reduced, it will remain down after the use of drugs has been stopped. After a while in a hospital, an intelligent patient can be taught to take his own pressure at home. He must do this if he is to go on taking the powerful pressure reducers. If he were to take a big dose of the drugs at a time when his pressure was very low, the result might be disastrous.

Experts have said that it may be well for some stroke patients to keep their hypertension because a high pressure can best keep blood flowing

143

through narrowed arteries in the heart and neck and brain. In the cases of women, I often do not worry about a systolic pressure between 165 and 190 mm. Hg because so many women will tolerate such a pressure for many years. Certainly, a *malignant type of hypertension* should be treated strenuously before it has had a chance to produce a hypertensive encephalopathy, with a marked destruction of the brain and the eyes.

If the patient is diabetic, he must, of course, have the best of treatment. Obesity plus diabetes plus hypertension plus a family history of strokes and heart attacks in the forties and fifties makes a bad combination.

DISTRESSING AND PROBABLY UNWISE OVER-DEPRIVATIONS OF THE PATIENT. I have never been enthusiastic about taking away a person's table salt, unless, perhaps, he has some edema. Also, I see little sense in taking away his red meat, or the little wine or beer that he may like to drink with his supper. Many old people are more annoyed than helped with irksome diets and treatments. If a person who has had a stroke is a heavy drinker, I would, of course, like to see him "go on the wagon," and if he is a chain-smoker of cigarettes, I would very much like to see him quit, but he may not be able to do this—in which case I will not annoy him.

If his blood cholesterol is very high, it may help him to go on a diet of low fat, with more vegetable oils than hard fats. This should somewhat lower his level of blood cholesterol. Unfortunately, no one can say for sure that the lowering of his cholesterol level will save him from more little and big strokes.

SHOULD THE PATIENT AVOID WORK OR PLAY? Some physicians probably coddle their old patients too much. Certainly I have seen hundreds of patients with a stroke or a coronary thrombosis do very well at work, and perhaps walking to the office every day. Work and exercise can be good for a man. Some heart specialists keep their heart patients in bed as long as possible, while others, like Levene, get them up quickly. I like to permit a man to do *everything that he can do comfortably*. I beg his wife not to keep saying to him "Don't do that," or "don't eat that," or "take a taxi" to go a couple of blocks.

In this connection I love the story told by that very wise man, Dr. Abraham Myerson (*Speaking of Man*, p. 16) about his experience one day with his old father who had suffered a heart attack. Dr. Myerson told him to stay in bed, but next day he found him out on a park bench, chatting with his cronies. When the doctor reproached him for his rashness, the old man asked, with a twinkle in his eyes, "How much life will you guarantee me, O doctor, if I obey your orders? And how much of value shall I place on a month, six months, a year more of that chronic illness, extreme old age?" So the doctor smiled and left him with his friends.

THE PATIENT MAY DO WELL TO AVOID TANTRUMS OF ANGER. Some

persons whose symptoms become acute when they "blow their top" should be warned that the losing of their temper could do them harm. As an irascible old millionaire patient of mine, with a tremendous hypertension, once said to a man who was annoying him, "Quick, get the hell out of here, I can't afford to get mad at you!" This little story has helped many of my patients to behave better; they, too, saw that they could not afford to go into tantrums of rage.

THE PHYSICIAN HAD BETTER NOT EXAMINE THE ACUTELY ILL PATIENT TOO MUCH. As I said in Chapter 3, some enthusiasts now insist that every patient with a stroke be rushed to a hospital to be thoroughly examined, preferably with the angiographic technic. As these men say, the diagnosis of "stroke" is no diagnosis at all; a real diagnosis should tell exactly *what* happened—hemorrhage, thrombosis, or embolism—and exactly *where* it happened—either in the neck or in a certain part of the brain—and the physician should know whether or not an operation should promptly be attempted.

It is true that sometimes an operation does save the life of a man with a stroke, but nowadays I find a number of our ablest neurologists speaking out against the *routine* use of angiography. They say, why use this technic unless, in the particular case, it is likely to give information that will enable the physician to get a better therapeutic result by treating the patient more intelligently? Most angiographers seem now to agree that if the patient is a senile old man in poor shape physically, or if he has an aphasia and a hemiplegia, and especially if he is in coma, he should be left alone. The chances are about 98 in 100 that, with an immediate coma, he will be dead in a few days; and the chances of helping him with surgery are remote. A number of neurologists are writing now that they can make a good diagnosis of a stroke at the patient's bedside, in perhaps 8 in 10 cases.

If I ever, in my late eighties, get a bad stroke and immediately go into coma, I hope that the physician who attends me will not order every test that he can think of. I hope he gives me rest and peace in my own bed, because that is what I would prefer to have.

Some few men have felt it unwise to wait, but the fact that one can sometimes delay operation for a long time was noted by Drs. Wright and Crawford at the Panel Discussion (p. 837) where Dr. Crawford told of a woman who, for a year, had suffered with a partial paralysis of one side, and some aphasia. She recovered after removal of two internal carotid obstructions *12 months after her stroke.* Doubtless, such a miracle cannot always be counted on—but it *can* happen.

Drs. De Bakey, Crawford, Cooley and Morris, Jr. (1959) tried operating on a few patients who had suffered a severe arterial insufficiency, with coma and paralysis. In 3 cases, although the circulation was restored in one or more of the occluded vessels, relief came too late, and the patient died.

Scheinberg and Rice-Simons (1964) wrote that Champ Lyons, speaking at the 4th Princeton Conference on Cerebral Vascular Diseases, said that he felt that the immediate mortality of the operation was 6 per cent and the risk of worsening the symptoms by surgery was 11 per cent.

THE NEED FOR REASSURANCE. I feel that I am justified in reassuring many of my patients who show signs of recovering from either a little or a big stroke. Thousands of little strokes clear away, leaving very little if any recognizable residue. I tell patients about Pasteur, whose survival in good shape for 20 years after a big stroke I have described elsewhere in this book. I also can tell of many of my patients who, after a severe little stroke, lived another 10 or 20 years without getting into any more trouble.

THE PHYSICIAN MUST NOT DESERT HIS PATIENT. One of the things we physicians must *not* do is to desert a man who has had a little or big stroke. We can do so much to encourage him, and sometimes we can help him to get back his health.

THE PHYSICIAN CAN GREATLY HELP A LITTLE-STROKE PATIENT BY TALKING TO HIS FAMILY. Back in 1901, I learned how much a physician can often do to help a little-stroke patient with a damaged brain by explaining to the family what has happened, and why the man is behaving so erratically, and often in a way that is distressing to his loved ones. I remember well the fine woman who used to ask me every so often how much of her formerly able, sensible, kindly and loving husband's distressing behavior was due to cussedness and how much to his little strokes. And I would say, "It must all be due to illness, and hence you must try to be patient and forgiving."

Talking like this has often been very helpful to a patient, in that it has gotten him more kindly treatment from his family. I feel sorry for the children of a man whose character and behavior and appearance have been much changed for the worse by a little stroke. Not knowing that his brain has been badly injured, they become disgusted with him; they lose patience with him; they become ashamed of him; and they lose their old liking and love for him—which is sad to see.

Often a man's business partner and his lawyer must be talked to so that they will understand what has happened. Many a time I have helped a family and business associates to decide what to do with a man who, in his life-time, had built a business empire. Then, with a little stroke, he lost so much of his ability, his judgment, his drive, and his old kindliness with his associates, his employees and his customers that the business started to go rapidly down hill. In some cases of this type I have helped the man's associates to grapple with the problem of what to do—close their doors, or sell the business, or turn the management over to a son or an old partner. In many cases it would help much to declare a brain-injured man incompetent, but rarely can a wife or a son do such a distressing thing to the invalid who, with his loss of good sense, is losing much money.

To show what a physician can sometimes do to help people in such trouble, I will tell here of what I had to do once for the family of a man aged 55 who, with his three sons, for years had done well with a factory in which they made women's dresses. Then suddenly, after a bad dizzy spell, the father became difficult and stubborn. He refused to let his designer bring out new styles. As a result, within two years the business was wrecked, and the sons—baffled, exasperated, and unable to sell the out-dated product of the factory—quarreled with their father and left him. Fortunately, I was able to get the old man to see what had happened to his mind, and then I was able to talk him into turning over the business entirely to his sons. I then got the sons to come back and take charge of the factory, and within a year everyone was happy because the plant was going well again.

THE INADVISABILITY OF A PATIENT'S TRAVELING ABOUT IN SEARCH OF A CURE. Often I am asked by the wife and grown children of a man who has had a bad stroke—usually a severe little one that has left the patient mentally crippled—if they should use up their little savings, taking him around to one clinic after another. I beg them not to do this because I do not know of anyone who has a sure cure for a partly destroyed brain.

Sometimes one needs to reassure a person who has had two little strokes, and has been told by some old woman that he will soon get a third one, which will be fatal. This is not so: I have never had any reason to believe that a third stroke is particularly likely to be severe.

THE PROBLEM OF TAKING CARE OF A MENTALLY CONFUSED OLD PARENT. Every so often I am consulted by a man who is at his wits' end trying to take care of his old mother who, after several little strokes, has become difficult, unreasonable, and perhaps at times so confused she cannot recognize her son. The problem of taking care of such a parent is often so difficult to cope with when the son has wealth, that I can imagine how difficult it is when the son hasn't much money, and when he cannot bear to think of having his parent committed and sent into a state mental hospital.

Many a time I have seen the mother insist on living alone in the old family home in a suburb. There, every so often, she would fall to the floor and perhaps lie there until the milkman, or someone else, suspecting what had happened, forced his way in and rescued her. In many a case the son hired a woman to take care of the old lady, but the minute he turned his back she fired the helper. Sometimes, if the woman's children have enough money, she can be kept in a good nursing home.

INSOMNIA. Insomnia which plagues some persons who have had a little or big stroke should always be treated with a generous amount of some sedative—usually a barbiturate. If the physician is afraid of producing a habit, he can change from one sedative to another at intervals. In those cases of a very restless person, in which a barbiturate won't work, paraldehyde or chloral can be tried.

AN AGITATED DEPRESSION. In those few cases in which a little stroke has produced an agitated depression, the person should be sent into a mental hospital for heavy sedation, perhaps in a constant hot bath. W. Russell (1906) used paraldehyde to calm these persons.

PARKINSON'S SYNDROME. When a person has developed a Parkinson's syndrome, his physician can try the several drugs that tend to quiet the tremor, and to lessen the stiffness of the muscles. Some patients may be in good enough shape for treatment with Dr. Irving Cooper's operation, in which a tiny area of the brain is frozen. The operation is not recommended for patients who are senile, or are in bad shape physically, or are getting rapidly worse.

DRUGS TO HELP THE PERSON RECOVER. My old professor of medicine, in 1905, was a firm believer in the efficacy of iodides in the clearing away of nerve injuries. In 1910, the very able Dr. Mott, and in 1925, the great Sir Clifford Allbutt spoke of their faith in iodides. In view of the fact that many people, untreated, recover to a remarkable degree after a severe little stroke, it is hard to say—when someone on iodides gets well—that it was the drug that worked the cure. But twice I did have patients who I felt sure had had a miracle worked for them by Lipoiodine—the palatable preparation of iodine that I like to use. One patient was a middle-aged building contractor who, on a certain New Year's Eve, collapsed, and fell to the floor with a severe little stroke. The important point is that in the next 4 months—until the end of April—he showed no sign of improvement, and remained with his mental processes so disorganized that he was unable to go to his office. Then I saw him and after 6 weeks of taking each day a couple of tablets of Lipoiodine, he was so "cured" that he went back to work. He then ran his good-sized business for several years until he had another stroke. The other patient also went for months, getting no better; and then, on Lipoiodine, soon went back to his big office where he worked happily for many years.

THE USE OF ANTICOAGULANTS. Anticoagulants seem to have been most helpful in stopping the series of "stuttering strokes" that come sometimes with obstruction in the internal carotid artery.

Certainly, anticoagulants must not be given to a patient whose stroke has been due to a hemorrhage. Obviously, a strong coagulant must not be put in the hands of any but an intelligent and responsible person who will keep having his prothrombin time measured, at the beginning, every day or two, and later, every 3 weeks or so. The length of the interval will depend on whether the effect of the drug on the individual is steady or erratic. Recently, Dr. R. N. Baker discussed treatment with anticoagulants before the National Stroke Congress.*

The big question is: how far down should the prothrombin time be driven? For years, nearly every authority insisted on keeping it down around 15 per cent. But this meant that every year a number of patients, on the medication, bled to death. If the keeping of a patient's prothrombin time around 15 per cent would surely save him from getting another stroke or another coronary thrombosis, this dangerous form of treatment would have some justification, but now that some experts agree that the large dose will not give the person complete protection, and that he can still suffer a thrombosis in his heart or his brain, there is not much sense in giving the huge dose.

Under these circumstances it now seems wise to some men to keep the prothrombin time between 40 and 60 per cent. With a prothrombin time definitely below normal one would expect to give the patient *some* protection from thrombus formation, and this is what one wants. I am glad that the change has come in the giving of anticoagulants.

Among the men who have been enthusiastic or hopeful about the use of anticoagulants have been McDevitt, Groch, and Wright (1959), McDevitt, Carter, Gatje, Foley, and Wright (1958), Millikan and Seikert (1955), Millikan, Seikert, and Shick (1955), Millikan, Seikert and Whisnant (1958), Fisher and Cameron (1953), Foley and Wright (1956), Fisher (1955 and 1958), J. F. Borg (1962), R. Kuhn (1961), Van der Drift (1961), Wright (Page's *Strokes*, 1961, p. 104), O'Doherty (1963), and Aring (1964).

In doubt were Denny-Brown (1960), who noted that in many cases a series of episodes will stop coming *with no treatment*. Also, he said he had seen infarcts come in the brain and the heart in spite of anticoagulant treatment. Fisher (1961), Brain (1957), Marshall (1961), Marshall and Shaw (Discussion of Pickering's paper, 1959), and Charles Wells (1960) had doubts. Somewhat disillusioned were Fisher (1961), and Sheldon (1956). Sir Austin B. Hill, J. Marshall, and D. A. Shaw (1962) showed with controls that in their hands the treatment was not effective. In some cases it caused a big stroke due to a hemorrhage. Five fatal strokes occurred in 66 cases treated; and at necropsy on 3 treated patients, a cerebral hemorrhage was found to be the cause of death. Aring (1964) warned against giving anticoagulants to a patient recovering from a

---

* J. A. M. A., Nov. 1964, p. 36. (See also, Drs. Baker, Schwartz and Rose, Neurol. 14:258, 1964.)

cerebral hemorrhage. Helander and Levander (1959) found no effect of anticoagulant treatment in 286 cases of coronary disease.

The impression I have gained from much reading on this topic is that the latest studies with controls show that there are somewhat fewer recurrences of trouble in the treated patients.

TREATMENT WITH RELAXANTS AND VASODILATORS. As a number of neurologists have pointed out, vasodilators can not logically be used in the treatment of little strokes if one accepts the mass of evidence which indicates that such strokes, in persons past 60, cannot be due to spasm.

Another objection to giving relaxants and vasodilators such as papaverine, nicotinic acid, nitroglycerine, histamine, euphylline, cyclandelate, or 5 per cent CO_2 in oxygen, is that experiments on animals and men have shown that these drugs have very little effect on the arteries of the brain, and what little effect they can have is likely to be short-lived. Some observers, for instance Millikan, Siekert and Shick, saw no results from giving relaxants. Clifford Allbutt (1909) said that vasodilators do not help, while William Russell (1909), thought that sometimes they did. W. R. Brain (1957) doubted if they had any effect.

Several men have thought that large doses of papaverine, given intravenously, could produce some dilation of the arteries. (See Russek and Zohman, H. W. Jayne, P. Scheinberg, and M. S. Belle, 1962.) R. A. Lende (1960) thought the most helpful drug was pentolamine. Noyes and Kolb (1963) said that aminophylline might sometimes help. Incidentally, blood vessel relaxants, if they should lower the blood pressure, could—in some cases—do the patient harm. Carbon dioxide gas will dilate the blood vessels of the brain, but as Seymour said, I. S. Wright and E. H. Luckey (1955) were disappointed with the results.

In 1960, Dr. Seymour Eisenberg, with Mary F. Camp and Margie R. Horn, wrote that the drug nylidrin hydrochloride had been found to increase the blood-flow in the retinas by a third. Also, it usually increased the cerebral blood-flow by 43 per cent if it was given for more than 2 weeks, but the authors were not sure that this increase in blood-flow to the brain really helps people with cerebral vascular disease.

Some men have tried giving thyroid substance, but H. W. Kimmerling (1962) found it useless. Other men have given ovarian hormones. Some decided that aluminum nicotinate is stronger than nicotinic acid, but it is such a nauseant that few people can tolerate it. Van der Drift (1961) relied on cyclandelate.

OPERATIONS ON THE INTERNAL CAROTID ARTERY. In from 20 to 25 per cent of cases of a certain type of little stroke, which comes in a series, with perhaps a combination of temporary blindness in one eye with a brief aphasia, and temporary weakness in an arm, the angiographer can show a narrowing of part of an internal carotid artery. Then surgical intervention may work a miracle of healing. Unfortunately, some experts tell us that it does not always do this. Dr. Michael E. de Bakey* reported on 1,115 patients who underwent arterial reconstructive surgery for "cerebral arterial insufficiency," and said that 79 per cent were later either free from symptoms or so well improved that they could resume their former activity. The immediate mortality rate was only 6 per cent.

The Unwisdom of Performing an Unnecessary Operation, as for a Gallstone, on Persons Who Have Just Had a Fairly Severe Little Stroke. Seeing that in the last 50 years many persons who had a little stroke got mistakenly operated on for a gallstone or a uterine myoma, I have had many chances to observe how dangerous it is to give some of these people an anesthetic and then to operate. I learned this in 1915 when a friend of mine, one of the most liked surgeons in San Francisco, had a spell of illness which I was sure was due to a little stroke. But one of his friends, who was an enthusiast on "focal infection," had all of his remaining teeth extracted, and with this the surgeon got a big stroke and died.

A woman patient of mine with a typical severe little stroke was talked into letting a dental surgeon remove a harmless unerupted tooth in her maxillary bone. As soon as she was anesthetized, she got a big stroke and died.

It is cruel to remove all the teeth of a person who is suffering from a severe little stroke, if only because so often the person's mouth is later so sensitive that for some time prostheses cannot be worn.

Should the Physician Tell the Patient He (or She) Has Had a Little Stroke? I am sure he should. He might as well, if only because most of these people know what they had. If reminded, many can remember their very dizzy, frightening spell, and their conviction then that it was a stroke. They feel much relieved when the doctor discusses their problem with them frankly, and tries honestly to answer their questions. As many a stroke victim has said to me, "When my doctor never mentioned a little stroke, and seemed never to think of such a thing to explain my symptoms, I wondered if he was competent—if he knew his business."

As an able lawyer once said to me, "Today, I should be very sad because I have just learned from you that my brain has been damaged. For some time, of course, I have known it was damaged—probably so badly that I will never be able to practice law again. But, actually, now I am much relieved, and very grateful to you, because at last I know where I stand, I know what I have to face, and I have found someone who will talk to me honestly and logically. For the last six months I have been going from one physician to another, being given different diagnoses,

* J. A. M. A., 190:35, 1964.

none of which, so far as I could see, explained the distressing failure in my mental powers. Now your diagnosis of a little stroke makes sense—it fits with the sudden onset of my illness, and the fact that I am now too dull to read a brief."

Many physicians fear that if a patient is told that he has had a little stroke he will become frightened, demoralized, hopeless, and perhaps suicidal. But in the last half-century I can remember only two patients who did not calmly accept my diagnosis. One—a young woman—came back and asked me to give her "a more pleasant diagnosis." The other, also a young woman, promptly joined a group of people who deny the existence of illness.

WILL THE COMING OF NEW LITTLE STROKES NULLIFY TREATMENT? Often a patient feels rather hopeless about his little stroke because he so fears that another spell will come about the time when he is able to start work again. It is true that this can happen, but more often the person who pulls out from a little stroke goes for some years before he is struck down again. Often, when he does get several more little strokes, they are so mild as not to interfere with his health and ability to work.

A NOTE ON THE TREATMENT OF BIG STROKES

When an aging man falls to the ground with an aphasia, a hemiplegia, *and a coma,* one of the first questions before the physician is: Shall he accede to the (usual) wishes of the family, and let the patient stay in his own bed, at least for a few days, or shall he insist on rushing the man to a hospital, there to give the fellow every test known to science?

I agree with the angiologists who think that when a man has a big stroke with coma, it is wise to do what the man's nearest relatives want, and let him stay in his bed for at least a week, until he either dies or shows signs of possible recovery. To insist on running up a huge bill on a man in a coma, who has a 98 per cent chance of being dead in a week, makes for an angry family and bad public relations.

Often, also, the family sees clearly that it would do a senile old man no good to drag him back to life. He, himself, if given a choice, would prefer not to have to live on—mentally and physically crippled.

Russek, Benton, Brown, Zohman, Greene, Kara, Doerner, and Rusk (1953), and Russek, Zohman, and Russek (1954) reported that the giving of cortisone sometimes seems to help to bring a patient out of his first shock. Dr. Albert Haas says that giving oxygen can help greatly. Any concomitant failure of the heart must, of course, be treated.

After a severe stroke many persons crave death. Many times in the past I have had people, utterly miserable after a big stroke, who told me that they greatly craved the relief that would come with death. In some cases the "head feels wrong, and very distressing." Worse yet, the distress does not let up by day or by night. I remember one lovely woman, a relative of mine, who used to keep asking me every so often, "Oh, how much longer has this terrible mental suffering got to go on?" Naturally, when one day she got a big stroke and died, I was glad—in spite of all my affection for her—that an end had come to her great distress. During 6 years I had tried to find some sedative that would relieve the misery in her head, but I never found anything that would help.

Some physicians, when they have a patient like that—whose life is nothing but a burden—when she gets a pneumonia, do not give penicillin, unless the nearest of kin demand that this be done.

STELLATE GANGLION BLOCK. Some 15 years ago there was much excitement about using a stellate ganglion block to help people who had just suffered a big stroke. The only enthusiastic paper I have found so far was written by Gilbert and de Takats (1948) and they admitted that in some cases the blocking with procaine did no good. Also in favor of the block was Leriche (1952). Most other writers were either in doubt or definitely against the stellate block. Among these are Kety (1950), Denny-Brown (1951, 1961, p. 1472), Millikan, Lundy, and Smith (1953, they saw no effect), Millikan and Moersch (1953), Sir Francis Walshe (1963), Wilson, Rupp, Riggs, and Wilson (1951), Harmel, Hafkenschiel, Austin, Crumpton, and Kety (1949), and Scheinberg (1950).

Pallin and Deutsch (1951) reported a case in which stellate block apparently caused the patient's death.

I remember a neurosurgeon friend of mine, who nearly had to leave town when, as he was giving a prominent banker a stellate block, the man died. I imagine that many poor results and a few tragic results—like my friend's—caused enthusiasm for this treatment to die down.

DIET. Irvine H. Page (1964) published a highly informative article on atherosclerosis. He told how, in 1950, when he found he had a blood cholesterol level of 300 mg. and an elevated S_1 10-20-lipoprotein content, he tried a diet on himself. First he reduced the amount of fat in his diet to 15 per cent of total calories, and with this got a sharp fall in his plasma lipids, and a decided loss of weight. The trouble with this was that there came a distressing impairment of his disposition, and a "resultant contraction of his circle of friends"! He also suffered a good deal of depression. Then he tried adding vegetable fats to his diet, but these raised the levels of his serum cholesterol and his beta lipo-proteins. After a year, he stopped the experiment, convinced that a physician would do well to try his favorite dietary prescription on himself before forcing it on his patients. As Dr. Page said so wisely, a diet should not be adhered to if all it does is to make the patient's life miserable. It is useless to try for a cholesterol-free diet because we men and women can make large amounts of cholesterol in our bodies.

An excellent discussion of the dietetic treatment was written by I. S. Wright for the book *Strokes*, edited by Irvine Page. See pages 93 to 97, in Page's book for a list of foods with the percentage of saturated and unsaturated fats in them.

Other discussions of diet can be found in three books:

1. *A Low Fat, Low Cholesterol Diet*, by E. V. Dobbin, H. F. Gofman, H. C. Jones, L. Lyon, and C. B. Young, New York, Doubleday, 1951.

2. *Low-Fat Diet; Reasons, Rules and Recipes,"* by R. L. Swank, Eugene, Oregon, Univ. of Oregon Press, 1959.

3. *Eat, Drink and Lower Your Cholesterol*, by Dr. F. T. Zugibe, New York, McGraw-Hill, pp. 208, 1963.

A splendid summary of our knowledge up to 1958 in regard to the *Chemistry of Lipids as Related to Atherosclerosis* was compiled and edited by Irvine H. Page. Another good summary of the problem of arterial disease is to be found in Campbell Moses' book, *Atherosclerosis* (1963).

As I write this in 1965, Dr. Page sends me the manuscript of a paper he gave recently, summarizing beautifully the enormous amount of work that has been done on the chemistry of cholesterol and the theories about the relation of the substance to atherosclerosis. At the end he admits—as only a great scientist will do—that he knows rather less about it all than he did several years ago when he started studying the problem.

THE REHABILITATION OF PATIENTS LEFT INJURED BY STROKES. Everyone should know that today much can often be done to rehabilitate stroke victims and to make life useful again for persons who have been left unable to talk, and persons unable to walk. The great leader in this field of work has, of course, been Dr. Howard Rusk, of New York City.* After studying a patient for a few days to decide whether he or she has the necessary determination and desire to get well, and the will-power to succeed, Dr. Rusk's skilled workers will take over, and in some 7 or 8 weeks the person will be walking and perhaps talking.

Excellent is the chapter by Dr. Rusk in Dr. Page's book on strokes. With good illustrations it shows the many exercises and manipulations that are used. The chapter is based on a booklet *Strike Back at Stroke*, obtainable—for 40 cents—from the Superintendent of Documents, Washington 25, D.C.

A patient would do well to get a copy of Dr. Rusk's book, *Living With a Disability—at Home—at Work—at Play* (New York, Doubleday and Blakiston, 1953). Also, a copy of *Help Devices for Rehabilitation,* Du-

* 400 East 34th Street.

buque, Iowa, W. C. Brown Co., 1957. Excellent is the little paper-bound book written by Genevieve Smith, entitled *The Care of the Patient with a Stroke—A Handbook For the Patient's Family and the Nurse*, 1959. Mr. Springer, the publisher, tells me that he still has copies on hand.

Help in teaching the patient to talk again can be obtained from the American Speech and Hearing Association, 1001 Connecticut Ave., N.W. Washington 6, D.C. They have a directory that lists clinically-certified speech therapists. A helpful *Aphasia Rehabilitation Manual and Therapy Kit* was published by Martha L. Taylor and Morton Marks, M.D. (Saxon Press, 207 East 37th St., New York 16, 1955. Price $7.50). Excellent is Mary C. Longerich's *Manual for the Aphasic Patient*, 1958. A wife could use it to help her husband.

Very encouraging and instructive for all persons who are recovering from a stroke would, I am sure, be the reading of three recently published books written by able men who suffered a big stroke and are now rehabilitated. These books are *Stroke*, by Douglas Ritchie, the eminent British broadcaster (New York, Doubleday, 1961); *Comeback, the Story of my Stroke*, by R. E. Van Rosen, as told to Kendall Crossen (Indianapolis, Bobbs Merrill, 1963); and *Report on the Accident inside my Skull, Episode* by that great editor, Eric Hodgins (New York, Atheneum, 1964). These men have described so well their experiences and difficulties during their months and years of treatment and rehabilitation.

Some patients can get help from the Office of Vocational Rehabilitation, Department of Health, Education, and Welfare, Washington, 25, D.C. Information can be obtained also from the National Society for Crippled Children and Adults, 2023 W. Ogden Ave., Chicago 12, Illinois.

All physicians who are interested in this problem ought to read the book, *Strokes*, by Irvine Page and his co-workers (New York, Dutton, 1961); also the book, *Management of Strokes*, by K. W. Sheldon (Philadelphia, Lippincott, 1956); also H. A. Kaplan's book on *Cerebrovascular Diseases* (1961).

Fletcher H. McDowell (1965) has written a small book on the treatment of stroke. Also very helpful is the book (in paper back) *Up and Around*, U.S. Dept. of Health, Education and Welfare, Public Health Service (1964). (Price 50 cents from Supt. of Documents, Washington, D.C. 20402.) Similar and very helpful is the book, *Do it Yourself Again; Self-help Devices for the Stroke Patient*, published by the American Heart Association, 44 East 23rd St., New York City, 10010 (1965). On p. 45 are addresses of a number of organizations that can help the person to recover from a stroke.

It is Well to Keep Up Hope. Anyone who has to treat old people who have suffered from strokes should know about the work of G. W. Robinson (1942). He wrote that by giving good care and training, he and his associates were able to rehabilitate 35 of 50 persons, all of them over the age of 60. He helped many with leptazol-produced convulsions. See also E. W. Lowman (1948) who told of getting 66 per cent of hemiplegics up and out of bed.

Bibliography

Abercrombie, J.: Pathological and Practical Researches on Diseases of the Brain and the Spinal Cord, Philadelphia, 1843.

Acheson, J., and Hutchinson, E. C.: Observations on the natural history of transient cerebral ischaemia, Lancet 2:871-874, 1964.

Adams, R. D.: Mechanisms of apoplexy as determined by clinical and pathological correlation, J. Neuropath. Exp. Neurol. 13:1-13, 1954.

Adams, R. D., and Cohen, M. E.: Hypertensive encephalopathy, Bull. New Eng. Med. Center, 9:180-190; 222-230; 261-273, 1947. Three parts: Part II is Adams and Cohen.

Adams, R. D., and van der Eecken, H. M.: Vascular diseases of the brain, Ann. Rev. Med. 4:213-252, 1953.

Aging, Neurologic and Psychiatric Aspects of the Disorders, Proc. Assoc. Res. Nerv. Ment. Dis. 35:307, 1956.

Alajouanine, T., Lhermitte, F., and Gautier, J. C.: Transient cerebral ischemia in atherosclerosis, Neurology 10:906-914, 1960.

Alexander, L., and Putnam, T. J.: Pathological alterations of cerebral vascular patterns, in Circulation of brain and spinal cord: a symposium on blood supply, Assoc. Res. Nerv. Ment. Dis. 18:471-543, 1938.

Allbutt, T. C.: Diseases of the Arteries, Including Angina Pectoris, London, Macmillan, 1915.

————: Arteriosclerosis, a Summary View, London, Macmillan, 1925.

Allen, E. B.: Psychiatric aspects of cerebral arteriosclerosis, New Eng. J. Med. 245:677-684, 1951.

Allen E. V., Barker, N. W., and Hines, E. A., Jr.: Peripheral Vascular Diseases, Philadelphia, Saunders, 1946.

Alman, R. W., and Fazekas, J. F.: Disparity between low cerebral blood flow and clinical signs of cerebral ischemia, Neurology 7:555-558, 1957.

Alpers, B. J.: Clinical Neurology, ed. 2, Philadelphia, Davis, 1950.

————: President's address, Trans. Am. Neurol. Assoc. 84:1-10, 1959.

————: Tice's System of Med. 10:133-134, 1962.

Alvarez, W. C.: Patients who are incapacitated by a little indigestion, Med. Clin. N. Am. 15:1409-1417, 1932.

————: Unrecognized "strokes" and the gastroenterologist, Am. J. Dig. Dis. Nutr. 2:90-92, 1935.

————: Small unrecognized strokes: a cause of puzzling indigestion, Proc. Staff Meet. Mayo Clinic, 10:293-295, 1935.

————: Dyspepsia—organic, reflex and functional, Proc. Interstate Postgrad. Med. Assem. N. Am. 210-216, 1937.

————: The survival of tissues after the death of an animal, Quart. Rev. Biol. 12:152-164, 1937. (Large bibliography.)

————: Useful hints in the treatment

of gastro-intestinal disease, Ohio Med. J. 33:1085-1092, 1937.

———: What is the matter with the patient who is chronically tired? J. Missouri Med. Assoc. 38:365-368, 1941.

———: Small unrecognized strokes: a common cause of illness in older persons, J. Michigan Med. Soc. 43:389-392, 1944.

———: Cerebral arteriosclerosis with small commonly unrecognized apoplexies, Geriatrics 1:189-216, 1946.

———: Cerebral arteriosclerosis with repeated thrombosis of small intracranial arteries, Oxford Medicine 6, Chap. II-A, 68 (1)-68 (22), 1947.

———: Cerebral arteriosclerosis with little strokes that cause a slow death, Am. J. Nurs. 47:160-170, 1947.

———: Small commonly unrecognized strokes, Postgrad. Med. 4:96-101, 1948.

———: Care of the dying, J.A.M.A. 150:86-91, 1952.

———: The little strokes, J.A.M.A. 157:1199-1204, 1955.

———: More about little strokes, Geriatrics 10:555-562, 1955.

———: The man with little strokes, Practitioner 175:508-510, 1955.

———: The management of persons with little strokes, Geriatrics 12:421-425, 1957.

———: The abdominal symptoms of little strokes, Geriatrics 12:164-170, 1957.

Alzheimer: Die Seelenstörungen auf arteriosclerotischer Grundlage, Allge. Z. Psychiatrie psychisch-gerichtliche Med. 59:695-711, 1902.

Alzheimer, A.: Histologische Studien zur Differentialdiagnose der progressiven Paralyse, Jena, 1904.

———: Über eigenartige Krankheitsfälle des späteren Alters, Z. Neurol. Psych. 4:365-385, 1911.

Amberg, E.: The advisability of eliminating the terms Meniere's disease and Meniere's symptoms from otologic nomenclature, Am. J. Med. Sci. 132:115-123, 1906.

Anderson, F. N.: Correlation of clinical and pathologic diagnosis in hemiplegia, Arch. Neurol. Psychiat. 19:564-566, 1928.

Anderson, W. A. D.: Pathology, ed. 4, St. Louis, Mosby, 1961.

Anitschkow, N.: Das Wesen und die Entstehung der Atherosklerose, Ergebn. Inn. Med. Kinderheilk 28:1-46, 1925.

Aring, C. D.: Vascular diseases of the nervous system, Brain 68:28-55, 1945.

———: Place of neurology in medical firmament, J. Assoc. Am. Med. Coll. 21:220-222, 1946.

Aring, C. D., and Merritt, H. H.: Differential diagnosis between cerebral hemorrhage and cerebral thrombosis. A clinical and pathologic study of 245 cases, Arch. Intern. Med. 56:435-456, 1935.

Arnason, A.: Apoplexie und ihre Vererbung, Acta Psychiat. Neurol. (bound in) Suppl. 7, pp. 7-180, 1935.

Askey, J. M.: Hemiplegia following carotid sinus stimulation, Am. Heart J. 31:131-137, 1946.

Ask-Upmark, E.: The carotid sinus and the cerebral circulation (bound in as Suppl. 6), Acta Psychiat. Neurol. pp. 1-374, 1935.

Baker, A. B.: Hemorrhagic encephalitis, Am. J. Path. 11:185-235, 1935.

———: Structure of small cerebral arteries and their change with age, Am. J. Path. 13:453-461, 1937.

Baker, A. B., Refsum, S., and Dahl, E.: Cerebrovascular disease. IV. A study of a Norwegian population, Neurology 10:525-529, 1960.

Baker, A. B., and Iannone, A.: Cerebrovascular disease. VII. A study of etiologic mechanisms, Neurology 11:23-31, 1961.

Baker, R. N.: Anticoagulants in stroke therapy, J.A.M.A. 190:36, 1964.

Baker, R. N., Schwartz, W., and Rose, A. S.: The transient ischemic stroke: a report of a study and an analysis of the problem, Neurology 14:258, 1964. (Abstract)

Barber, H.: A form of senile seizure, Brit. Med. J. 1:492, 1928.

Barnes, A. R.: Cerebral manifestations of paroxysmal tachycardia, Am. J. Med. Sci. 171:489-495, 1926.

Barrett, A. M.: Modern Trends of Nervous and Mental Disease, Philadelphia, Lea & Febiger, 1913 (quoted).

Barrett, J. W.: Sudden temporary loss of vision probably of circulatory origin, Ophthalmic Rev. 21:281-283, 1902.

Bastian, H. C.: Paralyses—Cerebellar, Bulbar, and Spinal, London, 1886.

Bayliss, W. M., Hill, L., and Gulland, G. L.: On intra-cranial pressure and the cerebral circulation, J. Physiol. 18:334-362, 1895.

Bean, W. B.: Infarction of the heart. III. Clinical course and morphological findings, Ann. Int. Med. 12:71-94, 1938.

Bean, W. B., Flamm, G. W., and Sapadin, A.: Hemiplegia attending acute myocardial infarction, Am. J. Med. 7:765-771, 1949.

Bean, W. B., and Reed, C. T.: Central nervous system manifestations in acute myocardial infarction, Am. Heart J. 23:362-376, 1942.

Beever, C. E., and Gunn, R. M.: Trans. Ophthal. Soc. U. K. 19:75-87, 1899.

Behrend, A., and Riggs, H. E.: Cerebral complications following surgical operation: prevention and treatment, Am. J. Surg. 53:296-299, 1941.

Benson, A. H.: Recurrent temporary visual obstructions from retinal vascular spasm, Trans. Ophthal. Congr. Edinburgh, 1894 (quoted).

Berlin, L., Tumarkin, B., and Martin, H. L.: Cerebral thrombosis in young adults, New Eng. J. Med. 252:162-166, 1955.

Bielchowsky, M., and Brodmann, K.: Zur feineren Histologie und Histopathologie der Grosshirnrinde, J. Psychol. Neurol. 5:173-199, 1905.

Birse, S. H., and Tom, M. I.: Incidence of cerebral infarction associated with ruptured intracranial aneurysms: a study of 8 unoperated cases of anterior cerebral aneurysm, Neurology 10:101-106, 1960.

Blumgart, H. L., Schlesinger, M. J., and Davis, D.: Studies on the relation of the clinical manifestations of angina pectoris, coronary thrombosis, and myocardial infarction to the pathologic findings; with particular reference to the significance of the collateral circulation, Am. Heart J. 19:1-91, 1940.

Bodechtel, G.: Gehirnveränderung bei Herzkrankheiten, Z. Neurol. Psychiat. 140:657-709, 1932.

Borg, J. F.: Long-term anti-coagulant therapy in chronic coronary artery disease, Geriatrics 17:372-378, 1962.

Boshes, B.: Neurologic and psychiatric aspects of aging, Mod. Med. 26:71-79, 1958.

Boshes, B. and Hummel, W. L.: Differential diagnosis in patients with co-existing neurologic and neurosurgical disorders, Neurology 6:804-807, 1956.

Bouckaert, J. J., and Heymans, C.: Carotid sinus reflexes. Influence of central blood-pressure and blood supply on respiratory and vasomotor centres, J. Physiol, 79:49-66, 1933.

————: On the reflex regulation of the cerebral blood flow and the cerebral vasomotor tone, J. Physiol. 84:367-380, 1935.

Boyd, W.: Textbook of Pathology, ed. 7, Philadelphia, Lea & Febiger, 1961.

Brain, W. R.: Diseases of the Nervous System, London, Oxford Univ. Press, 1955.

————: Order and disorder in the cerebral circulation, Lancet 2:857-862, 1957.

————: Clinical Neurology, ed. 2, London, Oxford Univ. Press, 1964.

Bremer, F.: Les spasmes vasculaires en neurologie, Rev. d'oto-neuro-ocul. 6: 297-316, 1928.

Bright, R.: Cases illustrative of the effects produced when the arteries and brain are diseased; selected chiefly with a view to the diagnosis in such affections, Guy's Hosp. Rep. 1:9-40, 1836.

Brissaud, E.: Maladies de l'hemisphere cérébrale, in Charcot, Bouchard and Brissaud's Traité de Méd. 6:134-158, Paris, 1894.

Broadbent, W.: Correspondence, Brit. Med. J. 2:1380-1381, 1909.

Browning, W.: Arterio-sclerosis and the nervous system, Trans. Med. Soc. State of New York, pp. 103-108, 1903.

Burr, C. W.: Transitory mental confusion and delirium in old age, J.A.M.A. 57: 2117-2119, 1911.

Burton, A. C.: Peripheral circulation, Ann. Rev. Physiol. 15:213-246, 1953.

Byrom, F. B: The pathogenesis of hypertensive encephalopathy and its relation to the malignant phase of hypertension. Experimental evidence from the hypertensive rat, Lancet 2:210-211, 1954.

————: The significance of hypertensive encephalopathy. Lectures on the Scientific Basis of Medicine 8:256-268, 1958-1959, Athlone Press, Univ. London, 1960.

Canstatt, C.: Die Krankheiten des höheren Alteres, Erlanger, 1839, 2 vols. (quoted).

Carmichael, E. A., Doupe, J., and Williams, D. J.: The cerebro-spinal fluid pressure of man in the erect posture, J. Physiol. 91:186-201, 1937.

Carter, A. B.: Cerebral Infarction, New York, Macmillan, 1964.

Cerebrovascular diseases, conference on, Wright, I. S. 1954. See Luckey, E. H. (ed.). Grune and Stratton, 1955.

Chao, W. H., Kwan, S. T., Lyman, R. S., and Loucks, H. H.: Thrombosis of left internal carotid artery, Arch. Surg. 37:100-111, 1938.

Charcot, J. M.: Clinical Lectures on Senile and Chronic Diseases, 1868, London, New Sydenham Soc., 1881.

———: Oeuvres Completes. Lecon sur les Maladies du Systeme Nerveux, vol. 1, Paris, 1886.

Chase, W. H.: Hypertensive apoplexy and its causation, Arch. Neurol. Psychiat. 38:1176-1189, 1937.

———: Cerebral thrombosis, hemorrhage and embolism: pathological principles, Proc. Assoc. Res. Nerv. Ment. Dis. 18:365-378, 1938.

Chiarie, H.: Über das Verhalten des Teilungswinkels der Carotis Communis bei der Enderarteritis chronica deformans, Ver. Deutsch. Ges. Path. 9:326-330, 1905.

Chorobski, J., and Penfield, W.: Cerebral vasodilator nerves and their pathway from the medulla oblongata with observations on the pial and intra-cerebral vascular plexus, Arch. Neurol. Psychiat. 28:1275-1289, 1932.

Clark, E. R.: Discussion of W. H. Chase, 1938 (q. v.).

Clarke, E.: Apoplexy in the Hippocratic writings, Bull. Hist. Med. 37:301-314, 1963.

Clarke, J. M.: On recurrent motor paralysis in migraine, Brit. Med. J., June 25 Suppl., 1534-1538, 1910.

———: The Bradshaw Lecture: Nervous affections of the 6th and 7th decades of life, Lancet 2:1016-1021; 1069-1073, 1915.

Classification and Outline of Cerebrovascular Diseases: Report of Committee of Advisory Council for National Institutes of Neurological Diseases and Blindness, Neurology 8:395-434, 1958.

Cloake, P. C. P.: Cerebral thrombo-angiitis obliterans, in Feiling's Modern Trends in Neurology, p. 477, New York, Hoeber, 1951.

Clough, P. W.: Editorial: Intermittent insufficiency of the cerebral arterial circulation, Ann. Intern. Med. 49:223-228, 1958.

Clow, H. E.: A study of 100 patients suffering from psychosis with cerebral arteriosclerosis, Am. J. Psychiat. 97:16-26, 1940.

Cobb, S.: The cerebral circulation. IX. The relationship of the cervical sympathetic nerves to cerebral blood supply, Am. J. Med. Sci. 178:528-536, 1929.

———: The cerebral circulation. XIII. The question of "endarteries" of the brain and the mechanism of infarction, Arch. Neurol. Psychiat. 25:273-280, 1931.

———: The cerebrospinal blood vessels, in Penfield, W., ed.: Cytology and Cellular Pathology of the Nervous System, vol. 2, p. 575, Philadelphia, Hoeber, 1932 (quoted).

———: The cerebral circulation. XXV. Remarks on clinical physiology, Ann. Intern. Med. 7:292-302, 1933.

———: A Preface to Nervous Disease, Chap. 6, pp. 78-94, Baltimore, Wood, 1936.

———: Cerebral circulation. XXVII. A critical discussion of the symposium, Assoc. Res. Nerv. Ment. Dis. 18:719-752, 1938.

Cobb, S., and Finesinger, J. E.: Cerebral circulation. XIX. The vagal pathway of the vasomotor impulses, Arch. Neurol. Psychiat. 28:1243-1256, 1932.

Cobb, S., and Hubbard, J. P.: Cerebral hemorrhages from venous and capillary stasis, a report of 5 cases with autopsy, Am. J. Med. Sci. 178:693-709, 1929.

Cole, S. L., and Sugarman, J. N.: Cerebral manifestations of acute myocardial infarction, Am. J. Med. Sci. 223:35-40, 1952.

Collier, J.: Recent work on aphasia, Brain 31:523-549, 1908.

Connolly, R. C.: The incidence of cerebral ischemia in spontaneous subarachnoid hemorrhage, J. Neurol. Neurosurg. Psychiat. 24:294, 1961.

Cooper, A.: Some experiments and observations on tying the carotid and vertebral arteries and the pneumogastric, phrenic and sympathetic nerves, Guy's Hosp. Rep. 1:457-475, 1836.

Corday, E., Rothenberg, S. F., and Putnam, T. J.: Cerebral insufficiency: an explanation of some types of localized cerebral encephalopathy, Arch. Neurol. Psychiat. 69:551-570, 1953.

Corday, E., Rothenberg, S., and Wiener, S. M.: Cerebral vascular insufficiency, an explanation of the transient stroke, Arch. Intern. Med. 98:683-690, 1956.

Courville, C. B.: Asphyxia as a consequence of nitrous oxide anesthesia, Medicine, 15:129-245, 1936.

Cowdry, E. V.: Arteriosclerosis, a Survey of the Problem, New York, Macmillan, 1933.

———, ed.: Problems of Aging, ed. 2, Baltimore, Williams & Wilkins, 1942.

Crawford, E. S., De Bakey, M. E., and Fields, W. S.: Roentgenographic diagnosis and surgical treatment of basilar artery insufficiency, J.A.M.A. 168:509-512, 1958.

Crawford, E. S., De Bakey, M. E., Blaisdell, F. W., Morris, G. C., Jr., and Fields, W. S.: Hemodynamic alterations in patients with cerebral arterial insufficiency before and after operation, Surgery 48:76-94, 1960.

Crawford, E. S., De Bakey, M. E., Morris, G. C., Jr., and Fields, W. S.: Treatment of stroke by arterial reconstructive operation, Southern Med. J. 54:476-485, 1961.

Crevasse, L. E., Logan, R. B., and Hurst, J. W.: Syndrome of carotid artery, Circulation 18:924-934, 1958.

Critchley, M.: Arteriosclerotic parkinsonism, Brain 52:23-83, 1929.

———: The anterior cerebral artery and its syndromes, Brain, 53:120-165, 1930.

———: Goulstonian Lectures: The neurology of old age, Lancet 1:1119-1127; 1221-1230; 1331-1336, 1931.

———: Discussion on the mental and physical symptoms of the presenile dementias, Proc. Roy. Soc. Med. 26: 1077-1091, 1933.

———: Neurologic changes in the aged, J. Chronic Dis. 3:459-477, 1956. (Marvelous bibliography.)

Currier, R. D., Giles, C. L., and Westerberg, M. R.: The prognosis of some brain-stem vascular syndromes, Neurology 8:664-668, 1958.

Curschman, H.: Ueber vasomotorische Krampzustände bei echter Angina Pectoris, Deutsch. med. Wschr. 32: 1527-1531, 1906.

Daly, E. O.: A case of recurring attacks of transient aphasia and right hemiplegia, Brain, 10:233-236, 1887.

David, N. J., and Heyman, A.: Factors influencing the prognosis of cerebral thrombosis and infarction due to atherosclerosis, J. Chronic Dis. 11: 394-404, 1960.

Davison, C., and Brill, N. Q.: Essential hypertension and chronic hypertensive encephalopathy, Ann. Intern. Med. 12:1766-1781, 1939.

De Bakey, M. E., Crawford, E. S., Cooley, D. A., and Morris, G. C., Jr.: Surgical considerations of occlusive disease of innominate, carotid, subclavian and vertebral arteries, Ann. Surg. 149:690-710, 1959.

De Bakey, M. E., Crawford, E. S., Morris, G. C., Jr., and Cooley, D. A.: Surgical considerations of occlusive disease of the innominate, carotid, subclavian, and vertebral arteries, Ann. Surg. 154:698-725, 1961.

De Bakey, M. E., Crawford, E. S., and Fields, W. S.: Surgical treatment of patients with cerebral arterial insufficiency associated with extracranial arterial occlusive lesions, Neurology II, no. 4, part 2:145-149, 1961.

De Bakey, M. E.: The surgical treatment of cerebrovascular insufficiency, Surg. Procedures 1:2-12, 1964.

Dejerine, J., and Roussy, G.: Le syndrome thalamique (1), Rev. Neurol. 14:521-532, 1906.

Delafield, F., and Prudden, T. M.: A Textbook of Pathology, ed. 16, rev. by F. C. Wood, Baltimore, Wood, 1936.

Démange, E.: Tremblement sénile et ses rapports avec la paralysie agitante, Rev. Méd. 2:58-80, 1882.

———: Étude Clinique at Anatomopathologique sur la Vieillese, Paris, 1886.

de Mussy, N. G.: Étude clinique sur les indurations des Artères, Archiv. gén. méd. 2:129-150, part 2, 292-326, 1872.

Denny-Brown, D.: Symposium on specific methods of treatment; treatment of recurrent cerebrovascular symptoms, and the question of vasospasm, Med. Clin. N. Am. 35:1457-1474, 1951.

———. Shattuck Lecture: The changing pattern of neurologic medicine, New Eng. J. Med. 246:839-846, 1952.

———: Recurrent cerebrovascular episodes, Arch. Neurol. 2:194-210, 1960.

Denny-Brown, D., Horenstein, S., and Fang, H. C. H.: Cerebral infarction produced by venous distension, J. Neuropath. Exp. Neurol. 15:146-180, 1956.

Denny-Brown, D., and Meyer, J. S.: The cerebral collateral circulation. II. Production of cerebral infarction by ischemic anoxia and its reversibility in early stages, Neurology 7:567-579, 1957.

Denst, J.: Pathologic changes in the brain in coma following other anesthesia, Neurology, 3:239-249, 1953.

de Takats, G.: The controversial use of cervical sympathetic block in apoplexy, Ann. Intern. Med. 41:1196-1210, 1954.

———: Sympathetic block in apoplexy, Surgery 38:915-927, 1955.

deVries, E.: Acute diseases of the brain due to functional disturbance of the circulation: laminated cortical disease, Arch. Neurol. Psychiat. 25:227-254, 1931.

Dickinson, C. J., and Thomson, A. D.: A post-mortem study of the main cerebral arteries with special reference to the cause of strokes, Clin. Sci. 20: 131-142, 1960.

Dobbin, E. V., Gofman, H. F. Jones, H. C., Lyon, L., and Young, C. B.: A Low Fat, Low Cholesterol Diet, Garden City, Doubleday, 1951.

Do It Yourself Again; Self-help Devices for the Stroke Patient, New York, Am. Heart Assoc., 1965.

Dozzi, D. L.: Cerebral embolism as a complication of coronary thrombosis, Am. J. Med. Sci. 194:824-829, 1937.

Duff, G. L., and McMillan, G. C.: Pathology of atherosclerosis, Am. J. Med. 11:92-109, 1951.

Duffy, P. E., and Jacobs, G. B.: Clinical and pathological findings in vertebral artery thrombosis, Neurology 8:862-869, 1958.

Dukes, H. T., and Vieth, R. G.: Cerebral arteriography during migraine prodrome and headache, Neurology 14:636-639, 1964.

Eastcott, H. H. G., Pickering, G. W., and Rob, C. G.: Reconstruction of internal carotid artery in a patient with intermittent attacks of hemiplegia, Lancet 2:994-996, 1954.

Easton, J.: Human Longevity: Recording the Name, Age, Place of Residence, and Year of the Decease of 1712 Persons Who Attained a Century and Upwards, London, 1799.

Ebert, R. V., Stead, E. A., Jr., and Gibson, J. G.: Response of normal subjects to acute blood loss, with special reference to the mechanism of restoration of blood volume, Arch. Intern. Med. 68:578-590, 1941.

Echlin, F. A.: Vasospasm and focal cerebral ischemia; an experimental study, Arch. Neurol. Psychiat. 47:77-96, 1942.

Ecker, A., and Riemenschneider, P. A.: Arteriographic evidence of spasm in cerebral vascular disorders, Neurology 3:495-502, 1953.

Edgeworth, F. H.: On transitory hemiplegia in elderly persons, Scot. M. S. J. 18:414-418, 1906. (Also vol. 19)

Editorial: Mental status in old age, Lancet 1:84, 1942.

Editorial: Little strokes, New Eng. J. Med. 246:154-155, 1952.

Editorial (H. J. L. M.): Question of cerebral angiospasm, Ann. Int. Med. 36:1129-1135, 1952.

Edwards, E. A., and Biguria, F.: A comparison of skiodan and diodrast as vasographic media, with special reference to their effect on blood pressure, New Eng. J. Med. 211:589-593, 1934.

Elliott, F. A.: Symposium on cerebrovascular diseases, Proc. Roy. Soc. Med. 52: 544-547, 1959.

Ellis, A.: Malignant hypertension, Lancet 1:977-980, 1938.

Engel, G. L.: Fainting: Physiological and Psychological Considerations, Springfield (Ill.), Thomas, 1950.

Engel, G. L., Romano, J., and McLim, T. R.: Vasodepressor and carotid sinus syncope; clinical, electroencephalographic and electrocardiographic observations, Arch. Intern. Med. 74: 100-119, 1944.

Evans, J., and McEachern, D.: The circulatory changes in cerebral vascular occlusion and in cerebral cicatrization, Proc. Assoc. Res. Nerv. Ment. Dis. 18:379-393, 1938.

Faris, A. A., Poser, C. M., Wilmore, D. W., and Agnew, C. H.: Radiologic visualization of neck vessels in healthy men, Neurology 13:386-396, 1963.

Fay, T.: A typical facial neuralgia; a syndrome of vascular pain, Ann. Otol. 41:1030-1062, 1932.

Fazekas, J. F., Kleh, J., and Finnerty, F. A.: Influence of age and vascular disease on cerebral hemodynamics and metabolism, Am. J. Med. 18:477-485, 1955.

Fazekas, J. F., Alman, R. W., and Bessman, A. N.: Cerebral physiology of the aged, Am. J. Med. Sci. 223:245-257, 1952.

Ferrier, D.: Cerebral amblyopia and hemiopia, Brain 3:456-477, 1880.

————: The regional diagnosis of cerebral disease, *in* Allbutt, T. C., and Rolleston, H. D. (eds.): System of Medicine 8:37-162, New York, Macmillan, 1911.

Ferris, E. B., Jr., Capps, R. B., and Weiss, S.: Relation of the carotid sinus to the autonomic nervous system and the neuroses, Arch. Neurol. Psychiat. 37:364-384, 1937.

Fields, W. S., Crawford, E. S., and De Bakey, M. E.: Surgical considerations in cerebral arterial insufficiency, Neurology 8:801-808, 1958.

Fields, W. S., Edwards, W. H., and Crawford, E. S.: Bilateral carotid artery thrombosis, Arch. Neurol. 4:369-383, 1961.

Finesinger, J. E.: Cerebral circulation. XVIII. Effect of caffeine on cerebral vessels, Arch. Neurol. Psychiat. 28:1290-1325, 1932.

Finesinger, J., and Putnam, T. J.: Cerebral circulation. XXIII. Induced variations in volume flow through the brain perfused at constant pressure, Arch. Neurol. Psychiat. 30:775-794, 1933.

Fink, K.: Akute transitorische Erblindung post-partum, Zbl. Gynaek, 48:1188-1191, 1924.

Fischer, O.: Miliare Nekrosen mit drusigen Wucherungen der Neurofibrillen, eine regelmässige Veränderung der Hirnrinde bei seniler Demenz, Mschr. Psych. Neurol. 22:361-372, 1907.

Fisher, C. M.: Occlusion of the internal carotid artery, Arch. Neurol. Psychiat. 65:346-377, 1951.

————: Disease of the cerebral arteries.

Clinical picture of cerebral arteriosclerosis, Minnesota Med. 38:839-851, 1955.

————: Cerebrovascular diseases: pathophysiology, diagnosis, and treatment, J. Chronic Dis. 8:419-447, 1958.

————: The use of anticoagulants in cerebral thrombosis, Neurology 8:311-332, 1958.

————: Anticoagulant therapy in cerebral thrombosis and cerebral embolism. A national cooperative study, interim report, Neurology II: 119-131, No. 4 Pt. 2, 1961.

————: Lacunes: small, deep cerebral infarcts, Neurology 15:774-784, 1965.

————: Pure sensory stroke involving face, arm and leg, Neurology 15:76-80, 1965.

Fisher, M., and Cameron, D. G.: Concerning cerebral vasospasm, Neurology 3:468-473, 1953.

Fleming, H. W., and Naffziger, H. C.: Physiology and treatment of transient hemiplegia, J.A.M.A. 89:1484-1487, 1927.

Florey, H.: Microscopical observations on the circulation of the blood in the cerebral cortex, Brain 48:43-64, 1925.

Fog, M.: The cerebral circulation. Reaction of the pial arteries to a fall in blood pressure, Arch. Neurol, Psychiat. 37:351-364, 1937.

Foix, C., and Ley, J.: Contribution à l'étude du ramollissement cérébral envisagé au point de vue de sa frequence et son siège et de l'état anatomique des arteres du territoire necrose, J. Neurol. Psychiatrie, 658, Nov. 1927 (quoted).

Foix, C., and Nicolesco, I.: Contribution à l'étude des grands syndromes de désintegration sénile cérébro-mesencephalique, Presse méd. 31:957-963, 1923.

Foley, J. M.: Hypertensive and arteriosclerotic vascular disease of the brain in the elderly, Proc. Assoc. Res. Nerv. Ment. Dis. 35:171-197, 1956.

Foley, J. M., and Horenstein, S.: Bilateral acute cerebral infarction following occlusion of internal carotid artery, Trans. Am. Neurol. Assoc. 80:129-132, 1955.

Foley, W. T., and Wright, I. S.: The use of anticoagulants, an evaluation, Med. Clin. N. Am. 40:1339-1353, 1956.

Forbes, H. S.: The cerebral circulation.

I. Observation and measurement of pial vessels, Arch. Neurol. Psychiat. 19:751-761, 1928.

Forbes, H. S., and Cobb, S.: Vasomotor control of cerebral vessels: the circulation of the brain and spinal cord; a symposium on blood supply, Publ. Assoc. Res. Nerv. Ment. Dis. 18:201-217, 1938.

Forbes, H. S., Finlay, K. H., and Nason, G. I.: Cerebral circulation. XXIV. A. Action of epinephrine on pial vessels: B. Action of pituitary and Pitressen on pial vessels; C. Vasomotor response in the pia and the skin, Arch. Neurol. Psychiat. 30:957-979, 1933.

Forbes, H. S., Nason, G. I., and Wortman, R. C.: Cerebral circulation. XLIV. Vasodilation in the pia following stimulation of the vagus, aortic and carotid sinus nerves, Arch. Neurol. Psychiat. 37:334-350, 1937.

Forbes, H. S., and Wolff, H. G.: Cerebral circulation. III. The vasomotor control of cerebral vessels, Arch. Neurol. Psychiat. 19:1057-1086, 1928.

Fowler, E. F., and de Takats, G.: Side effects and complications of sympathectomy for hypertension, Arch. Surg. 59:1213-1233, 1949.

Fox, in a letter to the editor described the case of a minister with typical little strokes, Brit. Med. J. 1:1201, 1895.

Freeman, D. G., Petrobelos, M. A., and Henderson, J. W.: Neurologic symptoms and signs in 347 cases of verified brain tumor, Neurology 3:437-452, 1953.

Freyhan, F. A., Woodford, R. B., and Kety, S. S.: Cerebral blood flow and metabolism in psychoses of senility, J. Nerv. Ment. Dis. 113:449-456, 1951.

Friedberg, C. K., and Horn, H.: Acute myocardial infarction not due to coronary artery occlusion, J.A.M.A. 112:1675-1679, 1939.

Frøvig, A. G.: Bilateral obliteration of the common carotid artery: thromboangiitis obliterans? Contribution to the clinical study of obliteration of carotids and to the elucidation of cerebral vascular circulation, Acta psychiat. et neurol., suppl. 39, pp. 1-79, 1946.

Fuller, S. C.: A study of the miliary plaques found in brains of the aged, Am. J. Insan. 68:147-219, 1911.

Fulton, J. F.: Discussion of Wechsler, Trans. Am. Neurol. Assoc. 61:83, 1935 (q. v.).

Gellerstedt, N.: Zur Kentniss der Hirnveränderungen bei der normalen Altersinvolution, Upsala Läkeref. Förh. 38:193-408, 1933.

Gibbs, F.: Cerebral blood flow preceding and accompanying experimental convulsions, Arch. Neurol. Psychiat. 30:1003-1010, 1933.

Gilbert, N. C., and de Takats, G.: Emergency treatment of apoplexy, J.A.M.A. 136:659-665, 1948.

Gildea, E. F., and Cobb, S.: The effects of anemia on the cerebral cortex of the cat, Arch. Neurol. Psychiat. 23:876-903, 1930.

Gillespie, R. D.: Discussion on the mental and physical symptoms of the presenile dementias, Proc. Roy. Soc. Med. 26, part 2: 1080-1084, 1933.

Gilman, S.: Cerebral disorders after open-heart operations, New Eng. J. Med. 272:489-498, 1965.

Glathe, J. P., and Achor, R. W. P.: Frequency of cardiac disease in patients with strokes, Proc. Staff Meets. Mayo Clinic, 33:417-422, 1958.

Gowers, W. R.: On a case of simultaneous embolism of central retinal and middle cerebral arteries, Lancet 2:794-796, 1875.

————: Manual of Disease of Nervous System, London, 1888.

————: Sudden cerebral lesions, Brit. Med. J. 2:1-6, 1907.

Grasset, J., et Rauzier, J.: Traité Pratique des Maladies du Système Nerveux, 1: 54-68, Paris, Masson et cie, 1894.

Greenfield, J. G.: The pathology of Parkinson's disease, *in* Critchley, M. (*ed.*): James Parkinson, 1755-1824, London, Macmillan, 1955.

Gregory, M. S.: Psychosis in old age, Bull. N. Y. Acad. Med. 2nd series 4: 1227-1240, 1928.

Grimson, K. S., Orgain, E. S., Rowe, C. R., Jr., and Sieber, H. M.: Caution with regard to the use of hexamethonium and apresoline, J.A.M.A. 194: 215-220, 1952.

Griswold, G.: Irregular apoplectic attacks due to other causes than hemorrhage and embolism, J.A.M.A. 3:57-59, 1884.

Groch, S. N., Hurwitz, L. J., and Mc-

Dowell, F.: A report of 4 patients, bilateral carotid artery occlusion disease, Arch. Neurol. 2:130-133, 1960.

Groch, S. N., Hurwitz, L. J., Wright, I. S., and McDowell, F.: Bedside diagnosis of carotid artery occlusive disease, New Eng. J. Med. 262:705-707, 1960.

Groedel, F. M., and Hubert, G.: Pseudoapoplektische and pseudoembolische cerebrale Zirculationstörungen auf ischämisches Basis, Deutsch. med. Wschr. 51: 1023-1025, 1925.

Grossmann, L. W.: Hysterical (?) hemiplegia, Med. Rec. 62:595, 1902.

Grünthal, E.: Klinisch-anatomisch vergleichende Untersuchungen über den Greisenblödsiem, Z. Neurol. Psychiat. 111:763-818, 1927.

Gull, W. W., and Sutton, H. G.: On the pathology of the morbid state commonly called Bright's disease with contracted kidney, Medico-Chir. Trans. 55:273-318, 1872.

Gulland, G. L.: The occurrence of nerves on intracranial blood vessels, Brit. Med. J. 2:781-782, 1898.

Gurdjian, E. S., Lindner, D. W., Hardy, W. G., and Webster, J. E.: Cerebrovascular disease: an analysis of 600 cases, Neurology 10:372-380, 1960.

Hackel, W. M.: Über den Bau und die Altersveränderungen der Gehirnarterien, Virchow Arch. Path. Anat. 266: 630-639, 1928.

Hamlin, H.: Life or death by EEG, J.A.M.A. 190:112-114, 1964.

Harding, F., and Knisely, M. H.: Settling of sludge in human patients: a contribution to the bio-physics of disease, Angiology 9:317-341, 1958.

Harmel, M. H.: Hafkenschiel, J. H., Austin, G. M., Crumpton, C. W., and Kety, S. S.: The effect of bilateral stellate ganglion block on the cerebral circulation in normotensive patients, J. Clin. Invest. 28:415-418, 1949.

Hassin, G. B.: The nerve supply of the cerebral blood vessels, Arch. Neurol. Psychiat. 22:375-391, 1929.

Head, H., and Holmes, G.: Sensory disturbances from cerebral lesions, Brain 34:102-254, 1911.

Heard, J. D.: The significance of transient cerebral crises and seizures, as occurring in arteriosclerotics, Edinburgh Med. J. 5:417-427, 1910.

Helander, S., and Levander, M.: The primary mortality and the 5-year prognosis of cardiac infarction, Acta Med. Scand. 163, fasc. 4:289-304, 1959.

Herbut, P. A.: Pathology, Philadelphia, Lea & Febiger, 1955, and (ed. 2) 1959.

Herrick, J. B.: Clinical features of sudden obstruction of the coronary arteries, J.A.M.A. 59:2015-2020, 1912.

Heyman, A., Patterson, J. L., Jr., Duke, T. W., and Battey, L. L.: The cerebral circulation and metabolism in arteriosclerotic and hypertensive cerebrovascular disease, New Eng. J. Med. 249:223-229, 1953.

Heymans, C., Bouckaert, J. J., Jourdan, F., Nowak, S. J. G., and Farber, S.: Survival and revival of nerve centers following acute anemia, Arch. Neurol. Psychiat. 38:304-307, 1937.

Hicks, S. F., and Warren, S.: Infarction of the brain without thrombosis; an analysis of one hundred cases with autopsy, Arch. Path. 52:403-412, 1951.

Hill, A. B., Marshall, J., and Shaw, D. A.: Cerebrovascular disease: trial of long-term anticoagulant therapy, Brit. Med. J. 2:1003-1006, 1962.

Hill, L.: The Physiology and Pathology of Cerebral Circulation, London, 1896.

———: Experimental pathology of cerebral circulation, *in* Allbutt, T. C., and Roleston, H. D. (*eds.*): System of Medicine 8:13-37, New York, Macmillan, 1910.

Himler, L. E.: Psychiatric aspects of aging, J.A.M.A. 147:1330-1331, 1951.

Hitzig, E.: Der Schwindel, *in* Specielle Pathologie und Therapie von Nothnagel 12:1-101, 1898.

Hobhouse, E.: Correspondence, Brit. Med. J., pp. 1313-1314, Oct. 30, 1909.

Holtzman, M., Panin, N., and Ebel, A.: A list of symptoms of injury to the different blood vessels of the brain, Am. J. Phys. Med. 38:133-135, 1959.

Horine, E. F., Weiss, M. M., and Beard, M. F.: Arteriolar studies in patients with hypertensive heart disease without hypertension, Am. J. Med. Sci. 184:206-213, 1932.

Howell, T. H.: Senile deterioration of the central nervous system; a clinical study, Brit. Med. J. 1:56-58, 1949.

Huber, G. C.: Observations on the innervation of the intracranial vessels, J. Comp. Neurol. 9:1-25, 1899.

Huchard, Henri, "La Maladie de l'hypertension arterial," Rev. gén. Clin. et Ther., 1891 (Quoted)

Huchard, Henri, Is said to have written in 1893, and 1899. (Quoted)

Huchard, H., "Arteriosclerosis". Abstract of discussion. Brit. M. J. 2:1076 (one page), 1909.

Huchard, H., "Maladie du coeur, Arteriosclerose"; Paris, 1910.

Hultquist, G. T., "Über Thrombose und Embolie der Arteria carotis und hierbei vorkommende Gehirnstörungen," Jena, Fischer, 1942.

Humphry, G. M., Old Age., Cambridge, 1889.

Hunt, J. R., The role of the carotid arteries in the causation of vascular lesions of the brain, with remarks on certain special features of the symptomatology, Amer. J. M. Sci., 147:704-713, 1914.

Hürthle, Karl, "Untersuchungen über die Innervation der Hirngefässe," Arch. f.d. ges. Physiologis, 44:561-618, 1889.

Hutchinson, J. N., "Symmetrical acrosphacelus without Raynaud's Phenomena," Arch. Surg., 7:201-209, 1896.

Inman, T. G., "Cerebral Thrombosis and abrupt slowing of the Cerebral Circulation," JAMA, 75:1765-1768, 1920.

Jackson, J. H.: On temporary paralysis after epileptiform and epileptic seizures: a contribution to the study of dissolution of the nervous system, Brain 3: 433-451, 1880.

Jacobson, D. E.: Einige sonderbare Fälle von Hemiplegie ohne entsprechendes Herdleiden im Gehirn, Deutsch. Z. Nervenheilk 4:235-269, 1893.

Jakob, A.: Ueber eigenartige Erkrankungen des Zentralnervensystems mit bemerkenswertem anatomischen Befunde, Z. Neurol. Psychiat. 64:147, 1921 (quoted).

James, G. W. B.: Cerebral arteriosclerosis, Proc. Roy. Soc. Med., sect. psychiat. 19, part 3:30-45, 1926.

Jane, J. A., Yashon, D., and Sugar, O.: Cerebral vascular disease; an analysis of present knowledge and presentation of an investigative technique and attitude, Arch. Intern. Med. 116:392-399, 1965.

Janeway, T. C.: A clinical study of hypertensive cardiovascular disease, Arch. Intern. Med. 12:755-798, 1913.

Jayne, H. W., Scheinberg, R. M., and Belle, M. S.: The effect of intravenous papaverine hydrochloride on the cerebral circulation, J. Clin. Invest. 31: 111-114, 1952.

Jelliffe, S. E.: The thalamic syndrome, Med. Record 77:305-310, 1910.

Jelliffe, S. E., and White, W. A.: Diseases of the Nervous System, a Textbook of Neurology and Psychiatry, ed. 6, Philadelphia, Lea & Febiger, 1935.

Jervis, G.: The presenile dementias, Chap. 10 *in* Kaplan, O. J. (ed.): Mental Disorders in Later Life, ed. 2, pp. 262-288, Stanford, Stanford Univ. Press, 1956.

Johnson, W. A., and Kearns, T. P.: Sludging of blood in retinal veins, Am. J. Ophthal. 54:201-204, 1962.

Johnson, W. M.: Medical management of older patients, J.A.M.A. 175: 649-653, 1961.

Jones, R. A.: Discussion, *in* Proc. Roy. Soc. Med. 26:1087-1088, 1933.

Jones, E.: Obstruction of internal carotid, Quart. J. Med. 3:233-250, 1909.

Joynt, R. J., and Benton, A. L.: The memoir of Marc Dax on aphasia, Neurology 14:851-854, 1964.

Kallmann, F. J.: Genetic aspects of mental disorders in later life, Chap. 3 *in* Kaplan, O. J. (ed.): Mental Disorders in Later Life, ed. 2, pp. 26-46, Stanford, Stanford Univ. Press, 1956.

———: Heredity in Health and Mental Disorder, p. 315, New York, Norton, 1953.

Kallmann, F. J., Feingold, L., and Bondy, E.: Comparative adaptational, social, and psychometric data on the life histories of senescent twin pairs, Am. J. Hum. Genet. 3:65-73, 1951.

Kallmann, F. J., and Sander, G.: Twin studies on aging and longevity, J. Hered. 39:349-357, 1948.

Kameyama, M., and Okinaka, S.: Collateral circulation of the brain, with special reference to atherosclerosis of the major cervical and cerebral arteries, Neurology 13 (suppl.): 279-286, 1963.

Kashida, D.: Über Gehirnarteriosklerose des früheren Alters und über die Kombination von corticalen, pyramidalen und extrapyramidalen Symptomen bei der Gehirnarteriosklerose, Z. Neurol. Psychiat. 94:659-702, 1925.

Kearns, T. P., and Hollenhorst, R. W.: Venous-stasis retinopathy of occlusive disease of the carotid artery, Proc. Staff Meet. Mayo Clinic 38:304-312, 1963.

Keith, N. M., van Wagener, H. P., and Kernohan, J. W.: The syndrome of malignant hypertension, Arch. Intern. Med. 41:141-188, 1928.

Kendell, R. E., and Marshall, J.: Role of hypotension in the genesis of transient focal cerebral ischaemic attacks, Brit. Med. J. 2:344-348, 1963.

Kenk, R., and Nall, M. L.: Physiology of the circulation of the brain. An annotated bibliography, 1938-1948, Physiol. Rev. (suppl. 1): 1-437, 1952.

Kennedy, F.: Allergic manifestations in the central nervous system, Trans. Am. Neurol. Assoc. 61:49-51, 1935.

Kennedy, F., Wortis, S. B., and Wortis, H.: The clinical evidence for cerebral vasomotor changes, Publ. Assoc. Res. Nerv. Ment. Dis. 18:670-681, 1938.

Kernohan, J. W., Anderson, E. W., and Keith, N. M.: The arterioles in cases of hypertension, Arch. Intern. Med. 44: 395-423, 1929.

Kernohan, J. W., Parker, H. L., and Loveshin, L. L.: [Periarteritis nodosa], Proc. Staff Meet. Mayo Clinic 24:43-52, 1949.

Kety, S. S.: Circulation and metabolism of the human brain in health and disease, Am. J. Med. 8:205-217, 1950.

————: Human cerebral blood flow and oxygen consumption as related to aging, J. Chronic Dis. 3:478-486, 1956.

Kety, S. S., Hafkenschiel, J. H., Jeffers, W. A., Leopold, I. H., and Shenkin, H. A.: The blood flow, vascular resistance, and oxygen consumption of the brain in essential hypertension, J. Clin. Invest. 27:511-514, 1948.

Kety, S. S., and Schmidt, C. F.: Nitrous oxide method for the quantitative determination of cerebral blood flow in man: theory, procedure and normal values, J. Clin. Invest. 27:476-483, 1948.

Kimmerling, H. W.: Concepts, theory and treatment of athersclerosis, J. Am. Geriat. Soc. 10:865-876, 1962.

Kinnier, Wilson S. A.: Cerebral arteriospasm, *in Bruce*, A. N. (ed.) Neurology, vol. 2, chap. 72, pp. 1096-1099, Baltimore, Williams & Wilkins, 1941.

Kirgis, H. D., Llewellyn, R. C., and Peebles, E. M.: Functional trifurcation of the internal carotid artery and its potential clinical significance, J. Neurosurg. 17:1062-1072, 1960.

Klabanoff, S. G., Singer, J. L., and Wilensky, H.: Psychological consequences of brain lesions and ablations, Psychol. Bull. No. 1, 51:1-41, 1954.

Knapp: A discussion, temporary paralysis, J. Nerv. Ment. Dis. 31:190, 1904.

Knisely, M. H., Block, E. H., Eliot, T. S., and Warner, L.: Sludged blood, Science 106:431-440, 1947.

Knisely, M. H., Warner, L., Harding, F.: Ante-mortem settling. Microscopic observations and analyses of the settling of agglutinated blood-cell masses to the lower sides of vessels during life; a contribution to the bio-physics of disease, Angiology 11:535-588, 1960.

Kocher, T.: Hirnerschütterung, Hirndruck und chirurgische Eingriffe bei Hirnkrankheiten, Specielle Pathologie und Therapie von Nothnagel, 9, part 3, sub-part 2:1-457, Wien, 1901.

Kornfeld, D. S., Zimberg, S., and Malm, J. R.: Psychiatric complications of open-heart surgery, New Eng. J. Med. 273:287-292, 1965.

Krapf, E.: Die Seelenstörungen der Blutdruckkranken, Vienna, 1936. Also J. Ment. Sci. 83:534-541, 1937.

Krehl, L.: The Principles of Clinical Pathology (Hewlett, A. W., trans.), p. 538, Philadelphia, Lippincott, 1907.

Kubik, C. S., and Adams, R. D.: Occlusion of the basilar artery; a clinical and pathological study, Brain 69:73-121, 1946.

Kuhn, R. A.: New Hope for Stroke Victims, New York, Appleton, 1960.

————: Strokes: big and little, Curr. Med. Digest 28:51-62, 1961.

Kussmaul, A., and Tenner, A.: Nature and Origin of Epileptiform Convulsions Caused by Profuse Bleeding (Bronner, E., trans.), London, New Sydenham Society, 1859.

Lambert, E. H., and Wood, E. H.: The problem of blackout and unconsciousness in aviators, Med. Clin. N. Am. 30:833-844, 1946.

Langwill, H. G.: Transitory hemiplegia, with notes of 2 cases, Scot. Med. J. 18:509-516, 1906.

Lauder Brunton: Intermittent closing of cerebral arteries [correspondence], Brit. Med. J. 2:1313; 1380, 1909.

Leary, T.: Experimental atherosclerosis in the rabbit compared with human (coronary) atherosclerosis, Arch. Pathol. 17:453-492, 1934.

————: The genesis of atherosclerosis, Arch. Pathol. 32:507-555, 1941.

Lende, R. A.: Local spasm in cerebral arteries, J. Neurosurg. 17:90-103, 1960.

Lennox, W. G., Gibbs, F. A., and Gibbs, E. L.: The relationship in man of cerebral activity to blood flow and blood constituents, J. Neurol. Psychiat. 1: 211-225, 1938.

Léri, A.: Le cerveau sénile, Rev. Neurol. 14:756-764, 1906.

————: Chapter in Marie, P.: La Pratique Neurologique, Paris, Masson, 1911.

Leriche, R.: Les Thromboses Artérielles, Paris, Masson, 1946.

————: Rational principles in treatment of spontaneous arterial occlusions, Angiology 2:430-433, 1951.

————: Essais de traitement de l'ictus cérébral et de ses sequelles paralytiques, Presse Méd. 60:153-155, 1952.

————: Treatment of embolism of cerebral vessels, Brit. Med. J. 1:231-235, 1952.

Leriche, R., and Fontain, R.: Rev. Chir. 55:755, 1936 (quoted).

Letter written to the Lancet by a woman: A death of a mind—a study in disintegration, Lancet 1:1012-1015, 1950.

Lewis, T.: Experiments relating to the peripheral mechanism involved in spasmodic arrest of the circulation in the fingers, a variety of Raynaud's disease, Heart 15:7-101, 1929.

Lewis, T., and Pickering, G. W.: Observations upon maladies in which the blood supply to digits ceases intermittently or permanently, and upon bilateral gangrene of digits; observations relevant to so-called "Raynaud's disease," Clin. Sci. 1:327-366, 1934.

Leyden, E.: Beiträge und Untersuchungen zur Physiologie und Pathologie des Gehirns, Virchow Arch. Path. Anat. 37:519-559, 1866.

————: Ueber periodisches Erbrechen (gastrische Krisen) nebst Bemerkungen ueber nervose Magenaffectionen, Z. klin. Med. 4:605-615, 1882.

Lhermitte, F.: Les ideés nouvelles sur la génese de l'hemiplegie transitoire et du ramollissement cérébral, Encephale 23: 27-39, 1928.

Liebow, I. M., Newill, V. A., and Oseasohn, R.: Incidence of ischemic heart disease in a group of diabetic women, Am. J. Med. Sci. 248:403-407, 1964.

Lindgren, S. O.: Course and prognosis in spontaneous occlusions of cerebral arteries, Acta psychiat. neurol. Scand. 33:343-358, 1958.

Lindstrom, P. A., and Brizze, K. R.: Relief of intractable vomiting from surgical lesions in the area postrema, J. Neurosurg. 19:228-236, 1962.

Lisa, J. R., and McPeak, E.: Acute miliary infarction of the heart, Ann. Intern. Med. 65:919-932, 1940.

Little Strokes, Booklet No. 689, U. S. Dept. Health, Education, and Welfare, Public Health Service, and the National Institute of Neurological Diseases and Blindness.

Longerich, M. C.: Manuals for the Aphasic Patient, New York, Macmillan, 1958.

Louis, S., and Lewis, B.: Sensory disorders in occlusion of internal carotid and middle cerebral arteries, Neurology 13 (suppl.): 693-696, 1963.

Lowman, E. W.: Rehabilitation of the hemiplegic patient, J.A.M.A. 137:431-436, 1948.

Lucas (1894): Quoted by Stengel, 1908 (q. v.).

Lundie, R. A.: Transient blindness due to spasm of the retinal artery, Ophthal. Rev. 25:129-140, 1906.

Maclachlan, D.: A Practical Treatise on the Diseases and Infirmities of Advanced Life, London, 1863.

Marie, P.: Leçons de Clinique Médicale 8:296, 1894-1895.

————: Collected Works, vol. 1, p. 71, 1901.

————: Congestion et anémie cérébrale, in Brouardel et Gilbert: Traite de Med. 8:531-551; 695-726, 1901.

————: Des foyers lacunaires de disintégration et de différents autres états cavitaries du cerveau, Rev. Med. 21: 281-298, 1901.

————: La Pratique Neurologique, p. 170, Paris, Masson, 1911.

Marks, H. H.: Characteristics and trends

of cerebral vascular disease, *in* Hoch, P. H., and Zubin, J. (eds.): Psychopathology of Aging, New York, Grune & Stratton, 1961.

Marshall, J.: The natural history of transient ischemic cerebro-vascular attacks, Quart. J. Med. 33:309-324, 1964.

Marshall, J., and Shaw, D. A.: The natural history of cerebrovascular disease, Brit. Med. J. 1:1614-1617, 1959.

McDevitt, E., Carter, S. A., Gatje, B. W., Foley, W. T., and Wright, I. S.: Use of anticoagulants in treatment of cerebral vascular disease. Ten-year experience in treatment of thromboembolism, J.A.M.A. 166:592-597, 1958.

McDevitt, E., Groch, S. N., and Wright, I. S.: A cooperative study of cerebrovascular disease methodology and a preliminary report on the use of anticoagulants, Circulation 20:215-233, 1959.

McDowell, F. H.: Treatment of stroke, vol. 2, Modern Treatment Series, New York, Hoeber, 1965.

McGaffin, C. G.: An anatomical analysis of 70 cases of senile dementia, Am. J. Insan. 66:649-656, 1910.

McMullen, J. B.: The surgical treatment of cerebral arterial insufficiency, J. Lancet 83:236-242, 1963.

McNally, W. D.: Sixty-three deaths from carbon monoxide poisoning in private garages, Arch. Path. Lab. Med. 5:43-48, 1928.

McNaughton, F. L.: The innervation of the intracranial blood vessels and dural sinuses; the circulation of the brain and spinal cord: a symposium on blood supply, Proc. Assoc. Res. Nerv. Ment. Dis. 18:178-200, 1938.

Meager, R. H., and Ingraham, F. D.: The relation of the cervical sympathetic trunk to cerebral angiospasm, Arch. Neurol. Psychiat. 22:570-574, 1929.

Mehnert: Ueber die topographische Verbreitung der Angiosklerose nebst Beiträgen zur Kenntnis des normalen Baues der Aeste des Aortenbogens und einiger Venenstämme, Diss. inaug. Dorpat, 1888 (quoted from Chiari, 1905, q. v.).

Mendel, E.: Ueber die apoplexia cerebri sanguinea, Berlin. klin. Wchnschr. 28: 577-582, 1891.

Merritt, H. H.: Cerebral vascular lesions, *in* Blumer: The Practitioner's Library

of Medicine and Surgery, vol. 9, chap. 23, pp. 657-682, 1936.

Merritt, H. H., and Aring, C. D.: The differential diagnosis of cerebral vascular lesions, Proc. Assoc. Res. Nerv. Ment. Dis. 18:682-695, 1938.

Merritt, H. H.: Vascular disorders of the nervous system, *in* Beeson and McDermott, *eds.*: Cecil & Loeb Textbook of Medicine, ed. 11, Philadelphia, Saunders, 1963.

Meyer, A.: Symposium on arteriosclerosis. Arteriosclerosis and mental disease, Trans. Med. Soc. State of N. Y., 109-114, 1903.

Meyer, J. S., Waltz, A. G., and Gotch, F.: Pathogenesis of cerebral vasospasm in hypertensive encephalopathy. I. Effects of acute increases in intraluminal blood pressure. II. The nature of increases irritability of smooth muscle of pial arterioles in renal hypertension, Neurology 10:859-867, 1960.

Meyer, S.: Circulatory changes following occlusion of the middle cerebral artery, and their relation to function, J. Neurosurg. 15:653-673, 1958.

Michel, J.: Lehrbuch d. Augenheilkunde, Wiesbaden, 1884.

Miller, J. L.: Hypertension and the value of the various methods for its reduction, J.A.M.A. 54:1666-1669, 1910.

Millikan, C. H.: A classification and outline of cerebrovascular disease, Neurology 8:395-434, 1958.

Millikan, C. H., Lundy, J. S., and Smith, L. A.: Evaluation of stellate ganglion block for acute focal cerebral infarcts: preliminary report of observations on 87 patients, J.A.M.A. 151:438-440, 1953.

Millikan, C. H., and Moersch, F. P.: Factors that influence prognosis in acute focal cerebrovascular lesions, Arch. Neurol. Psychiat. 70:558-562, 1953.

Millikan, C. H., and Siekert, R. G.: Studies in cerebrovascular disease. I. The syndrome of intermitten insufficiency of the basilar arterial system, Proc. Staff Meet. Mayo Clinic 30:61-68, 1955.

———: Studies in cerebrovascular disease. IV. The syndrome of intermittent insufficiency of the carotid arterial system, Proc. Staff Meet. Mayo Clinic 30:186-191, 1955.

Millikan, C. H., Siekert, R. G., and Shick,

R. M.: Studies in cerebrovascular disease. III. The use of anticoagulant drugs in the treatment of insufficiency or thrombosis within the basilar arterial system, Proc. Staff Meet. Mayo Clinic 30:116-126, 1955.

——: Studies in cerebrovascular disease. V. The use of anticoagulant drugs in the treatment of intermittent insufficiency of the internal carotid arterial system, Proc. Staff Meet. Mayo Clin. 30:578-586, 1955.

Millikan, C. H., Siekert, R. G., and Whisnant, J. P.: Anticoagulant therapy in cerebral vascular disease—current status, J.A.M.A. 166:587-592, 1958.

Moersch, F. P.: Nervous and mental phenomena associated with paroxysmal tachycardia, Brain 53:244-258, 1930.

Moniz, E.: L'encephalographie arterielle, son importance dans la localization des tumeurs cérébrals, Rev. Neurol. 2:72-90, 1927.

——: Die Cerebrale Arteriographie und Phlebographie, Berlin, Springer, 1940.

——: Thrombosis y otras obstrucciones de las carotidas, Barcelona, Salvat, 1941 (quoted).

——: Intermittent cerebral circulation, Imprensa med. 8:5, 1942 (quoted from Ecker and Riemenschneider, 1953, q. v.).

Moniz, E., Lima, A., and de Lacerda, R.: Hemiplegies par thrombose de la carotide interne. Presse med. 45:977-980, 1937.

Monroe, R. T.: Diseases in Old Age. A Clinical and Pathological Study of 7941 Individuals Over 61 Years of Age, Cambridge, Harvard Univ. Press, 1951.

Montz, A. R.: Sudden death, New Eng. J. Med. 223:798-801, 1940.

Moorhead, T. H.: Intermittent closing of cerebral arteries (correspondence), Brit. Med. J. 2:1715, 1909.

Moses, C.: Atherosclerosis, Mechanisms as a Guide to Prevention, Philadelphia, Lea & Febiger, 1963.

Mott, F. W.: Arterial Degenerations and Diseases, in Allbutt, T. C., and Rolleston, H. D. (eds.): System of Medicine 6:608-620, New York, Macmillan, 1910.

Muir, R.: Textbook of Pathology, ed. 7, London, Arnold, 1958.

Müller, O., and Siebeck, R.: Über die Vasomotoren des Gehirns, Z. exp. Pathol. Therap. 4:57-87, 1907.

Murray, J. F.: Types and effects of heart disease in cerebrovascular disorders, Stanford Med. Bull. 15:78-82, 1957.

Nall, M. L., and Ferguson, F. C.: Physiology of the circulation of the brain—an annotated bibliography. Part II. Report literature, 1938-1952, Physiol. Rev., suppl. 2, 36:1-148, 1956.

Nascher, I. L.: Geriatrics. The Diseases of Old Age and Their Treatment, p. 85, London, 1919.

Nedzel, A. J.: Histologic changes following vascular spasm in central nervous system (Pitressin episodes), Arch. Path. 28:697-711, 1939.

——: Vascular Spasm, Experimental Studies, Champaign, Univ. Illinois Press, 1943.

Nettleship, E.: Repeated paroxysmal failure of sight in connection with heart disease, Brit. Med. J. 1:889-891, 1879.

Neubürger, K.: Über streifenformige Erkrankungen der Grosshirninde bei Arteriosklerose, Z. Neurol. Psychiat. 101:452-469, 1926.

Newton, T. H., Adams, J. E., and Wylie, E. J.: Arteriography of cerebrovascular occlusive disease, New Eng. J. Med. 270:14-18, 1964.

Nöllenburg, W.: Statistische Untersuchungen über die Erblichkeit der Lebenslänge, Z. Konstitutionsl. 16:707, 1932 (quoted from Kallmann, 1956, q. v.).

Nordmann, M.: Kreislaufstörungen und Pathologische Histologie, Ergebnisse der Kreislaufforschung, vol. 4, Dresden, 1933.

Nothnagel, H.: Die vasomotorischen Nerven der Gehirngefässe, Virchow Arch. Path. Anat. 40:203-213, 1867.

——: Angina pectoris vasomororia, Deutsch Archiv. klin. Med. 3:309-322, 1867.

Noyes, A. P., and Kolb, L. C.: Modern Clinical Psychiatry, ed. 6, Philadelphia, Saunders, 1963.

Noyes, H. D.: Textbook on Diseases of the Eye, p. 547, New York, Wood, 1890.

Obersteiner, H.: Die Innervation der Gehirngefässe, Neurol. Centralbl. Leipzig 16:356, 1897.

O'Doherty, D. S.: Internal carotid artery occlusive disease, GP 27:108-115, 1963.

Oppenheim, G.: Über "drusige Nekrosen" in der Grosshirnsrinde, Neurol. Centralbl. 28:410-413, 1909.

Oppenheim, H.: Lehrbuch der Nervenkrankheiten, ed. 5, 2 vols., 1908; trans. into English by Bruce, A., Edin., Schulze, 1911.

Oppenheimer, B. S., and Fishberg, A. M.: Hypertensive encephalopathy, Arch. Intern. Med. 41:264-278, 1928.

Osler, W.: Oliver Wendell Holmes, Bull. Hopkins Hosp. 5:85-88, 1894.

———: The cerebral complications of Raynaud's disease, Am. J. Med. Sci. 112: 522-529, 1896.

———: Address on arteriosclerosis, Brit. Med. J. 2:1800, 1909.

———: Transient attacks of aphasia and paralyses in states of high blood pressure and arterio-sclerosis, Canad. Med. Assoc. J. 1:919-926, 1911.

Page, I. H.: Atherosclerosis, Circulation 10:1-27, 1954.

———: Chemistry of Lipides as Related to Atherosclerosis, Springfield (Ill.), Thomas, 1958.

———: Arterial Hypertension, Philadelphia, Davis, 1960.

———: The Pathogenesis of Atherosclerosis as of January 1961, N. Y. Heart Assoc. Conference on Atherosclerosis, Jan. 24, 1960, pp. 5-17.

Page, I. H., Wright, I. S., Weiss, E., Crawford, E. S., De Bakey, M. E., and Rusk, H. A.: Strokes, How They Occur And What Can Be Done About Them, New York, Dutton, 1961.

Pal, J.: Ueber Gefässkrisen und deren Beziehung zu den Magen unde Bauchkrisen der Tabiker 50:2135-2139, 1903.

———: Gefässkrisen, Leipzig, 1905.

———: Ueber die zerebralen Insult und den Angiospasmus der Hypertoniker, Wien. klin. Wschr. 44:1297-1299, 1931.

Pallin, I. M., and Deutsch, E. V.: Death following stellate ganglion block, Ann. Surg. 133:226-233, 1951.

Panel discussion on advances in the diagnosis and treatment of cerebrovascular disease, Irving S. Wright, Moderator, J. Am. Geriatrics Soc. 8: 823-837, 1960.

Parker, G.: A letter on intermittent closing of cerebral arteries, Brit. Med. J. 2:1499, 1909.

———: The causes of transient cerebral paralyses, Bristol M. Chir. 27:15-27, 1909.

Parker, H. L., and Kernohan, J. W.: The central nervous system in periarteritis nodosa, Proc. Staff Meet. Mayo Clinic 24:43-48, 1949.

Paterson, J. D.: Capillary rupture with internal hemorrhage in the causation of cerebral vascular lesions, Arch. Path. 29:345-354, 1940.

Peabody, G. L.: Relations between arterial disease and visceral changes, Trans. Assoc. Am. Phys. 6:154-178, 1891.

Pearl, R., and Pearl, R. DeW.: The Ancestry of the Long-lived, Baltimore, Hopkins, 1934 (quoted from Kallmann, 1956, q. v.).

Pelz, A.: Ueber transitorische Aphasie bei Migräne, Deutsch med. Wschr. 42: 1095-1097, 1916.

Penfield, W.: Intracerebral vascular nerves, Arch. Neurol. Psychiat. 27:30-44, 1932.

———: The evidence for a cerebral vascular mechanism in epilepsy, Ann. Intern. Med. 7:303-310, 1933.

———: Discussion of Wechsler, Trans. Am. Neurol. Assoc. 61:83, 1935.

———: The circulation of the epileptic brain, Procs. Assoc. Res. Nerv. Ment. Dis. 18:605-637, 1938.

———: Epilepsy automation and the centrencephalic integrating system: patterns of organization in the central nervous system, Publs. Assoc. Res. Nerv. Ment. Dis. 30:513-528, 1952.

Perera, G. A.: Development of hypertensive manifestations after the disappearance of hypertension, Circulation 10:28-29, 1954.

Petrén, K.: Ueber den Zusammenhang swischen anatomisch Bedingter und functioneller Gangstörung (besonders in der Form von trepidander Abasie) im Greisenalter, Arch. Psych. 33:818-871, 1900. And *ibid.*, 34:444-489, 1901.

Pick, A.: Ueber die Besiehungen der senilen Hirnatrophie zur aphasia, Prag.

m. Wschr. 17:165, 1892 (quoted from Jervis, 1956, q. v.).

———: Zur Symptomatologie des atrophischen Hinterhauptlappen, Arb. Deutsche Psych., Univ. Klin. in Prag., 1908 (quoted).

Pick, L.: Zur Symptomatologie der linkseitigen Schlüfenlappenotrophie, Mschr. Psych. Neurol. 16:378-388, 1904.

Pickering, G. W.: The cerebrospinal fluid pressure in arterial hypertension, Clin. Sci. 1:397-413, 1933-1934.

———: Transient cerebral paralysis in hypertension and in cerebral embolism. With special reference to the pathogenesis of chronic hypertensive encephalopathy, J.A.M.A. 137:423-430, 1948.

———: Vascular spasm, Lancet 2:845-850, 1951.

———: The genetic factor in essential hypertension, Ann. Intern. Med. 43:457-464, 1955.

———: Symposium on cerebrovascular disease, Proc. Roy. Soc. Med. 52:540-542, 1959.

Pickering, G. W., Wright, A. D., and Heptinstall, R. H.: The reversibility of malignant hypertension, Lancet 2:952-956, 1952.

Pickworth, F. A.: Mental disorder and its relation to deficient oxidation in the brain tissue, p. 91 *in* The Mott Memorial Volume, Contributions to Psychiatry, Neurology and Sociology, Dedicated to the Late Sir Frederick Mott, London, Lewis, 1929.

———: A new method of study of the brain capillaries and its application to the regional localization of mental disorder, J. Anat. 69:62-71, 1934.

Pincock, J. G.: The natural history of cerebral thrombosis, Ann. Intern. Med. 46:925-930, 1957.

Plassmann, S.: Durchblutungs-Schaden und ihre Gehandlung, 1943 (quoted by Leriche in Thromboses Artérielles, q. v.).

Platt, R.: Heredity in hypertension, Quart. J. Med. 16:111, 1947 (quoted).

Pool, J. L.: Cerebral vasospasm, New Eng. J. Med. 259:1259-1264, 1958.

Pool, J. L., Bridges, T. J., Clark, K., and Yohr, M. D.: Pletysnographic studies of cerebral circulation. Evidence for cranial nerve vasomotor activity, J. Clin. Invest. 37:763-772, 1958.

Pool, J. L., Jacobson, S., and Fletcher,

T. A.: Cerebral vasospasm—clinical and experimental evidence, J.A.M.A. 167:1599-1601, 1958.

Proceedings of International Conference on Vascular Disease of the Brain, Neurology 11, no. 4, part 2:8-176, 1961.

Purves-Stewart, J.: The Diagnosis of Nervous Diseases, ed. 9, Baltimore, Williams & Wilkins, 1945.

Putnam, T. J.: The cerebral circulation; some new points in its anatomy, physiology and pathology, J. Neurol. Psychopathol. 17:193-212, 1937.

———: Lesions of "encephalomyelitis" and multiple sclerosis. Venous thrombosis as the primary alteration, J.A.M.A. 108:1477-1480, 1937.

Rankin, J.: Cerebral vascular accidents in patients over the age of 60. I. General considerations, Scot. Med. J. 2:127-136, 1957; II. Prognosis, *ibid.*, 200-215.

Ray, B. S., and Dunning, H. S.: Transient monocular blindness accompanying thrombosis of the internal carotid artery: report of 3 cases treated by superior cervical ganglionectomy, Trans. Am. Neurol. Assoc. 44-46, 1953.

Raynaud, M.: Nouvelles recherches sur la nature et le traitement de l'asphyxie locale des extrémités, Arch. générales de médecine 1:5-21, 1874.

———: L'asphyxie locale et de la gangrene, symétrique des extrémités, Paris, 1862 (quoted from Pickering, Lancet, 1951, p. 850, q. v.).

Raynor, R. B., and Ross, G.: Arteriography and vasospasm. The effects of intracarotid contrast media on vasospasm, J. Neurosurg. 17:1055-1061, 1960.

Reiner, L.: Mesenteric arterial insufficiency and abdominal angina, Arch. Intern. Med. 114:765-772, 1964.

Reitan, R. M.: Intellectual functions in aphasic and non-aphasic brain-injured subjects, Neurology 3:202-212, 1953.

Report by an *ad hoc* committee established by the Advisory Council for the National Institute of Neurological Diseases and Blindness, Public Health Service: A classification and outline of the cerebrovascular diseases (with a foreword by Pearce Bailey), Neurology 8:395-434, 1958.

Resch, J. A.: Intracranial vascular syndromes, Geriatrics 19:684-688, 1964.

Rhein, J. H. W., Winkelman, N. W., and Patten, C. A.: Mental conditions in the aged, Archiv. Neurol. Psychol. 20:329-335, 1928.

Ricker, G.: Die Enstehung der pathologisch-anatomischen Befunde nach Hirnerschütterung in Abhängigkeit vom Gefässnervensystem des Hirnes, Virchow Arch. Path. Anat. 226:180-212, 1919.

————: Die Methode der direkten Beobachtung der lokalen Kreislaufsstörungen und die Verwertung pathologisch-anatomischer Befunde in den Kreislaufsorganen für die Pathologie derselben, Emil Abderhalden Handb. der biologischen Arbeitsmethoden, Abt. 8, Exper. Morphol. Teil 1, erste Hälfte, pp. 509-560, 1924.

————: Pathologie als Naturwissenschaft — Relationspathologie, Berlin, Springer, 1924.

Ricker: Sklerose und Hypertonie der Innervierten Arterien, Berlin, Springer, 1927.

Riegel, F., and Jolly, F.: Ueber die Veränderungen der Piagefasse in Folge von Reizung sensibler Nerven, Virchow. Arch. Path. Anat. 52:218-230, 1871.

Riser, M., and Sorel, R.: Etudes sur la circulation cérébrale. Les spasmes des artères cérébrales chez le sujet normal, Comp. rend. Soc. Biol. 104:295-297, 1930.

Riser, M. P., and Planques,: Les spasmes vasculaires en neurologie Etude clinique et expérimentale, Encephale 26:501-528, 1931.

Roberts, H. J.: Difficult Diagnosis, Philadelphia, Saunders, 1958.

Robinson, G. W., Jr.: Psychiatric geriatrics. The possibilities in the treatment of mental states of old age, J.A.M.A. 116:2139-2141, 1941.

————: The abnormal mental reactions of old age, J. Missouri State Med. Assoc. 39:36-40, 1942.

————: Mental states in old age, Lancet 1:84, 1942.

Robinson, R. W., Cohen, W. D., Higano, N., Meyer, R., Lukowsky, G. H., McLaughlin, R. B., and MacGilpin, H. H., Jr.: Life-table analysis of survival after cerebral thrombosis—ten year experience, J.A.M.A. 169:1149-1152, 1959.

Rochester, D.: The early diagnosis and symptoms of arterio-sclerosis, Trans. Med. Soc. State of N. Y., 86-91, 1903.

Roger, G., Vidal, F., and Tessier, P. J.: Cerveau senile, Chap. 6 in Nouveau traité de Medicine 19:430, 1920.

Rolleston, H. D.: Some Medical Aspects of Old Age, Being the Linacre Lecture, 1922, St. John's College, Cambridge, London, Macmillan, 1922.

Rook, A. F.: Coughing and unconsciousness: the so-called laryngeal epilepsy, Brain 69:138-148, 1946.

Rosenberg, E. F.: The brain in malignant hypertension; a clinicopathologic study, Arch. Intern. Med. 65:545-586, 1940.

Rosenblath: Ueber die apoplektiforme, nichtembolische and vorwiegend unblutige Hirnerweichung and über "artero-capillary fibrosis," Z, klin. Med. 106:482-527, 1927.

Rothenberg, S. F., and Corday, E.: Etiology of the transient cerebral stroke, J.A.M.A. 164:2005-2008, 1957.

Rothschild, D.: Pathologic changes in senile psychoses and their psychobiologic significance, Am. J. Psychiat. 93:757-788, 1937.

————: Neuropathologic changes in arteriosclerotic psychoses and their psychiatric significance, Arch. Neurol. Psychiat. 48:417-436, 1942.

————: The role of the pre-morbid personality in arteriosclerotic psychoses, Am. J. Psychiat. 100:501-505, 1944.

————: Senile psychoses and psychoses with cerebral arteriosclerosis, in Kaplan, O. J. (ed.): Mental Disorders in Later Life, ed. 2, pp. 289-331, Stanford, Stanford Univ. Press, 1956.

Roy, C. S., and Sherrington, C. S.: On the regulation of the blood supply of the brain, J. Physiol. 11:85-108, 1890.

Rusk, H. A., Taylor, E. J., Zimmerman, M., and Judson, J.: Living With a Disability, at Home, at Work, at Play, New York, Blakiston, 1953.

Russek, H. I., Benton, J. G., Brown, H., Zohman, B. L., Greene, L., Kara, A., Doerner, A. A., and Rusk., H. A.: Cortisone as an adjunct in the rehabilitation of the hemiplegic patient, Am. J. Med. Sci. 225:147-152, 1953.

Russek, H. I., and Zohman, B. L.: Papaverine in cerebral angiospasm (vascular encephalopathy), J.A.M.A. 136: 930-932, 1948.

Russek, H. I., Zohman, B. L., and Russek, A. S.: Cortisone in the immediate therapy of apoplectic stroke, J. Am. Geriat. Soc. 2:216-222, 1954.

Russell, W.: Arterial hypertonus and arteriosclerosis: their relations and significance, Lancet 1:1519-1524, 1901.

———: Cerebral manifestations of hypertonus in sclerosed arteries, Practitioner 76:306-316, 1906.

———: Arterial Hypertonus, Sclerosis and Blood Pressure, Edinburgh and London, 1907.

———: A post-graduate lecture on "intermittent closing of cerebral arteries; its relation to temporary and permanent paralysis," Brit. Med. J. 2:1109-1110, 1909.

———: Correspondence on intermittent closing of cerebral arteries, Brit. Med. J. 2:1580, 1909.

Sachs, E.: Discussion of Wechsler, Trans. Am. Neurol. Assoc. 61:84, 1935, q. v.

Saphir, O.: A Text on Systemic Pathology, vol. 2, New York, Grune & Stratton, 1959.

Savage, G.: Mental disorders associated with old age, J. Nerv. Ment. Dis. 51: 217-230, 1920.

Savory, W. S.: Case of a young woman in whom the main arteries of both upper extremities and of the left side of the neck were throughout completely obliterated, Trans. Med. Chir. Soc. London 39:205-219, 1856.

Schaller, W. F., Tamaki, K., and Newman, H.: Nature and significance of multiple petechial hemorrhages associated with trauma of the brain, Arch. Neurol. Psychiat. 37:1048-1076, 1937.

Scheinberg, P.: Cerebral blood flow in vascular disease of the brain. With observations on the effects of stellate ganglion block, Am. J. Med. 8:139-147, 1950.

———: Cerebral circulation in heart failure, Am. J. Med. 8:148-152, 1950.

Scheinberg, P., Blackburn, I., Rich, M., and Saslaw, M.: Effects of aging on cerebral circulation and metabolism, Arch. Neurol. Psychiat. 70:77-85, 1953.

Scheinberg, P., and Rice-Simons, R. A.: The treatment of recurring cerebral

ischemic phenomena, Geriatrics 19: 887-893, 1964.

Schmidt, C. F.: The present status of knowledge concerning the intrinsic control of the cerebral circulation and the effects of functional derangements in it, Fed. Proc. 3:131-139, 1944.

———: The Cerebral Circulation in Health and Disease, Springfield (Ill.), Thomas, 1950.

Schmidt, C. F., and Pierson, J. C.: The intrinsic regulation of the blood vessels of the medulla oblongata, Am. J. Physiol. 108:241-263, 1934.

Schmidt, C. F., Kety, S. S., Strauss, W. L., Jr., Batson, O. V., Starr, F., Davies, P. W., Brink, F., and Bronk, D. W.: Minutes of the Conference on Cerebral Blood Flow and Metabolism, U. S. National Research Council, Div. of Med. Sci. Bull on Shock, pp. 230-241, 1944.

Schmoll, E.: Ueber motorische, sensorische und vasomotorische Symptome verursacht durch Koronarskelerose— und sonstige Erkrankungen linkseitigen Herzhälfte, Munchen. med. Wschr. 54:2027-2030, 1907.

Schneck, S. A.: On the relationship between ruptured intracranial aneurysm and cerebral infarction, Neurology 14: 691-702, 1964.

Schneider, C.: Pick's disease, Mschr. Psychiat. Neurol. 65:230-275, 1927.

———: Pick's disease, Arch. Neurol. Psychiat. 19:543-544, 1928.

Schonfeld A.: Über Vorkommen und Bedeutung der drusigen Bildungen (Sphärotrichie) in der Hirnrinde, Mschr. Psychiat. Neurol. 36:342-278, 1914.

Schwartz, P.: Die Arten der Schlaganfälle des Gehirns und ihre Entstehung, Berlin, Springer, 1930.

Schwiegk, H.: Wiederbelebung durch einen künstlichen Kreislauf, Klin. Wschr. 24:104-111, 1946.

Shahbrom, E., and Levy, L.: The role of systemic blood pressure in cerebral circulation in carotid and basilar artery thromboses, Am. J. Med. 23: 197-204, 1957.

Sharp, J. G.: A series of cases of transient aphasia, hemiplegia, and hemiparesis due to arterial spasm, Lancet 2:836-866, 1915.

Sheldon, K. W.: Management of Strokes, Philadelphia, Lippincott, 1956.

Shenkin, H. A., Novak, P., Goluboff, B. Soffe, A. M., and Bortin, L.: The effects of aging, arteriosclerosis and hypertension upon the cerebral circulation, J. Clin. Invest. 32:459-465, 1953.

Shock, N. W.: Physiological aspects of mental disorders in later life, Chap. 4 *in* Kaplan, O. J. (*ed.*): Mental Disorders in Later Life, ed. 2, pp. 47-97, Stanford, Stanford Univ. Press, 1956.

Shoemaker, W. T.: Obstruction of the central retinal artery, Am. J. Med. Sci. 127:677-684, 1904.

Siekert, R. G., and Millikan, C. H.: Studies in cerebrovascular disease. II. Some clinical aspects of thrombosis of the basilar artery, Proc. Staff Meet. Mayo Clinic 30:93-100, 1955.

Silverman, D.: Serial electroencephalography in brain tumors and cerebrovascular accidents, Arch. Neurol. 2: 122-129, 1960.

Smith, G. W.: Care of the Patient with a Stroke—a Handbook for the Patient's Family and the Nurse, New York, Springer, 1959.

Smith, P.: Reflex amblyopia and thrombosis of the retinal artery, Ophthal. Rev. 3:1-21; 33-47; 129-147, 1884.

————: Intermittent closing of cerebral arteries (correspondence), Brit. Med. J. 2:1380, 1909.

Sodeman, W. A.: Pathologic Physiology, ed. 3, Philadelphia, Saunders, 1961.

Southard, E. E.: Anatomical findings in senile dementia: a diagnostic study bearing especially on the group of cerebral atrophies, Am. J. Insan. 66: 673-708, 1910.

Spielmeyer, W.: Vasomotorish trophische Veranderungen bei zerebraler Arteriosklerose, Mschr. Psychiat. Neurol. 68: 605-620, 1928.

————: Kreislaufstörungen und Psychosen, Z. Neur. Psychiat. 123:536-573, 1930.

Staemmler, M.: Zur Lehre von der Entstehung des Schlaganfalles, Klin. Wschr. 15:1300-1306, 1936.

————: Ueber Veränderungen der kleinen Hirngefässe in apoplektischen Erweichungsherder und ihre Beziehungen zur Traumatischen Spätapoplexie, Beitr. Path Anat. 78:408-429, 1927.

Steegman, A. T.: Encephalopathy following anesthesia. Histologic study of four cases, Arch. Neurol. Psychiat. 41:955-977, 1939.

Stengel, A.: Nervous manifestations of arteriosclerosis, Am. J. Med. Sci. 135: 187-199, 1908.

Stephens, J. H.: Haemorrhagic leucoencephalitis, Scot. Med. J. 2:154-161, 1957.

Stevenson, L. E.: A case of Raynaud's disease, Lancet 2:917-918, 1890.

Stöhr, P.: Über die Innervation der Pia Mater und des Plexus chorioideus des Menschen, Z. Anat. Entwicklungsgesch., Abth. I., 63:562-607, 1922.

————: Mikroscopische Anatomie des Vegetativen Nervensystems, p. 177, Berlin, 1928.

Stürup, H.: Coronary thrombosis and other forms of circulatory insufficiency coinciding with cerebral apoplexy, Acta med. Scandinav. 144:189-196, 1952.

Survey Report of Cerebral Vascular Study Group: Institute of Neurological Diseases and Blindness of National Institutes of Health for the Classification and Outline of Cerebrovascular Disease, 1958.

Swank, R. L.: Low-fat Diet; Reasons, Rules and Recipes, Eugene, Univ. Oregon, 1959.

Symonds, C., and Mackenzie, I.: Bilateral loss of vision from cerebral infarction, Brain 80:415-455, 1957.

Symposium on central nervous system control of circulation, proceedings, Washington, D. C., No. 1-3, 1959, Physiol. Rev., suppl. 4, 1960.

Taylor, J.: Occlusion of the cerebral vessels, *in* Allbutt, T. C. and Rolleston, H. D. (*eds*): System of Medicine 8: 290-307, New York, Macmillan, 1911.

Taylor, M. L., and Marks, M.: Institute of Physical Medicine and Rehabilitation, N. Y. University Bellevue Medical Center, 1955.

Thoma, R.: Ueber die Elastizität der Arterien und die Angiomalacie, Virchow Arch. Path. Anat. 236:243-269, 1922.

Thomas, C. B.: Constriction of pial vessels in the unanesthetized cat produced by stimulation of the cervical sympathetic chain, Am. J. Physiol. 108: 241-263, 1934.

Thomas, H. M.: Diseases of the cerebral blood vessels, Chap. 12 *in* Osler, W., and McCrae, T.: Modern Medicine, Its Theory and Practice, ed. 3, vol. 6, pp. 305-388. Philadelphia, Lea & Febiger, 1928.

Thompson, G. W.: A case of obliteration of a retinal artery following attacks of temporary amblyopia, Trans. Ophthal. Soc. U. K. 22:177-180, 1902.

Thompson, R. K., and Smith, G. W.: Experimental occlusion of the middle cerebral artery during arterial hypotension, Trans. Am. Neurol. Assoc. 76: 203-207, 1951.

Tilney, F.: The aging of the human brain, Bull. N. Y. Acad. Med. 4:1125-1143, 1928.

Tooth, H. H.: Cerebral hemorrhage, *in* Allbutt, T. C. and Rolleston, H. D. (eds.): System of Medicine 8:307-334, New York, Macmillan, 1911.

Torkildsen, A., and Penfield, W., Ventriculographic interpretation, Arch. Neurol. Psychiat. 30:1011-1024, 1933.

Trousseau, A.: Tremblement senile et paralysis agitans, Chap. 47 *in* Clinique Médicale de l'Hotel-Dieu, ed. 7., vol. 2, pp. 280-292, Paris, 1885.

Up and Around, U.S. Dept. Health, Education and Welfare, Public Health Service, 1964 (price, 50¢).

Ustvedt, H. J.: Mortality from cerebrovascular accidents in Norway in relation to mortality from cardio-vascular-renal disease, Acta med. Scand., fasc. 4, 163:305-327, 1959.

van Buskirk, C.: Intracerebral vascular disease, Chap. 10 *in* Baker, A. B. (ed.): Clinical Neurology, ed. 2, vol. 2, pp. 564-615, New York, Hoeber-Harper, 1962.

Van Rosen, R. E. (as told to Crossen, K.): Comeback, the Story of My Stroke, Indianapolis, Bobbs-Merrill, 1963.

van der Drift, J. H.: Ischemic cerebral lesions, Angiology 12:401-418, 1961.

Vander Eecken, H. M., and Adams, R. D.: Anatomy and functional significance of meningeal arterial anastomoses of human brain, J. Neuropath. Exper. Neurol. 12:132-157, 1953.

Viamonte, M., Jr., and Parks, R. E. (eds.): Progress in Angiography, Springfield (Ill.), Thomas, 1964.

Villaret, M., and Cachere, R.: Les Embolies Cerebrales, Paris, 1939.

Volhard, F., and Farr, T.: Die Brightsche Nierenkrankheit; Klinik, Pathologie und Atlas, Berlin, Springer, 1914.

Volhard, F.: Uremia, Chap. 39, *in* Berglund, H., and Medes, G.: The Kidney in Health and Disease, Philadelphia, Lea & Febiger, 1935.

Vunas, Börje: Sympathetic vasodilator system and blood flow, Physiol. Rev., suppl. 4, 69-80, 1950.

Wagenmann, A.: Beitrag zur Kentniess der Circulationsstörungen in den Netzhautgefässen, Arch. Ophthal. 44:219-249, 1897.

Wahal, K. M., and Riggs, H. E.: Changes in the brain associated with senility, Arch. Neurol. 2:151-159, 1960.

Walshe, F.: Diseases of the Nervous System, ed. 10, Baltimore, Williams & Wilkins, 1963.

Warthin, A. S.: The pathology of the aging process, Bull. N. Y. Acad. Med. 4:1006-1046, 1928.

————: Old Age, The Major Involution, the Physiology and Pathology of the Aging Process, New York, Hoeber, 1929.

Wartman, W. B.: The incidence and severity of arteriosclerosis in the organs from 500 autopsies, Am. J. Med. Sci. 186:27-35, 1933.

Weber, E.: Ueber die Selbstandigkeit des Gehirns in der Regulirung seiner Blutgehalt, Jahresbericht Neurol. Psychiat. 12:124-127, 1908.

Weber, F. P.: Agnosia of hemiplegia and of blindness after cerebral embolism, Lancet 1:44-46, 1942.

Weber, F. P., and Gruber, R.: Recurrent temporary amblyopia of angiospastic origin and the association of retinal angiospasm with other vasomotor neuroses, Internat. Clinics, series 18, 2:111-123, 1908.

Wechsler, I. S.: Abdominal pain as a symptom of disease of the brain, J.A.M.A. 105:647-650, 1935.

————: Abdominal pain as a symptom of disease of the brain, Trans. Am. Neurol. Assoc. 61:81-84, 1935.

Weibel, J., Fields, W. S., Crawford, E. S., De Bakey, M. E., and Beall, A. C.: Clinical evaluation of conray for angiography in patients with cerebrovascular disease, Am. J. Roentgen. 90: 1281-1286, 1963.

Weiss, E.: The emotions and strokes, *in* Page, I. H., *et al.*: Strokes, How They Occur and What Can Be Done About Them, New York, Dutton, 1961.

Weiss, S.: The regulation and disturbance of the cerebral circulation through extracerebral mechanisms, Proc. Assoc. Res. Nerv. Ment. Dis. 18: 571-604, 1938.

————: Instantaneous physiologic death, New Eng. J. Med. 223:793-797, 1940.

Weiss, S., and Baker, J. P.: The carotid sinus reflex in health and disease. Its role in the causation of fainting and convulsions, Medicine 12:297-354, 1933.

Wells, C. E.: Cerebral circulation, the clinical significance of current concepts, Arch. Neurol. 3:319-331, 1960.

Wertham, F. I.: The incidence of growth disorders in 923 cases of mental disease, Arch. Neurol. Psychiat. 21:1128-1140, 1929.

Wertham, F., and Wertham, F. E.: The Brain as an Organ, Its Postmortem Study and Interpretation, New York, Macmillan, 1934.

Westphal, K.: Über die Enstehung des Schlaganfalles: II. Klinische Untersuchungen zum Problem der Enstehung des Schlaganfalles, Deutsch. Arch. klin. Med. 151:31-95, 1926.

Westphal, K., and Bär, R.: Über die Enstehung des Schlaganfalles: I. Pathologisch—Anatomische Untersuchungen zur frage der Enstehung des Schlaganfalles: Same journal pp. 1-30.

Wilbrand, H., and Saenger, A.: Die Neurologie des Augens, vol. 3, part 2, Wiesbaden, 1906.

Wilder, J.: Zur Klinik der cerebralen und peripheren Angiospasmen, Z. Neurol. Psychiat. 105:752-796, 1926.

Williams, D.: Quoted by McNaughton, p. 196, 1938, q. v.

Williamson, O. K.: An address on the symptoms which precede and are associated with general arterio-sclerosis, Practitioner 101:241-259, 1918.

Wilson, G., Rupp, C., Jr., Riggs, H. E., and Wilson, W. W.: A study of 542

cases of acute CVA demonstrated at autopsy, J.A.M.A. 145:1227-1229, 1951.

Windscheid, Prof.: Die Beziehungen der Arteriosklerose zu Erkrankungen des Gehirns, Munchen. med. Wschr. 49: 345-347, 1902.

Wolff, H. G.: The cerebral circulation, Physiol. Rev. 16:545-596, 1936.

————: The cerebral blood vessels—anatomical principles. The comparative anatomy of the cranial circulation, Assoc. Res. Nerv. Ment. Dis. 18: 29-68, 1938.

Wolff, H. G., and Forbes, H. S.: Cerebral circulation. Vasomotor control of cerebral vessels. IV. The action of hypertonic solutions, part I, Arch. Neurol. Psychiat. 20:73-83, 1928.

Wolkoff, K.: Über atherosklerose der Gehirnarterien, Beitr. Path. Anat. 91:515-553, 1933.

Woltman, H. W.: Arteriosclerosis of the nervous system. An analysis of 59 cases with cord changes, Med. Clin. N. Am. 5:511-520, 1921.

————: Cerebrospinal arteriosclerosis, Minnesota Med. 5:102-107, 1922.

————: The effects of arteriosclerosis on the central nervous system, Chicago Med. Soc. Bull. 52:363-375, 1949.

Worcester, A.: The Care of the Aged, the Dying, and the Dead, ed. 2, Springfield (Ill.), Thomas, 1950.

Wright, I. S., and McDevitt, E.: Cerebral vascular diseases: their significance, diagnosis, and present treatment, including the selective use of anticoagulant substances, Ann. Intern. Med. 41:682-698, 1954.

Ziegler, L.: Discussion of Wechsler, Trans Am. Neurol Assoc. 61:84, 1935, q. v.

Zugibe, F. T.: Eat, Drink and Lower Your Cholesterol, New York, McGraw-Hill, 1963.

Zülch, K. J.: Störungen des intrakraniellen Druckes Handb. Neuro-Chirugie, vol. 1, part 1, pp. 208-303, 1959 (quoted from van der Drift, 1961, q. v.).

Index of Authors

179

Index of Subjects